Europe in the Era of Two World Wars

Europe in the Era of Two World Wars

FROM MILITARISM AND GENOCIDE TO CIVIL SOCIETY, 1900–1950

Volker R. Berghahn

PRINCETON UNIVERSITY PRESS

PRINCETON AND OXFORD

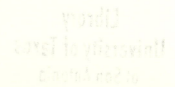

First published in Germany under the title *Europa im Zeitalter der Weltkriege—*
Die Entfesselung und Entgrenzung der Gewalt © 2002 Fischer Taschenbuch
Verlag in der S. Fischer Verlag GmbH, Frankfurt am Main

English translation © 2006 by Princeton University Press
Published by Princeton University Press, 41 William Street,
Princeton, New Jersey 08540
In the United Kingdom: Princeton University Press,
3 Market Place, Woodstock, Oxfordshire OX20 1SY

Library of Congress Cataloging-in-Publication Data

Berghahn, Volker Rolf.
[Europa im Zeitalter der Weltkriege. English]
Europe in the era of two World Wars : from militarism and genocide
to civil society, 1900–1950 / translated by V.R. Berghahn.
p.   cm.
Includes bibliographical references and index.
ISBN-13: 978-0-691-12003-4 (cloth : alk. paper)
ISBN-10: 0-691-12003-X (cloth : alk. paper)
1. Political violence—Europe—History—20th century.
2. Totalitarianism—History—20th century.
JC328.6.B4713   2002
940.5—dc22   2005043241

British Library Cataloging-in-Publicatin Data is available

This book has been composed in Caledonia

Printed on acid-free paper. ∞

pup.princeton.edu

Printed in the United States of America

1   3   5   7   9   10   8   6   4   2

Contents

Europe in the Era of Two World Wars

On 31 December 1899, the end of the nineteenth century and the beginning of the twentieth century were celebrated all over Europe. The decades that had just come to a close had brought a turn for the better in large parts of the European continent and the British Isles. This at least was how it appeared to newspaper columnists and essayists, to the speakers and audiences at the New Year's celebrations. There were splendid fireworks and church bells rang in the new century.

There was much that the Europeans could look back on with some pride. Industrialization had advanced impressively. To the branches of the First Industrial Revolution (coal, iron, textiles) had been added those of the second wave (electrics, chemicals, manufacturing engineering). The states of Europe had considerably expanded their overseas possessions, and there had been a slow but steady rise in living standards. The visual arts, literature, music, theater, and architecture had produced works that have remained world famous to this day. Europe had never been more powerful and glittering than in those decades.[1]

To be sure, in all countries there were also darker sides, and social critics and cultural pessimists wrote about poverty, decadence, and decay. However, the overall mood in all nations was optimistic, and many believed that the new century would bring further improvements in their material well-being and in politics and culture. If nothing else, the continuing technological progress would secure economic growth and further uplift ever larger numbers of people, as had happened in the nineteenth century.

If those revelers on New Year's Eve 1900 had, on the following day, been put into quarantine for the next ninety years to be given to read, upon their release, two books that were published in the 1990s, they would have found both the titles and the contents hard to believe. The first book, *The Age of Extremes*, is by the internationally respected historian Eric Hobsbawm. It first appeared in Britain in 1994 and was subsequently translated into many other languages. The second book, by Mark Mazower, is *Dark Continent* and, like Hobsbawm's volume, it received much praise.[2]

Hobsbawm prefaces his first chapter with an array of quotations, most of whose authors view the twentieth century as an age of catastrophe. Thus, the British philosopher Isaiah Berlin who had studied his times closely, spoke of "the most terrible century in Western history." To the French ecologist René Dumont it was a "century of massacres and wars." The British novelist William Golding thought it represented the "the most violent century in human history." The Italian historian Leo Valiani alone had something more positive to say when he wrote that the twentieth century demonstrated "that the victory of the ideals of justice and equality is always ephemeral, but also that, if we manage to preserve liberty, we can always start all over again. There is no need to despair, even in the most desperate situations."[3]

Although Hobsbawm does not completely refute Valiani's verdict, for him the century was nevertheless one of extremes, of "religious wars" and intolerance. In contrast to the "long nineteenth century," he also considers it a short one, lasting only from 1914 to 1989. He does not deny that Europe experienced a period of reconstruction and prosperity after 1945. But from 1974 on developments appear to him to be again much more uncertain and ominous. Accordingly, the book is shaped like a triptych on which the years 1914–45 are depicted as an "age of catastrophe." Following the "golden" 1950s and 1960s, Hobsbawm argues, there came a third period in which the future once again looked problematical, though not necessarily apocalyptic.[4] Of course his analysis ends in the early 1990s and he has not extended it into the current century.

All in all, the years 1945–73 are thus to him an epoch that deviated from the century's norm, positing that those years might well be viewed as the extraordinary ones. Those years witnessed worldwide changes that were profound and irreversible. This does not mean, though, that Hobsbawm intends to dissociate himself from the title of his book. To make this point he mentions just one statistic: according to recent estimates, the twentieth century, with all its wars (civil and otherwise), cost 187 million lives, more than 10 percent of the population of 1900. Even though the world had become more prosperous and infinitely more productive, in the end he comes back to the point that the short century that, in his view, came to a close in 1989 did not culminate in a celebration of what had been achieved with the end of the cold war but with a feeling of unease. Finally, that twentieth century was different at the end from its beginning in three respects: it was no longer Eurocentric; its economy was transnational and global; and, perhaps most unsettling, it saw "the dissolution of the old patterns of human social relationships" and hence a generational rupture.

Mark Mazower similarly leads the reader into the history of a "dark continent" whose inhabitants vacillated between periods of tolerance and racist policies of extermination.[5] To him Europe is the cradle of democracy and liberty, but also the source of expansionism, war, and gigantic ideological conflicts and revolutions. He refers approvingly to Thomas Masaryk's dictum after World War I that Europe had become "a laboratory atop a vast graveyard." Unlike Hobsbawm, Mazower conceives of the twentieth century as being divided into two halves. The first half was the epoch of catastrophes, whereas the second half offers more ground for some optimism. Nor, in his view, were the genocidal policies that reappeared in the Balkans in the 1990s harbingers of a disastrous future.

Still, as far as Europe is concerned, he remains a skeptic. He claims to be an agnostic in terms of the future of European integration and the European Union. Contrary to Hobsbawm, who never abandoned his Marxist sympathies, he avers that politics cannot be reduced to some economic base. This is why he sees the need to preserve the European nation-state. Capitalism alone would never the able to generate "feelings of belonging capable of rivaling the sense of alliance felt by most people to the state in which they live." This leads him to conclude that "if the Europeans can give up their desperate desire to find a single workable definition of themselves and if they can accept a more modest place in the world, they may come to terms more easily with the diversity and dissension which will be as much their future as their past."[6]

The following chapters of this book pursue different and less far-reaching aims than Hobsbawm's and Mazower's volumes. This may be seen, to begin with, from its more limited time frame. Furthermore, it focuses on a major theme of the 1914–45 period: the unleashing and subsequent escalation of violence that during a relatively short period of some thirty years cost over seventy million lives in Europe alone. Of course, we shall also have to examine other events and developments during those decades. But my main objective is to analyze in particularly concentrated form the orgy of violence that swept through Europe and to see if it is possible to capture, at the same time, the mentalities of the men of violence who were responsible for millions of deaths. I confess that it may well be a vain hope that it will be possible, through this focus, to make more comprehensible what to many still seems incomprehensible about this period. There can be little doubt that the years 1914–45 were an "age of extremes" and that Europe became a "dark continent." But why did this happen?

Another point to be examined here is no less important. History is never just a one-way street. There are always alternatives, and this is also true of Europe in this epoch when violence at times appeared to have become its dominant feature. The alternative to the epoch of violence for the first time assumed more concrete shape in the decades before 1914. It was sidelined thereafter by horrendous wars and civil wars, except for a brief period in the mid-1920s. Only after 1945 did the alternative finally break through in Europe, leading to a period of peace and prosperity that the region basically enjoyed up to the 1970s and, *pace* Hobsbawm, even beyond until the late 1990s. The alternative I am thinking of is the model of an industrial society that, within a democratic-constitutional political framework, peacefully consumes the mass-produced goods that it has manufactured.

This, it seems, was the powerful alternative vision of twentieth-century European history that stood in sharp contrast to the society that the men of violence established in Europe between 1914 and 1945 and that brought death and untold misery to millions of people. Like the former, this latter type was based on the idea of a highly organized industrial society that deployed the most modern technologies. But it was geared to the mass production of military goods and their use in wars of territorial conquest and exploitation. Dominated by the men of violence, people did not peacefully consume the goods they had produced; rather they were, in an orgy of violence, themselves "consumed" by the weapons they had produced.

At first glance it therefore looks as if this book is returning to ancient hypotheses concerning the development of European society. Is this perhaps a copy of Werner Sombart's *Traders and Heroes* or Joseph Schumpeter's idea of a basically pacific capitalism whose victory is slowed down, though not prevented from achieving ultimate triumph, by the opposition of militaristic and aristocratic elites who continue to pursue their age-old policies of conquest? The following chapters, it is true, contain indirect references to this interpretation of European history. There is also Herbert Spencer who, writing in the later nineteenth century, postulated the existence of two societal types: a "militant" and an "industrial" one. Like other liberals, Spencer predicted the long-term victory of the latter type. Finally, mention should be made of Alfred Vagts who, in 1937–38, published an influential book devoted to the problem of militarism in modern societies. He juxtaposed this militaristic type not with pacifism but, significantly enough, with what he called civilianism.[7]

The arguments of these social scientists and historians were taken up again by scholars after World War II. First there was the debate on the driving forces behind militarism in the twentieth century, followed by work on the question of civil-military relations in the context of both European and non-European societies. More recently, these debates have been transformed again into research on the character and dynamics of "civil society." While this has been a fruitful approach to understanding how modern industrial societies "tick," there has also been justified criticism. The Giessen University sociologist Helmut Dubiel has complained that the "notion of 'civil society' lost all its theoretical and empirical contours." He is unhappy about the vagueness of the concept and feels that "today it is perhaps more a catch-all term for a reservoir of problems and questions that a disarmed Marxism has left behind." What to Dubiel is even more unfortunate is that the "theory of civil society does not take account of 'uncivil' phenomena such as power, domination, and violence." Instead its protagonists adhered to a "naively optimistic anthropology," according to which "modern societies are normally characterized by openness, freedom from violence, solidarity, and justice." However, according to Dubiel, it is only through the "experience of 'uncivil' societal conditions" that the notion of civil society becomes more tangible. At the end of his deliberations he arrives at four basic forms of the uncivil: "a) despotism/totalitarianism; b) corruption; c) ethnocentrism; d) barbarism."[8]

In our subsequent analysis of systems of domination that are geared toward war and violence we will repeatedly encounter these four basic forms and, in the process, will also come across the no less interesting question of the recivilization of such systems. The rule of the men of violence reached its climax in Europe during World War II before they were defeated in 1945 (and to some extent defeated themselves). In inflicting this defeat, the United States played a crucial role. Without its contribution, that war would likely not have been decided in favor of the Allies. Nor would we have seen the (renewed) rise of a civil society in Europe of which America was its most powerful protagonist.

The history of Europe in the twentieth century cannot be written and understood without reference to the history of the United States. It was America's weight that tipped the scales against the two Central European monarchies, Germany and Austria-Hungary, in 1918. Having retreated from the European scene in the early 1920s, Washington came back in 1924 to help with the reconstruction of the continent. It withdrew again in the wake of the great crash of 1929, until World War II drew the United States once more into a decisive role in defeating the Axis Powers, Germany, Italy, and Japan. In 1945, determined not to repeat the mistakes of the early 1920s, Washington for the second time participated in a major way in the financing and organizing of Europe's postwar reconstruction, or at least of the western half of the once "dark continent," in ways that stabilized civilian societies similar to the ones that had emerged in North America.

This transatlantic connection was comprehensive. It was political, military, economic-technological, and sociocultural, and it was first forged in the period before 1914. For it was at that point that America came to represent, at least in broad outline, the civilian alternative to the regimes that would soon overwhelm Europe with their policies of violence. Later, this alternative became articulated more clearly in declarations and programs. The Fourteen Points of President Woodrow Wilson in October 1918 are perhaps the most important example during the first round. A quarter of a century later, the principles of a different world can be found in the Atlantic Charter of August 1941 or in the Charter of the United Nations.

The American vision of the future that these documents juxtaposed with the concepts of the men of violence was based on the fundamental insight that a civil society would lack stability and the capacity for gradual rational reform unless it was based on a constant proliferation of material prosperity and wealth. If Dubiel is correct that work on civil society has frequently lost sight of the problem of alternative "uncivil" systems, debates on a democratic political culture similarly seem to overlook that the latter will be built on sand if it is not accompanied by the tangible experience of growing welfare. Where prosperity and economic opportunity exist and people's income is sufficiently large to enable them to improve the quality of their life both materially and intellectually, the men of violence who want to deploy mass-produced military goods for wars of conquest that devour those human beings en masse will be frustrated. In this sense this book revolves around the confrontation between military and civilian ways of organizing society. The former assumed massive proportions in World War I and again in World War II until Europe finally broke through to a civilian consumer society after 1945.[9]

It cannot be stressed too strongly that this type of society is not naively seen here as the be all and end all of human social organization. However important its victory over the militaristic societies of conquest was for the development of Europe after 1945, we shall also have to raise the question of the costs. The satisfaction that was felt over the emergence of a civilian society that brought prosperity and peace was not just marred by the fact that the eastern half of Europe fell under Stalin's rule. The communists, it is true, also promised higher living standards but during the cold war in fact concentrated on the development of heavy industry because the Soviet bloc could not marshall the resources to provide both.

No less important, the spreading of "prosperity for all" in Europe and the United States after World War II created problems for the non-Western world that have not been solved to this day. To begin with, violence was exported to the Third World, many of whose people lived on a starvation diet. Worse, the emergence of islands of prosperity in a world of hunger and poverty created tensions and conflicts abroad, and in turn began to threaten the stability of the civilian industrial societies of the West. If Europe's social question of the nineteenth century had, after major conflicts, been settled after 1945 by securing the participation of the industrial proletariat in both politics and consumption, that same social question assumed global proportions in the second half of the twentieth century. Globalization that on closer inspection was a continuing process of Americanization and that generated a simple-minded optimism in the 1990s had a dark side whose dangerous dimensions have become much clearer in recent years.

However, these questions must not distract us from our main focus: the first half of the twentieth century. Two very different concepts of how to organize a modern industrial society existed in Europe in those decades. Examining their fundamentals and dynamics is central to understanding the gigantic struggle of two world wars from which the United States rose in 1945 as the hegemonic power of the West. The account of European history in the era of the two world wars is preceded by a chapter that deals with a period that was full of hope and during which few people anticipated how catastrophic World War I would be. But even during those years, the Europeans were sitting on a volcano that was being fed by the explosive power of colonialism. It was in the colonies that the orgy of violence that consumed millions of lives began and that ricocheted back into Europe in 1914.

CHAPTER ONE

Europe before World War I, 1895–1914

INDUSTRIAL ECONOMY AND CIVIL SOCIETY

Considering its political, economic, and sociocultural consequences, it is no surprise that World War I has been called the "primordial catastrophe" (*Urkatastrophe*) of the twentieth century.[1] In the light of what happened during the war and in the two decades after its end in 1918, the escalation of physical violence presents historians with great problems, and to this day they are struggling to find plausible explanations. Europe had not seen mass death on such a scale since the Thirty Years War of the seventeenth century. Millions of people perished, not to mention the destruction of material assets in a wave of violence that finally came to a cataclysmic end in 1945, ushering in a more peaceful period, at least for western Europe and the United States, though not for other parts of the world.

As far as Europe is concerned, its eastern half was separated off by the Iron Curtain, which became the front line between two extra-European superpowers commanding a huge arsenal of nuclear weapons. Despite this cold war between the West (First World) and the Soviet bloc (Second World) that at times seemed to be turning into a hot war, western Europe experienced an epoch relatively free of violence and devoted to material reconstruction and the creation of a new prosperity and political democracy. John Gaddis has called this era the "long peace." It was to a degree; the killing of innocent civilians that had increasingly become the hallmark of the years 1914–45 continued in the Third World, while countless opponents of Stalinist rule died in the gulags and prisons of the Second World.

In light of the rupture that the outbreak of World War I in August 1914 caused in the development of Europe, some historians have been tempted to introduce counterfactual speculations. They have asked how the historical process might have evolved if war had not broken out at that point. Such speculations have been particularly fashionable with respect to Russia and Germany. As to Russia, it has been asserted that the political and economic reforms introduced by the tsarist regime with the abolition of serfdom in the 1860s and later proceeded before and after the revolutionary upheavals of 1905 would have successfully continued. There would have been no 1917 Bolshevik revolution and consequently no Lenin and no Stalin. In short, Russia's development and hence that of world history would have taken a different and, in any case, less violent path through the period covered in this book.[2]

Similar arguments have been advanced with regard to Germany: without World War I, no defeat in 1918, no Hitler, and no Holocaust. In a variation of Manfred Rauh's hypothesis that Germany found herself on the road to parliamentarism, Margaret Anderson concluded that without the catastrophe of World War I the peaceful democratization of the imperial monarchy would have unfolded successfully.[3] A nonviolent "leap" into a parliamentary constitutionalism would have occurred, as in 1918: "Perhaps the death of the Kaiser at eighty-three would have sped a regime change—in 1941— analogous to Spain's after the death of Franco at the same age in 1975." She is circumspect enough to add that "we cannot know."[4]

While counterfactuals once again appear to have become quite popular, more recently promoted with respect to World War I by Niall Ferguson,[5] it is probably more fruitful to start with other trends that were disrupted by World War I. Thus it may be said with much greater certainty that the dynamic expansion of industry and of the world trading system would have continued without the catastrophe of 1914. This industrial economy, it is true, being exposed to the vagaries of a capitalistically organized market for goods and services, underwent repeated upswings and recessions. Still, economic historians generally agree that even the years of the so-called Great Depression of 1873–95 in effect amounted to a period of retarded growth. Overall trade and industry increased even during those years of a widely perceived downturn. Continued growth was particularly marked in the branches of the so-called Second Industrial Revolution, that is, chemicals, electrical engineering, and machine manufacturing. Most important, from 1895, the world economy entered a boom period that, with a few short recessions, lasted until just before World War I.

Here are a few statistics relating to Europe's basic industries on which the prosperity of the new branches could be built. These figures also reflect the changing economic balances between the nations that were also affected by the dynamics of industrial expansion. In Britain, then the leading industrial country, annual iron production reached 6.5 million tons in the early 1870s, four times that of Germany (1.6 million tons) and more than five times that of France (1.2 million tons), with Russia trailing far behind at a level of 375,000 tons. By 1913 annual production of the German empire had not only increased almost tenfold (14.8 million tons), but it had also overtaken that of Britain (9.8 million tons). France's production had grown fourfold, but with 4.7 million tons the country was not that far ahead of Russia (3.9 million tons). As to coal mining, Britain was able to double its production between 1880 and 1913 and thus retain its lead over Germany (191 million tons, plus 87.5 million tons of lignite). In annual steel production, however, there was a marked change. In 1890, Britain was still well ahead of Germany (3.6 millions tons versus 2.2 million). In 1913, however, the Germans outproduced the British by a factor of three (18.6 million versus 6.9 million).

The expansion of industry—especially after 1895—left agriculture well behind. Thanks to rapid population growth, demand for agricultural produce rose in most regions of Europe, but farming was no longer as profitable as it had been in the 1850s and 1860s. In the years before 1914, the largest gains could be made in the industrial and commercial sectors. Agriculture fell behind. This development is reflected in the migratory patterns from the rural parts to the urban centers and the momentous growth of the industrial cities. They attracted millions of workers who were hoping to find a better life than their current one as land laborers on the large estates in East Prussia, Italy, and Ireland, or as smallholders on farmsteads that could barely support a family. Millions more Europeans emigrated to North America and other parts of the world.

Finally, the rapid expansion of domestic and foreign trade has to be considered. The volume of European exports doubled between 1870 and 1900 and—except for two brief recessions in 1900–1901 and 1907–1908—followed an upward trend. By 1913, two-thirds of trade took place among the nations of Europe. Some 13 percent of all goods went to North America. Import and export figures doubled and trebled. Africa and Asia participated in this internationalization of the world economy to the tune of 15 percent. However, as will be seen when we look more closely at the age of imperialism and colonialism, the terms of trade with the European powers were extremely unfavorable and largely imposed by the metropolitan countries, often accompanied by ruthless methods of political domination.

However much Europe as a whole benefited from the dynamic expansion of its industries and its global trading relations, the gains were very unevenly distributed among the domestic populations. It was above all the industrial and commercial bourgeoisie that was able to accumulate wealth. Their lifestyles and urban residences began to compete with those of the nobility, especially at the many smaller courts of Central Europe. There is the description of the British prime minister William Gladstone, who was quite used to the splendor of British upper-class social life in London. Having attended a party at the residence of the Berlin private banker Gerson Bleichroeder, he gave the following description of what he had seen: "The banqueting hall, very vast and very lofty, and indeed the whole mansion is built of every species of rare marble, and where it is not marble it is gold. There was a gallery for the musicians who played Wagner, and Wagner only, which I was very glad of, as I have rarely had the opportunity of hearing that master. After dinner, we were promenaded through the splendid saloons—and picture galleries, and the ball-room fit for a fairy-tale, and sitting alone on the sofa was a very mean-looking little woman, covered with pearls and diamonds, who was Madame Bleichroeder and whom he had married very early in life when he was penniless. She was unlike her husband, and by no means equal to her wondrous fortune."[6]

In comparison to the wealth of the upper-middle classes, the circumstances of the working class were, to be sure, much more modest. Still, in most European countries living standards were also rising among these strata. Many families could not only afford better nutrition and hygiene but were increasingly able to enjoy pleasures of the "little man," such as tobacco and beer. Wages gradually rose and work hours in industry and commerce were slowly reduced from twelve to eleven or ten. This meant that many men and women, who had escaped the much more restrictive routines of labor in agriculture, gained more leisure time. There was more time to socialize with family and friends that was also reflected in the expansion of associational life. Ultimately, there was hardly a hobby in pre-1914 Europe that people could not pursue within an association or club in conjunction with like-minded people. In this sense, the currently much debated idea of a civil society may be said to have been fully developed well before World War I.

Sports became increasingly popular, but just as other clubs and associations tended to be segregated by social class, sports were also stratified. Soccer drew most of its supporters, active and passive, from the working class. The bourgeoisie, by contrast, preferred tennis, field hockey, and golf. But even among such traditionally aristocratic sports as horse racing popularization set in. And where equestrian sports were too expensive and exclusive, the British lower classes, for example, could go the local greyhound races hoping that by betting a few pennies on their favorite dog they might win some money. The idea of competition among clubs and teams created solidarities. Even if people were not actively engaged in a particular sport, they were keen to support their local team.[7]

The prosperity of the pre-1914 years stimulated other leisure activities: shopping and window shopping. While in the provinces shopping continued to be primarily the purchase of daily provisions and other goods in small specialized corner shops—at the same time an important means of local communication among neighbors—cities also had large department stores. These "palaces of consumption" used attractive displays and invited anonymous buying of often mass-produced clothes off the peg and household goods; or, during sales, they encouraged wandering in the aisles in search of a bargain. What was offered here at affordable prices was linked to another phenomenon that spread in the prewar years: rationalized factory production and the increasingly cunning marketing of cheap goods, particularly in the department stores.[8]

Many—though by no means all—of the innovations in the fields of mass production and selling had been developed in the United States, which had undergone a process of rapid industrialization in the final decades of the nineteenth century and by 1900 was among the most powerful industrial nations. Between 1860 and 1900, its railroad network had grown from 35,000 to 250,000 miles, which not only stimulated the iron and steel industries but also opened up a large domestic market with a rapidly growing population. This in turn encouraged rationalization of production. Above all, it was Frederick Taylor and the Scientific Management movement that, by introducing time-and-motion studies and other ideas, propagandized improvements in factory organization and added financial incentives for workers and white-collar management to increase productivity.[9] Engineers designed ever more fast-producing machines, while others labored to make the sales and accounting departments more efficient. Henry Ford, one of the pioneers of the automobile, developed not only the assembly line but also the idea of using a large part of the productivity gains of rationalized mass production to pay bonuses to his diligent workers and to reduce prices. Rather than pocketing all the profits himself, he passed rationalization gains on to the consumer.

His calculation was that even if average families did not have markedly more money in their pockets, their living standard would rise by virtue of the lower prices they would have to pay for goods, including those, such as consumer durables, that were hitherto out of reach. In this fashion, mass-produced items with reduced prices would be affordable to strata of society that had been spending their income on daily necessities. They might be able to buy a glass of beer, or a cigar, or visit to the local dance hall or cinema. Henry Ford was more ambitious, hoping to turn them all into owners of his popular car models that came off the assembly lines of his factories in Michigan. It was Ford's solution to the theory of domestic underconsumption that John A. Hobson had put forward at the turn of the century in his critique of costly British imperialism that, in his view, enriched the few and held back the prosperity of the many.

However, in this pre-1914 period there were also many obstacles to the realization of Ford's dream of creating a civilian mass-production and mass-consumption society that had little to do with imperialism. Looking at Europe, three must be mentioned here.

1. The trend toward a mass-based prosperity had a "civilizing" effect, as defined in our introduction, in regions of Europe that participated in the process of industrial and commercial expansion. Where this trend was powerful enough, earlier forms of violence and the relentless exertion of superior state power receded. Civilian mentalities and practices spread both in daily social intercourse and in political culture. This is not to downplay down the presence of violence in the urban and industrial societies of pre-1914 Europe, although it was in most cases no longer applied to arbitrarily kill and maim. Still, many families, whether middle class or working class, continued to be subjected to the superior muscle power of the husband and father. Where the majority of people in the urban centers were forced to live in one- or two-room apartments in huge blocks, the "rental garrisons," tensions

would often explode into physical attacks on the weaker family members. For pupils in schools and apprentices in the workshops, corporal punishment was common, never mind the bullying by fellow students in the schoolyard. Those arrested by the police on criminal or political charges could not expect to be treated with kid gloves, and in the judiciary the dominant principle was retribution, not rehabilitation. Striking workers had to flee from the blows of the police truncheon.

With the introduction of universal service millions of young men were recruited into a highly coercive institution devoted to the administration of violence in foreign and civil war. Army drill was harsh everywhere. Before 1914, all European nations were busily preparing for a foreign war that, in an increasingly tense political atmosphere, many thought might break out at any time. Production was not just for peaceful consumption but also for war and the extreme forms of violence that are the subject of subsequent chapters. And yet, notwithstanding arms races and mass armies, well-equipped with modern weapons, ordinary men and women went about their peaceful and nonviolent pursuits as before. In this sense, prewar Europe labored under a strange contradiction. In essence, a majority of citizens led civilian lives and consumed the nonmilitary goods that rising incomes afforded them. But this idea and its practice were permanently threatened by the production and stockpiling of armaments that, if used in a major war, would consume millions of soldiers and civilians.

2. The evolution of a civil society in Europe during the nineteenth century was initially carried forward by the middle classes and later also by the growing working-class movements. Time and again during those decades their aspirations collided with entrenched and institutionalized forms of compulsion that were most tangibly embodied in the universal service army as the *ultima ratio regum*, ready to be used not merely against foreign enemies but also against groups that challenged the socioeconomic and political status quo. And there was yet another contradiction rooted in the existing liberal-capitalist system. Although the prewar boom was clearly driven by the market forces capitalism had unleashed, it proved difficult to achieve a better distribution of the material gains. Those who, in the competition for greater personal prosperity, got the short end of the stick perceived the persistent social inequalities as unjust and unacceptable. Since this was increasingly also an age of political participation by the "masses" and of an expansion of the suffrage that proved irreversible, feelings of bitterness turned into protests. They found support from political parties that agreed with the criticisms of existing socioeconomic conditions and translated them into programmatic demands for change.[10]

Parts of the propertied classes and their intellectual and political mouthpieces who were alarmed by these developments began to promote the idea of gradual reform, and in this they were joined by some more moderate leaders of the working-class movement. They had given up the notion of bringing about a social revolution toward which their more radical comrades were working. In their view, reforms should help overcome the most glaring inequalities and offer a more equitable sharing of the wealth being generated. To be sure, on the Left there were many who deemed capitalism constitutionally incapable of accepting and implementing such reforms. For them a fundamental change rather than reformism offered the only chance to rectify the material condition of the "masses." They viewed capitalism as a brutal system of exploitation of wage earners by the owners of the means of production to which the only response was the creation of a counterforce and ultimately an overthrow.

Fear of a "revolution from below," in which memories of the upheavals of 1789 in France, of 1848, especially in Central Europe, and of the short-lived Paris Commune of 1870–71 played an important role, mobilized the opposition not only to left-wing revolutionaries but also against bourgeois reformists. Various people proposed countering the demands for shared prosperity, greater social equality, and political participation with a policy of violent containment. In their eyes it was the main task of the police and judiciary, and as a last resort the army, to arrest the growth of the working-class movement and, if necessary, even destroy it. Assuming that this superior force would secure ultimate victory over the forces of radical change, they were even prepared to contemplate the possibility of civil war. The result was a polarization of politics in Europe before 1914, particularly in Central Europe, and the use of the repressive apparatus of the state against political demonstrations and strikes. When the suffragettes took their protest to the streets, they were dispersed by the police. Industrial workers who struck to demand higher wages and better working conditions were likewise roughed up and imprisoned. Since the demonstrators did not give up easily, there were injuries and even fatalities.[11] In short, while the societies of Europe became more complex and diverse, tensions and levels of violence increased.

3. However, not all those who saw a strategy of gradual reform within a liberal-capitalist market and civil society as no more than an invitation to the "masses" to advance further claims to participation favored the notion of a use of violence that would simply put the clock back. There were also influential voices who wanted to divert left-wing criticism of the hierarchical structures and injustices at home into the international system. In their eyes, overseas possessions opened up not only opportunities for sending the disaffected and disgruntled abroad as settlers, while increasing support among those who stayed behind by holding up to them the prospect of imperial

prestige and global influence, but also by promising them higher living standards thanks to the material gains from trade with the colonies.

The British entrepreneur Cecil Rhodes articulated this concept bluntly in 1895 when he remarked: "My cherished idea is a solution for the social problem, i.e., in order to save the 40,000,000 inhabitants of the United Kingdom from bloody civil war, we colonial statesmen must acquire lands to settle the surplus population, to provide new markets for the goods produced by them in the factories and mines. The Empire is a bread and butter question. If you want to avoid civil war, you must become imperialists."[12] In Germany, the naval officer and later navy minister Alfred Tirpitz wrote in a similar vein a year later, "In my view, Germany will in the coming century quickly sink back from its position as a great power if we do not push on now energetically, without losing time, and systematically with those general maritime interests [of ours], to no small degree also because the great national task and the economic gains that will come with it constitute a strong palliative against educated and uneducated Social Democrats."[13]

There can be no doubt that the export of millions of migrants to the colonies and to North America before 1914 helped reduce social tensions at a time of high European birthrates and hence the potential for violent conflicts within the industrializing societies of Europe. Otherwise it might have been difficult to find employment for all of them at home. At the same time they acted as a "white bridge" with their former homelands who were deemed to require military and naval protection abroad. Those who stayed behind were told that the colonies contributed to rising prosperity, even if in fact it was rather more a minority of businessmen who actually reaped the benefits.

Considering that the costs of ruling and administering vast stretches of land overseas had to be borne by the broad masses of taxpayers, it is not surprising that critics like Hobson doubted at the turn of the century, just as many economic historians did later, that the colonies were profitable for the national economies of Europe as a whole. They thought it better to use expenditures spent on the upkeep of colonies for raising domestic incomes and for infrastructural improvements as a way of stimulating consumption at home. A typical nineteenth-century reformer, Hobson aimed to solve the "social question" not by following Rhodes's recipe but by avoiding civil war by improving the lot of the mass of the population at home. Surmounting underconsumption within Britain (and by implication in Europe more generally) was tantamount to promoting internal and external peace and prosperous civilian lifestyles. Colonialism was for reformists like him merely grist for the mills of illiberal men who talked about putting up dams against the demands for greater social equality and political participation and were willing to use the physical power of the state.

However, the advocates of imperialism invented yet another justification for their quest. In their view, it was also a matter of bringing Christianity to the "primitive" peoples of Africa and Asia and with it an allegedly higher form of civilization. It was an argument that politicians, intellectuals, and churchmen liked to refer to in their speeches and writings. And here we are faced with yet another aspect of Europe's development before 1914 without a treatment of which it is difficult to understand why World War I broke out in August of that year and why the subsequent years saw an explosion of violence that badly undermined the beginnings, most clearly discernible in the United States, of a civilian society that peacefully consumed its mass-produced goods and had a political system that, despite many continuing injustices and inequalities, was in principle representative and constitutional.

THE CURSE OF ETHNONATIONALISM AND COLONIALISM

Historians and social scientists have debated at length the origins of modern imperialism and the emergence of colonial empires, especially from the eighteenth century onward. To avoid their critics' charge of putting forward crude generalizations and untenable theories, many of them more recently began to focus on the decades before 1914. The challenge was to explain why those decades witnessed a wild "scramble for colonies" in the course of which Africa and Asia were almost completely carved up among the European powers. At the same time the territories that were not directly occupied and settled remained or became part of so-called informal empires in which the metropolitan country wielded power and influence indirectly. Thus, the United States regarded large parts of Central and South America as their "backyard," even if they did not have their own troop contingents and administrators there. Instead they relied on the collaboration of local elite groups.

Searching for the deeper causes of the European "scramble for colonies" before 1914, scholars have pointed to the dynamic expansionist drive inherent in capitalist industrialism. The assumption was that from the years of retarded growth in the 1870s and 1880s businessmen were in constant search of opportunities abroad. When around 1895 the "Great Depression" was replaced by another period of rapid economic expansion and prosperity, the pressure to open up new markets and for raw materials intensified. Even if, as we have seen, most of the growth in trade took place among the industrial countries themselves, Africa and Asia remained important partly as recipients of European exports but above all as suppliers of raw materials at artificially low prices that the metropolitan industries turned into finished and high-value goods for the well-to-do classes but increasingly also for mass consumption.[14]

Apart from economic interests, nationalist and power-political rivalries must also be taken into consideration as propellants of the hectic acquisition of colonies in the late nineteenth century.[15] In light of the power and durability of the nation-state, much has also been written about nationalism as a force of societal and political integration. For a long time patriotic contemporaries but also subsequent generations of scholars viewed nationalism as a positive historical phenomenon. No doubt its achievements in overcoming localism and in bringing together people of diverse backgrounds, mentalities, and traditions have been impressive. This may be particularly true of the early phases of its development when it was still more cosmopolitan, accepting of ethnic difference, and hence less exclusive. Nationalism has also inspired many intellectuals and artists to produce major cultural works.[16]

However, if we contemplate the evolution of nationalism over the past two hundred years or so, the later balance sheet is rather more negative. Here the critics of the years before 1914 who advocated a tolerant internationalism and peaceful coexistence among the nations and warned against the dangers and the growing excesses of an exclusionary ethnonationalism that mushroomed in those decades have been proven right. What contributed to these excesses was the infusion of social Darwinist elements. There were those who, using Darwin's theory of the evolution of the species, began to interpret all human life as a ruthless "struggle for survival" in the course of which the strong subjugate the weak. For them it was but a small step to transpose this model not merely to the interactions of individual human beings but also to nations. Since the international system was basically anarchic and lacked any kind of central authority, nations were said to have no choice but to assert themselves within that system through power politics and the use of military force.[17]

The development of the science of genetics added a biological component to the notion of a power-political "struggle for survival." Even before the advent of social Darwinism, certain human communities and minority groups, inside and outside Europe, had been considered inferior. Genetics now gave this view a pseudoscientific foundation to support the notion of national superiority. Accordingly, the different European nations claimed to be genetically and culturally superior to their neighbors. Indeed, even within one's own society some intellectuals, academics, and politicians classified people as genetically inferior or superior. Here lie the origins of the pre-1914 eugenics movement that went as far as advocating the forced sterilization of men and women suspected of intergenerationally transmitted diseases and disabilities and of marginal people, the "asocials."

This became the credo of an ethnonationalism that, insofar as it was directed toward the inside, propagated both eugenicist and racist arguments against "asocials" and others, on the one hand, and ethnic minorities, on the other. Thus Jews, as an identifiable minority, became the target of a racist anti-Semitism in different parts of Europe. To be sure, they had previously been the victims of religious, social, and economic Judeophobia that had pervaded European society for centuries. It was rooted in the teachings of the Christian churches and Catholicism in particular that stigmatized Jews as the "murderers of Christ." Economic anti-Semitism also had a long tradition, turning Jews—especially in times of economic depression—into exploiters and usurers of impoverished non-Jewish peasants and craftsmen. Then came the pseudoscientific assertions of social Darwinism together with a biological racism that put them into a category as an allegedly inferior and dangerous group to justify their isolation and, as will be seen later, even their violent physical annihilation during the Holocaust.[18]

Judeophobes now invoked scientific research that "proved" Jews were genetically different and inferior. They were seen as "impurities" that poisoned the "blood" of the non-Jewish population. In short, Jews were not only used as scapegoats to explain personal or collective failure or economic difficulties by reference to the most outlandish conspiracy theories; they were also allocated an inferior place within a hierarchy of "races," a group that (like "asocials") endangered the genetic quality of the majority in whose midst they lived. Radical anti-Semites were prepared to use violent means to stop procreation and ultimately even to pursue the cold-blooded murder of all the Jews of Europe.

The notion that the world was divided into inferior and superior "races" was not only applied to the societies of Europe and its minorities, but also to Europeans' relations with the non-European world. Just as eugenics and anti-Semitism captured a growing section of the population in the years before 1914, people were also taken in by the classification of "races" on a global scale. In this picture, the idea that the "white races" were at the top of the scale proved particularly popular. Beneath them ranged the people of Asia and Africa, who were assumed to be culturally and economically as well as biologically inferior. Although by the end of the twentieth century all these theories were thoroughly discredited, the widespread acceptance of prejudices and stereotypes concerning the "primitive peoples" of other continents demonstrates how much headway social Darwinism and biological racism had made in Europe before World War I. Although in retrospect the ignorance of the complexities of non-European cultures' languages, religions, mentalities, and traditions was staggering, it was not confined to a few marginal scribblers whose pamphlets divided the world into superior and inferior "races." Slowly their ideas were becoming accepted by many Europeans as a way of imagining how humanity was structured.[19]

The final step the ethnonationalists took concerned their own national society in relation to their neighbors. It was self-evident to the Germans that they ranked above the British, French, or Italians, just as Italy, France, and Britain placed themselves above the Germans. Similarly, the Hungarians or Poles felt superior to their neighbors. To be sure, the Japanese or Chinese in the Far East had long established similar hierarchies, and their sense of superiority toward the Europeans helped them to ward off, at least for a while, European claims to domination and colonies in a kind of reverse ethnonationalism. If it did not work militarily or economically, it did so at least culturally. In Africa, by contrast, the invasion of ethnonationalist Europeans in the "scramble for colonies" was so profound that it not only destroyed the local economies and political systems but in many cases the culture and members of entire colonial societies.

The impact of European colonialism became the object of more extensive research after 1945. This research revealed, albeit slowly, just how devastating this impact had been on the non-European world, Africa in particular. We do not propose to go back to the centuries when millions of men and women were forced into slavery and shipped off to the Middle East or to South and North America. Here—as in this chapter more generally—our focus is on the decades before World War I and the policies of violence that Europeans pursued overseas at that time. Given that Britain had the largest colonial empire, London's practices of conquest and exploitation have long attracted historians' attention. They have analyzed how superior military technology was used to quell indigenous opposition to British colonial rule. There is the case of the Zulus of southern Africa who were mowed down by machine-gun fire when facing colonial troops with their spears and shields. The bloodbath was incredible, in some ways anticipating those on the western front during World War I.[20] The wars in East Africa are less well-known. The suppression of the so-called Maji-Maji uprising in German East Africa cost between 200,000 and 300,000 lives, if we include those who later died from the devastation and dislocation caused by Germany's colonial troops.[21] When we turn to the western parts of the continent there is the case of a small monarchy, Belgium, that deserves more detailed scrutiny before we turn to German policy in South-West Africa, today's Namibia.

In the early 1880s when other European nations acquired colonies all over the world, Leopold II, king of the Belgians, fixed his eyes on the inaccessible and largely unexplored Congo Basin. Through cunning diplomacy up to February 1885 and at the end of an international Congo conference held in Berlin, he succeeded in persuading the great powers, including the United States, to give him the huge territory of tropical rainforest in central Africa. Thanks to the energy of Henry Morton Stanley, the British explorer whom Leopold hired as his agent for the Congo, the king was able to conclude agreements with various indigenous tribes, which transferred land rights to him.[22]

What happened subsequently under Leopold's watch as "king sovereign" has been told most powerfully in Joseph Conrad's famous *Heart of Darkness*.

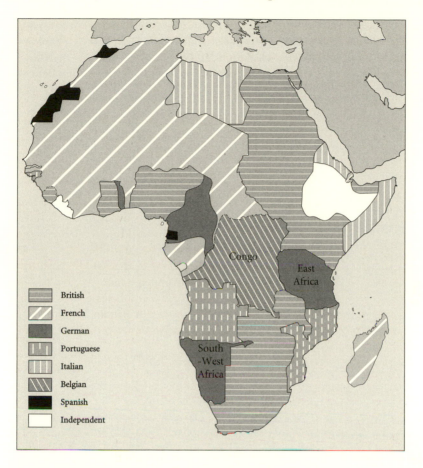

1. European colonial possessions in Africa before 1914

He summarized the conditions under Leopold's rule in four words: "The horror! The horror!" The motives of the king can be put even more simply: greed and the determination to exploit the region to the hilt for his gain. In addition to the mahogany and other precious woods, the Congo was rich in ivory and caoutchouc. The latter was much in demand before 1914 in Europe and North America where the bicycle boom increased demand for bicycle tubes followed, with the rise of the automobile, by a strong demand for car tires.

Although the inhabitants of the Congo time and again rose up against the brutality of Belgium's colonial troops, there was never, as in East or South-West Africa, a large-scale war. The millions of men, women, and children who died under Leopold's rule were victims of innumerable smaller expeditions and "pacifications" in the course of which torture, shootings, and killings with rifle butts were common. Those able to flee from the marauding troops often died from hunger or disease. Repeatedly abducted women and children were led away on what can only be described as death marches.

Details of those horrors are still difficult to come by. But we do have the following account by Ilanga, a woman from the eastern Congo who reported:

> The next morning soon . . . after the sun rose over the hill, a large band of soldiers came into the village, and we all went into the houses and sat down. We were not long seated when the soldiers came rushing in shouting, and threatening [chief] Niendo with their guns. They rushed into the houses and dragged the people out. Three or four came to our house and caught hold of me, also my husband Oleka and my sister Katinga. We were dragged into the road and were tied together with cords about our necks, so that we could not escape. We were all crying, for now we knew that we were to be taken away to be slaves. The soldiers beat us with the iron sticks from their guns and compelled us to march to the camp of Kibalanga, who ordered the women to be tied up separately, ten to each cord, and the men in the same way. When we were all collected—and there were many from other villages whom we now saw, and many from Waniendo—the soldiers brought baskets of food for us to carry, in some of which was smoked human flesh. . . . We then set off marching very quickly. My sister Katinga had her baby in her arms and was not compelled to carry a basket; but my husband Oleka was made to carry a goat. We marched until the afternoon when we camped near a stream, where we were glad to drink, for we were much athirst. We had nothing to eat, for the soldiers would give us nothing. . . . The next day we continued the march. . . . So it continued each day until the fifth day when the soldiers took my sister's baby and threw it in the grass, leaving it to die, and made her carry some cooking pots which they found in the deserted village. On the sixth day we became very weak from lack of food and from constant marching and sleeping in the damp grass, and my husband who marched behind us with the goat, could not stand up longer, and so he sat down beside the path and refused to walk more. The soldiers beat him, but he still refused to move. Then one of them struck him on the head with the end of his gun, and he fell upon the ground. One of the soldiers caught the goat, while two or three others stuck the long knives they put on the end of their guns into my husband. I saw blood spurt out, and then saw him no more, for we passed over the brow of a hill, and he was out of sight. Many of the young men were killed the same way, and many babies thrown into the grass to die."[23]

In her book *The Origins of Totalitarianism*, first published in 1951, Hannah Arendt offered an acute analysis of European colonialism and the racist-exterminationist forces behind it. Referring to Selwyn Jones's estimate, she wrote that some twelve million people perished in Leopold's Congo between 1890 and 1911.[24] More recently Adam Hochschild arrived at the figure of ten million dead during the period 1890–1920. Having closely studied the history of the Belgian Congo but also that of other parts of Africa, he concluded that "if you were to ask most Americans or Europeans what were the great totalitarian systems" of the twentieth century, "almost all would be likely to say: Communism and Fascism." However, there was, he continued, a third totalitarian system—"European colonialism—the latter imposed in its deadliest form in Africa. Each of the three systems asserted the right to control its subjects' lives; each was buttressed by an elaborate ideology; each perverted language in an Orwellian way; and each caused tens of millions of deaths."[25]

Writing in 1968, Helmut Bley similarly highlighted these elements of European colonialism in his study of German South-West Africa: "The balance of power in Africa opened the way for a dogmatizing [*Verabsolutierung*] of the ideas and methods of modern control." This, he added, led to a situation "in which the borderline with the totalitarian sphere had been transgressed" in South-West Africa. The colony "reached a stage in which all life chances of the Africans were subordinated to the will to rule and to the security interests" of the Europeans. Underlying these considerations was "the idea that the struggle would be conducted without the possibility of peace." Consequently, "the Germans set their system of domination in motion on the premise that the position as masters could not be justified and that giving a minimum of social and economic leeway would trigger a process of emancipation among the Africans." This is why they deployed "the socio-economic and socio-psychological insights of the time deliberately as instruments of domination." In this process, their point of orientation was rather more "the general notions of social conflict that they had adopted from Europe than a specific colonialist idea of racial inequality."[26]

Unlike in the Congo, violence escalated slowly in South-West Africa until it culminated in a genocidal war against the indigenous populations that was quite cold-bloodedly planned. In 1892 there had been a campaign against the Nama people. Thereafter, though, Theodor Leutwein, the governor and representative of the kaiser, tried hard to create a well-ordered system of governance in the colony in which the indigenous people would have a firm place, even if it was not one of equality. Unfortunately his efforts were undermined time and again by the demands of the white settlers from Germany. Their notions of legal titles to their properties clashed with the traditions of the semi-nomadic Herero who, by virtue of their own ancient traditions, had used the territory for the grazing of their large and roaming cattle herds. Wolfgang Eckart has described the situation as follows: "Reckless expropriations of land and the ruthless exploitation of the indigenous population through fraudulent usury had by the end of 1903 . . . created a state of affairs in which it was merely a question of time when the Herero would rise who had been pushed from their own land and soil and had been driven into economic dependency."[27]

When this point had finally been reached in 1904, the struggle of the Herero against the troops that Berlin dispatched ended in a catastrophe in which the victims were not merely the armed Herero warriors but also women, children, and the elderly. The Nama, whose fight in the south was more like a guerilla war, lost 35–50 percent of their people between 1892 and 1911; the figure for the Herero rose to almost 80 percent. Recent research has modified the older argument that the Germans brutally drove the Herero into the Omaheke Desert then hermetically sealed off the region and left entire families to die in the food- and waterless desert. Rather what seems to have happened is that some who fled eastward before the advancing German troops hoped to traverse the desert to Bechuanaland on paths that were known to them. But since there were so many of them, the relatively few watering holes on their way became overused and depleted, delivering thousands to their death. Others were slaughtered on the spot.

Those who fled westward and finally surrendered had their belongings and cattle confiscated before they were put into camps in which the death rate was around 45 percent. This meant that of some 15,000 captured Herero and 2,000 Nama a mere 7,700 survived.[28] There are no reliable figures on total losses, not least because the estimates of the size of the Herero population before the war vacillated between 35,000 and 100,000. German official statistics for 1911 give the total number of registered Herero as 15,000. If we merely use the lowest prewar estimates, this would mean that "more than a third of the Herero were killed or died as a result of the war."[29] The actual losses were probably much higher. This is also true of the Nama.

The behavior of the Germans raises two points that are relevant for the basic approach to this study in subsequent chapters and to the theme of violence. There is first of all the direct killing by the troops. Herero men, armed or unarmed, who fell into their hands were murdered without further ado. What differed from nineteenth-century conventional European warfare was that women and children were also summarily shot, often after abuse and torture. Those responsible for such actions appreciated that fundamental human norms were being violated and therefore tried to justify their actions. A white farmer who had shot a woman because she had stolen one of his sheep was asked by a judge why he felt it necessary to use lethal force. He replied: "Should we simply subject ourselves to theft?" His defense attorney then used the term "vermin" that, however ominous as a harbinger of the racism that was to come, was not unusual for this time and, as we have seen, related to the proliferating biological perceptions of human society. Planted in the mind of an ordinary white settler of European background, it was used to justify exploitation and murder.[30]

At the height of the campaign against the Herero other outrageous but typical rumors began to circulate about native women who cruelly mutilated white captives and dead soldiers. These rumors in turn were used to justify

German atrocities. A German military doctor has left a description of scenes that were widespread during this war: "Bloodily glittering bayonets in their hands, blood-splattered uniforms: around them piles of culled enemies, wailing women, screaming children, and bleating cattle."[31] The torturing of the survivors then continued in the camps. Joachim Zeller has recently published an essay on the Swakopmund Camp with horrific photos.[32] The title of his article ("Hundreds were driven to their deaths like cattle and [then] buried like cattle") is taken from a report by a missionary. The report added that it was hardly possible to exaggerate the "crudity" and the "brutal behavior as masters [*Herrentum*]" that its author had witnessed.

During the most murderous period the daily death toll at Swakopmund from undernourishment and hard slave labor was around thirty. Whoever survived these conditions continued to be without legal protection and was subjected to whipping. The rape of women was also common. As Zeller demonstrates by reference to the cynical descriptions at the bottom of his photos, camp supervisors had a "disdain for human beings that was motivated by racism." This disdain can also be seen in the way the skulls of fallen or murdered Hereros were treated. Herero women were forced to clean the skulls of skin with bits of broken glass. They were then collected for racist anatomical research and sent to institutes in Germany.

That something horrendous had happened in German South-West Africa in 1904 during the encounter between the Europeans and the indigenous populations can also be gauged from the ambivalent reports of some of the soldiers involved in the campaign. Here we find, next to descriptions of massacres, doubts about the "heroic" exploits of the colonial troops. With respect and even admiration they write about the tall and slender figures of the Herero warriors who did not fit the stereotypes of inferior "negroes" they had picked up back home. Physicians seem to have felt pangs of conscience as well. Wavering between pity and a heart of stone, one of them wrote: "They are a genuine calamity, those amputated blacks. They haven't learned anything, they cannot work, and if, after their wounds have healed, they are discharged into the street, they just starve to death. Consequently they stay here and are fed with the others. Soon the state will even have to build homes for cripples."[33]

However, in order to grasp what happened in Africa under European colonial rule, we must also deal, apart from the mentalities and attitudes of the perpetrators, with those of their superiors and commanding officers. To begin with, there is Leutwein's dilemma that reflects the failure of his attempt to establish order and stability between 1894 and the outbreak of the war ten years later and that explains why he was replaced by Lieutenant General Lothar von Trotha. "A persistent colonial policy," he wrote, "no doubt requires the killing of all prisoners capable of bearing arms." He himself would not resort to such methods. Nor, however, would he reprimand the person who would do so. After all, "colonial policy is basically an inhuman matter. And ultimately it can only lead to a deterioration of the rights of the indigenous population in favor of those who forced their way in. Whoever does not agree with this, must be an opponent of colonial policy in general—a position that is at least logical." At the same time, Leutwein continued, "it is not right, on the one hand, to deprive the natives of their land on the basis of questionable agreements and for this purpose to gamble with the life and health of fellow-citizens on the ground and, on the other, to praise [the virtues of] humanity in the Reichstag, such as some Reichstag deputies have done."[34]

Trotha, Leutwein's successor, was not hampered by such inhibitions. After his victory over the Herero in October 1904, he published a proclamation that bluntly articulated European inhumanity: "The Herero are no longer German subjects. They have been murdering, thieving; [they] have cut off the ears, noses, and other body parts and now no longer want to fight because of cowardice." Accordingly, "every Herero whether he is caught with or without a rifle, with or without cattle," was to be shot. He continued, "I shall no longer accommodate women and children, drive them back to their own people or give orders that they be shot at. . . . [Signed:] The great general of the powerful."[35]

These words, it must be admitted, were a bit too much for Germany's Reich chancellor Bernhard von Bülow, who had himself coined a few aggressive slogans when it came to selling German expansionist *Weltpolitik*. But Bülow's qualms did not prevent Trotha from issuing another order to his troops in which he promised his men a bonus for each Herero killed. Only when it came to women, he added, should they aim above the target's head. Since his order presumably meant that "no more male prisoners would be taken," his troops' violent practices were not to turn into "atrocities against women and children." In other words, he was not prepared to erase the line between combatants and civilians completely. However, as we have seen, in reality all Hereros were treated as outlaws to be liquidated. It did not make much difference that Bülow, sitting in Berlin, began to worry about the public criticism that Trotha's radicalism might unleash back home. Consequently, he asked the kaiser as supreme commander of all German troops to countermand Trotha's orders because they "contradicted all Christian and humanitarian principles."

The tension between those who wanted to uphold some standards of humanity and those who were prepared to abandon them—a tension, as we shall see, that began to weaken in the second half of World War I and had disappeared by the time of World War II—also emerges when we juxtapose Bülow's attitudes with those of Alfred von Schlieffen, chief of the General Staff. He, the father of the battle of annihilation (discussed below), was much more a kindred spirit of Trotha when he wrote that the commander of South-

West Africa needed to be supported if he "wants to destroy the entire [Herero] nation or drive it out of the territory. After what has happened, it will be very difficult for the blacks to live together with the whites, if the former are not to be kept permanently in a state of forced labor, i.e., in a kind of slavery." Consequently, "the race war that has broken out can only be concluded with the annihilation of one party."[36] A retrospective report, produced by the General Staff two years later, came to the conclusion, "The waterless Omaheke [Desert] was to complete what German arms had begun: the annihilation of the Herero people."

Such statements raise the question as to whether the war in South-West Africa was genocidal not merely in its practice at the front but also in intent when we consider the orders the troops received. Many historians have answered this question in the affirmative; others have rejected this notion. Gesine Krüger has recently tried to distance the atrocities in the colonies before 1914 somewhat from the Nazi "Final Solution of the Jewish Question" in World War II. However, by referring to the definitions of genocide that Zygmunt Bauman and other social scientists developed, she, too, concludes that what happened in German South-West Africa was genocide. Tilman Dedering has compared the behavior of the colonial troops to that of the Wehrmacht in eastern Europe during World War II.[37]

Two aspects must be added to these recent verdicts by historians in light of the criticism that the war against the Herero encountered in the Reichstag at the time. Both of them point to the violent experience Europe underwent in the future. The liberal economist Moritz Bonn wrote in 1909—and hence long before he had to flee from Hitler's dictatorship—"As long as there are still people who deem such policies as necessitated by Nature, the danger will persist that they may also be used in other places. If the mistakes of Trotha's colonial policy can be surrounded with a theoretical halo, nothing will protect us from it being repeated."[38] Bonn probably did not have the faintest notion then that Europe itself might one day be one of those "other places." Given that violence no longer had any boundaries, Bley pointed to the double boomerang effect of colonialism in and after World War I. In his view, the Germans approached South-West Africa initially with attitudes that "were rooted in the social unrest of contemporary Europe." Later the "methods of treating human beings" practiced in the colonies ricocheted back "into the motherland."[39]

Bley's thoughtful though depressing argument, derived form his study of colonialism, leads us back to Europe. Violence in the colonies, whether British, Belgian, German, French, or Italian, had assumed forms before 1914 that "consumed" not just combatants but also civilians. The next question to be investigated is what kinds of images of warfare Europeans developed concerning their own part of the world before total war hit them with real force after 1914.

PREMONITIONS OF TOTAL WAR

Given the complexities that marked the societies of pre-1914 Europe, it is not surprising that its inhabitants held very different views about a future war. At the one end of the spectrum stood the confirmed pacifists who worked for "a world without war." The size of their organizations varied considerably from country to country. Roger Chickering, in a book that deals with the German Peace Society but is to some extent conceived within a comparative framework, has advanced the hypothesis that the relative numerical weakness of pacifist movements in Germany before 1914 mirrored the much greater attractiveness of associations that—though not always actively promoting war—nevertheless agitated for the preparation of war in the form of ever more exorbitant armaments expenditures.[40] He adds that the balance was tilted less in favor of militaristic forces, for example, in Britain and France.

In addition to the small number of pure pacifists, there was a larger group of liberals who did not reject war and violence as a matter of principle, but viewed military conflicts as self-destructive and therefore impossible to justify rationally, at least as far as the great powers that had fully developed industries and were involved in international trade were concerned. In Britain, the "first industrial nation," Richard Cobden and John Bright argued as early as the mid-nineteenth century that war and industry were incompatible. Similar points were later made by liberals such as Herbert Spencer and Norman Angell, whose books were widely discussed and translated into other European languages. As mentioned in the introduction, Spencer had put forward the notion of two opposing types of society. The "militant" type was geared toward confrontation and struggle. It required centralization and the integration as well as subordination of the individual to the community. The other "industrial" type embodied a system in which the individuality of the citizen was defended and upheld against the state. Unlike the "militant" type, its raison d'être did not revolve around the preparation of war and violent expansion but around peaceful industrial production and trade.[41]

Angell in his best-selling *The Great Illusion: A Study of the Relation of Military Power in Nations to Their Economic and Social Advantage*, an expanded version of his *Europe's Optical Illusion* and published in 1910, added the idea that the interdependencies that industry, commerce, and banking had created between the nations had become so great that war between them was no longer thinkable. Such a war, he warned, would disrupt the flow of peaceful trade and the production of civilian goods to such an extent that even the victors in a military conflict would in effect be among the losers. This insight, he thought, would in the future keep the great powers from entering into war with each other. They would all recognize the greater benefits of peaceful exchange, consumption, and prosperity for all. If there were dangers of war they emanated, according to Angell, from countries that lagged behind the progressive nations in the development of trade and industry. Once they had joined the circle of the latter, major wars would be phenomena of the past.[42] In the meantime, structures of international law, mediation, and conflict resolution needed to be developed.

These views were diametrically opposed to those of other contemporaries who regarded war as something evitable in human affairs. They saw war as the "father of all things" that contained both destructive and creative forces. Next to them were those who believed that an anarchistic international system that lacked a central authority and was propelled by social Darwinist power politics required constant vigilance. However, contrary to the radical militarists, they justified the demand for relentless war preparation with defensive arguments. The problem was that in the last years before 1914 their positions were articulated more and more aggressively so that through their propaganda they contributed to the sharpening of international tensions. In these circumstances a serious diplomatic crisis could easily be deepened by the martial posturing of nationalist associations and the right-wing press. This would in turn put pressure on governments to rattle their sabers. Suddenly, the political decision makers would find themselves in a conflict that might spin out of control. A chain reaction of this kind was, as we shall see, in fact set in motion in July 1914.

Between the pacifists and liberals, on the one hand, and the militarists and social Darwinists, on the other, stood the majority of ordinary citizens who could be mobilized for a defense of the fatherland to ward off an unprovoked attack, but no more. Finally, there were the large number of workers whose basic attitudes toward society and politics had come under the influence of the growing socialist movements. Unless they explicitly subscribed to a social democratic reformism, they did not reject revolutionary violence in principle; but with respect to the danger of a major war, they tended to set their hopes in the solidarity of the workers' International. By appealing to the masses, The International would prevent a war between the advanced industrial countries in which the workers, drafted into the universal service armies, would be the cannon fodder and first victims of mass slaughter.[43]

It is instructive to look at the images of war discussed among the people of Europe and among military experts in the decades before 1914 against the backdrop of these divergent attitudes toward war and violence. As far as the overwhelming majority of the population is concerned, it is safe to assume that they believed the next war would be similar to the previous one. To be sure, this was a naive view that did not take into account the changes in technology and military organization that had since occurred. Although these changes had been considerable in the late nineteenth century, many Europeans nevertheless thought that a future war would look like the Franco-German conflict of 1870–71: there would be a clash of two large armies in which the stronger side would be victorious after a short while. These were the memories of the Franco-German war that were not applicable any longer, even at the end of that conflict. Yet, the fact that it had ultimately become a "people's war" was repressed by the myth of a short "cabinet war."

This myth is one of the reasons why Europe's men joined up in large numbers in the summer of 1914 when their leaders called on them to defend the fatherland. Almost all of them were convinced that they would be home again by Christmas of that year.[44] If they had had a better understanding of what industrialized warfare of the twentieth century would be like, the recruits would probably have volunteered much more reluctantly and many might even have resisted being sent to the front.

Popular conceptions of future warfare were not merely the product of discussions among the regulars in pubs or of increasingly hazy memories of the Franco-Prussian War. They also appeared in novels, in short stories, and in serialized accounts in magazines that were read by a growing number of ordinary citizens in pre-1914 Europe. But such fictionalized speculations hardly reflected what was to come in World War I. True, there were the studies of the *guerre en ballon* and the deployment of new weapons. In Britain around the turn of the century a genre emerged that focused on the impending invasion of the British Isles, whether by ship or through a tunnel that had been secretly dug under the English Channel. By and large, these stories were geared more toward satisfying a demand for heroic exploits or a widespread enthusiasm for modern technology and its feats. They rarely gave a realistic picture of industrialized warfare.

Apart from Albert Robidas's more ironic depictions, it was above all the well-known British writer H. G. Wells and the Polish-French banker and amateur historian Jean de Bloch who succeeded in painting a more accurate picture. Wells's predictions were suffused with social Darwinist ideas about struggle, but he recognized the destructive potential of modern military technology. In August 1909, for example, he published an article in *Mc-Clure's Magazine* in which he postulated that the invention of the airship would lead to tangible changes in the conduct of war. There were also visions of war "a mile above earth, between corps of artillery firing into huge bodies of inflammable gas, where the defeated plunge down to the ground a mass of charred pulp, [that] will become a thing too spectacularly horrible for conception. Will civilization permit it to exist? Or does this new machine mean the end of war?"[45]

However, the thinker who probably came closest to anticipating correctly the terrible reality of World War I was de Bloch. In no less than six volumes he not only examined the lethal power of weapons that had been developed since 1871, the machine-gun among them; his volumes also contain statistical analyses before he provides the following description of a future war between the great powers:

> At first there will be increased slaughter—increased on so terrible a scale as to render it impossible to get troops to push the battle to a decisive issue. They will try to, thinking that they are fighting under the old conditions, and they will learn such a lesson that they will abandon the attempt forever. Then, instead of a war fought out to the bitter end in a series of decisive battles, we shall have as a substitute a long period of continually increasing strain upon the resources of the combatants. The war, instead of being a hand-to-hand contest in which the combatants measure their physical and moral superiority, will become a kind of stalemate, in which, neither army being able to get at the other, both armies will be maintained in opposition to each other, threatening each other, but never able to deliver a final decisive attack."[46]

Although not many ordinary people read Bloch's lengthy depictions of the war that was to hit Europe in 1914, others were not naïve. In addition to the military, international lawyers had also considered the evolution of warfare since the early modern period. The first of them wrote in the wake of the Thirty Years War and its catastrophic consequences. For them, and for Hugo Grotius, one of the most eminent among them, there were two central questions: how and with what mechanisms might it be possible to prevent similar conflicts from happening again, and second, what principles and rules had to be put in place to regulate war if its outbreak could not be avoided and to contain excesses and atrocities of the kind that had devastated large parts of Central Europe between 1618 and 1648.[47]

It is significant that these questions relating to conflict prevention receded into the background during the eighteenth and nineteenth centuries. International lawyers were more concerned with establishing, refining, and enforcing new laws that would govern the treatment of wounded enemy soldiers, prisoners of war, and, not least, noncombatants. It had become increasingly clear that women, children, and the elderly were not firmly protected against wartime violence. There was also the question of who was a combatant and who was a civilian and of the criteria that differentiated them.

If the protection of civilians grew weaker in the years leading up to 1914, this was due not only to the fact that the borderline between combatants and noncombatants had already disappeared in the colonies, as we have seen in the treatment of indigenous people in Africa, it was also because military professionals began to recognize the increasing totality of a war that might occur in Europe in the future that would "inevitably" also engulf civilians. In Hans Morgenthau's later definition, in the eyes of some experts war had become even before 1914 a war of total populations against total populations for total stakes.[48]

Thus, the military responded differently than the populations of Europe, who were fascinated by serialized stories of underwater invasions or battles in the skies or who fantasized in the alehouse over their fifth glass of beer. Among these experts was Field Marshal Helmuth von Moltke, whose strategy had defeated the French in 1870–71 and who continued as chief of the General Staff in united Germany. He never forgot that that conflict had turned, in its final phases, into a "people's war" that had been propelled by the passions of modern nationalism. Its genie that had been let out of the bottle in the wars of liberation against Napoleon I in 1814–15 had more or less been successfully put back into the bottle at that point. But in the 1860s, if not before, it had reappeared. Worse from the point of view of upholding the idea of conventional warfare between two hostile armies, a "people's war" in 1870 was no longer just the mass mobilization of soldier-citizens; it had also seen the emergence of the franc-tireurs and the involvement of large parts of the civilian population.

This time around, Moltke still succeeded in curbing the outbreak of massive popular resistance and in enforcing the peace that the French signed at Versailles. But as the experience of the short-lived Paris Commune had also demonstrated, this was no longer the age of cabinet wars. Moltke took away a dramatic lesson from this experience: future wars between great powers must never be allowed to degenerate into a long war of attrition. Conflict had to be brief and geared toward the total destruction of the enemy within a limited time and by using the latest weapons, technology, and railroads. However, toward the end of his years of service Moltke had come to the pessimistic conclusion that, given its location in the heart of Europe and threatened by a war on two fronts, Germany had little prospect of winning a lightning war of annihilation. This meant that the more important task for him became securing and maintaining peace.[49]

His successors had listened attentively to the old field marshal as far as the strategic preparation of total war was concerned; but they could not follow him in the pacifist conclusions that he drew from his assessment of the geopolitical situation of the country.[50] This is why they continued to prepare for a European war and tried to escape from the danger of a war of attrition from which no one would emerge victorious by concentrating on the idea of a particularly brutal and swift hammer blow. Moltke's successors were Alfred von Schlieffen, whose attitudes toward annihilation we have cited above in connection with the war in South-West Africa, and the old field marshal's nephew of the same name. In two ways they drove German strategic thinking to the extreme. To begin with, Schlieffen, who after the French and Russians had concluded their alliance in 1893 reckoned with a war on two fronts, first conceived of an operations plan that his successor,

Helmuth von Moltke, then implemented in July 1914: under violation of Belgian neutrality and thereby circumventing the northern fortifications on France's eastern border, he proposed to defeat France in a lightning war. After this, he wanted to move his troops quickly to the east to annihilate the Russians in a second strike who, due to the slowness and inefficiency of the tsarist war machine, would not pose a serious immediate danger to Germany and its ally Austria-Hungary.

Second, Schlieffen, and Moltke even more so, became obsessed with the idea that the element of surprise was crucial, even if the projected mass mobilization of soldiers could not be kept secret for long. This required the meticulous preparation of the train timetables with the help of which tens of thousands of soldiers would be transported to the Belgian border in a very short time, but this also almost inevitably forced Moltke to prepare for a preventive war in which even the most elementary rules of existing international law would be pushed aside. To justify these violations he had to invoke the higher interest of the nation, whose survival was allegedly lethally threatened by the French and Russians. Accordingly, he accepted the invasion of small neutral countries, Belgium and Luxembourg, without long-winded declarations of war and the swiftest advance westward through Belgium. It was a strategy that tried to evade the consequences of a "people's war" in the age of the "people's war" by proceeding with devastating force and speed.

However, to understand the "primordial catastrophe" of the twentieth century that was unleashed in Europe in August 1914, one must realize that this kind of thinking also spread among the general staffs of the other great powers. The French spoke of the *attaque brusque*, and General Ferdinand Foch thought that the machine-gun was an excellent offensive weapon—until he had to recognize that in the age of industrialized warfare it was in fact a terrible weapon in the hands of the defense. Although Moltke assumed the Russian army was a lumbering juggernaut, tsarist officers, too, planned a war of annihilation. This was also true of Franz Conrad von Hötzendorf, the chief of the General Staff of the Habsburg forces.

How widespread these assumptions had become by the turn of the century can also be seen when we look at the evolution of naval strategy. As late as the mid-1890s the "cruiser school" still dominated naval thinking in Europe. In the age of imperialism, naval warfare would not occur in home waters but as raids against the coasts of faraway enemy colonies. This required the construction of fast cruisers. But once the concept of annihilation had swept the board in the armies of Europe, its radiating influence proved so powerful that it was slowly also adopted among the navies of the great powers. The cruiser, with its range and speed, was replaced by battleships with larger guns and heavier armor. They would meet in the home waters for a decisive do-or-die battle in which the war at sea would be decided virtually in one afternoon through the annihilation of the enemy fleet.[51]

This change in strategic thinking triggered naval arms races—above all the one between the British Royal Navy and the German Imperial Navy—in which one side tried to outbuild the other in the number of battleships. The Anglo-German race continued from the turn of the century until about 1911–12, when it became clear that London had in effect won the naval arms competition with Berlin. The fleet that Tirpitz had constructed was too weak to face the Royal Navy in that much vaunted decisive battle in the North Sea, as became clear in 1916 during the Battle of Jutland. However, the end of the Anglo-German naval arms race did not mean that the specter of a future war between the great powers receded into the background. Rather the competition was transferred to the European continent and turned into an arms competition on land. It strengthened the hand of the army general staffs and increased their propensity to contemplate a violent way out of the growing international impasse before 1914. They even contemplated a preventive campaign of annihilation before the other side had become too strong to make a lightning war victory unlikely. It might be said, therefore, that Moltke's and de Bloch's warnings were taken seriously, but in a somewhat paradoxical way: the "people's war" of attrition that everyone thought could no longer be won was to be avoided with the help of a swift all-or-nothing blow.

Ordinary citizens and the military thus had vastly different concepts about what a future European war might entail. The army and navy staffs had integrated into their plans not only the latest weapons developments and improved transport capacities but also the experience of the "people's war," and the lessons learned from the various colonial wars. The preparation for war was now focused on the application of overwhelming force, which would result in a short, ruthless, and total war.

However, what would happen if the strategy of annihilation proved too risky and if the danger of a war of attrition was greater than was militarily and politically acceptable? In that case would it not have been wiser to return to the elder Moltke's position of trying, at all costs, to secure and preserve peace? Against the background of this question we shall first have to investigate the situation just before the outbreak of war in 1914 before turning to the forms of violence that subsequently became the hallmark of World War I and to the escalation of which Europe saw no end until 1945.

CHAPTER TWO

Violence Unleashed, 1914–1923

MOBILIZATION, 1914

Scholarship on the outbreak of World War I had long been dominated by the view that all European nations slid over the brink into the abyss almost without realizing what was happening to them. In the 1960s, the Hamburg University historian Fritz Fischer once again raised a question that had been asked soon after 1918 by scholars on the Allied side: should the German government bear exclusive responsibility for the outcome of the July Crisis of 1914? His arguments triggered a vigorous international debate and stimulated a wave of fresh and in-depth research. Feeling that the Fischer debate focused too one-sidedly on Germany's share, other historians, a number of British and American scholars among them, subsequently investigated the responsibility of the other participant countries and their governments with great vigor. In this context, the policies of the Habsburg empire also attracted renewed attention.

Although recent work has concluded that Russia, Britain, and France also bear a certain responsibility for the events of 1914, the overall picture that emerged during the Fischer debate has not changed so greatly as to make another major revision necessary.[1] This has occurred despite the fact that Gregor Schöllgen and Klaus Hildebrand have tried to remind us of Britain's hegemonic position and the failure of the decision makers in London to integrate the rising and restive German empire into the international system.[2] But it seems that not even these arguments have overthrown the new scholarly consensus that those primarily responsible for unleashing World War I must be sought in Berlin and Vienna. Whoever wants to analyze the July Crisis of 1914 and the immediate origins of the conflict does not have to stop at each of the capitals of Europe but can confidently begin with the two Central European monarchies and their key decision makers. They were responsible for the sharpening of international tensions after the assassination of Archduke Ferdinand and his wife in Sarajevo on 28 June 1914. They also refused to de-escalate the crisis once it threatened to end in a shooting war although they held in their hands the diplomatic keys to do so.

What continues to be debated are the motives that drove Berlin and Vienna to pursue a policy of violence and to what extent the decision makers were of one mind as the crisis unfolded. In this respect, Fischer developed the hypothesis, which he put in ever more pointed terms in subsequent years, that from the start the aim was to trigger a major European war. After discovering documents relating to the so-called War Council of 8 December 1912, he even went so far as to assert that the conflict had been decided upon and subsequently prepared for after that fateful meeting in Berlin. The assassinations at Sarajevo, he continued, merely provided the hoped for pretext to strike and implement the Schlieffen Plan. Fischer even doubted that there were any civilian "doves" in the German government, and if there were, they were quickly shunted into the sidelines by the military "hawks." Once the objective of a general settling of accounts with France and Russia had been agreed upon between Berlin and Vienna, the causal line from the meeting between Wilhelm II and the Austrian envoy, Alexander Count von Hoyos, at which the former issued his infamous "blank check" to Vienna to the mobilization orders and declarations of war at the end of the month, ran, in Fischer's view, pretty straight.[3]

Other historians have pleaded for a more differentiated view of these events. They believe that a more moderate political strategy was agreed upon at the beginning of July. The plan was to initiate a limited offensive in the Balkans. It was supposed to start with an ultimatum to Serbia followed by a lightning campaign against Belgrade, in the course of which the precarious position of the multinational Habsburg empire, besieged as it was by its Slavic groups, would be restabilized. This scenario, drawn up by Germany's Reich chancellor Theobald von Bethmann Hollweg, was—so the argument continues—initially accepted by the military "hawks." It was based on the assumption that Russia and France would not intervene on the side of the Serbs. Only when this strategy turned out to be based on miscalculations— the other great powers could not be kept out of the Austro-Serbian conflict— did the generals seize the reins and inexorably steer Germany and Austria-Hungary into a great war.

Judging from the many new documents that have been unearthed in the context of the Fischer debate, this second interpretation seems to be the more plausible one. There is, first of all, the Viennese side of the picture in which Conrad, the chief of the General Staff, wanted to go to war against Serbia right after the assassinations at Sarajevo. But Emperor Francis Joseph, his minister president, Karl Count von Stürgkh, and his Hungarian counterpart, Stefan Count Tisza, decided to wait. In the meantime, news reached them from Berlin that Wilhelm II supported the Habsburg monarchy in its attempt to defend its vital interests and encouraged action against Belgrade. To find out if this was true, on 5 July Francis Joseph sent Count Hoyos to Berlin where the kaiser assured him that Germany would stand by its ally if it wanted to punish Serbia for its alleged part in the assassination.

In doing so, Wilhelm's advisors realized that there might be a chain reaction and hence a major war if Russia, in response to an Austro-Hungarian move against Serbia, felt obliged to honor its role as a protector of fellow

Slav countries such as Serbia. Moltke may have thought of an immediate escalation of this kind, but on 5 July he and his colleagues were prepared to wait and see if the limited war strategy would have the desired result of Serbian humiliation and Austro-Hungarian stabilization. When Admiral Eduard von Capelle visited Wilhelm II on 6 July, the day after the "blank check" had been issued, the latter told him that a Russian intervention was unlikely. The tsar would not wish to condone the assassinations. Nor was Russia militarily and financially prepared for a confrontation with Vienna and Berlin. France, in his view, would not become involved in a conflict in the Balkans. Bethmann, it is true, was more pessimistic than Wilhelm II and appreciated the dangers of a Balkan war from the start. However, he seems to have assumed that the limited war strategy had a good chance of success, provided Vienna created a swift fait accompli in Belgrade and then called an international conference to provide an imprimatur for the shift in the balance of power in the Balkans.[4]

This was also Moltke's understanding of the situation in early July. He did not interrupt his summer vacation and opined that Austria-Hungary would defeat Serbia quickly and make peace long before the other powers had a chance to intervene. Further indications that the German military was prepared to give Bethmann's plan a chance came from the Prussian war minister Erich von Falkenhayn and Alfred von Waldersee, the quartermaster general, when both of them left Berlin on 5 July to go on vacation. That Berlin did not think of an immediate great war is finally demonstrated by Wilhelm II himself. He, too, left Berlin immediately after his meeting with Hoyos to take his yacht on a long-planned cruise off the coast of Norway. The Reich chancellor and his civilian advisors were therefore left on their own to oversee the limited war strategy.

Its success depended, of course, primarily on a swift agreement on the text of the proposed ultimatum to Belgrade within the Austro-Hungarian camp. It would then be handed to the Serbs without delay, and the anticipated rejection would enable Vienna to justify an invasion that everyone expected to end in a quick victory. If, on the other hand, the handing over of the ultimatum took weeks rather than days, the other powers were bound to suspect that the two Central European monarchies were using the assassinations as a pretext to implement more ambitious aims. The trouble was that by the middle of July, the decision makers in Vienna still had not been able to agree on the text of the ultimatum. Tisza, above all, wanted to give Belgrade a list of demands and issue an ultimatum only if the Serbs refused to fulfill them. Moreover, he sought assurances that the emperor and his colleagues did not aim to destroy Serbia. This, in his view, was the only way to keep the Russians out since St. Petersburg would never permit the extinction of Serbia.

When these differences of opinion reached Berlin, Bethmann urged Vienna to expedite matters. It was at this time that he began to talk to Kurt Riezler, his private secretary, about a "leap into the dark" that the decisions of the first days of July amounted to. It was a risk that the Reich chancellor thought was still acceptable, especially if compared to the gamble that Moltke began two weeks later. At the same time it became increasingly clear that the German analysis of the possible responses of France and Russia had been very superficial. Still, it was presumably not completely illusory to assume that an early move by Vienna might keep the other great powers out of an Austro-Serbian conflict, even if the localization strategy involved the invasion of a sovereign country that was merely suspected of being behind the assassinations in Sarajevo. At this stage at least there was no firm proof of the involvement of Serb authorities. In short, when devising his plan on 5 July Bethmann certainly did not realize that it would take until 23 July, almost four weeks after Sarajevo, before the ultimatum was finally handed over in Belgrade.[5]

That Berlin grew increasingly nervous is evidenced not only by Bethmann's remarks and maneuvers, but also by those of Gottlieb von Jagow, the state secretary in the Foreign Ministry. He appeared insecure and incoherent when Rear Admiral Paul Behncke, the deputy chief of the Admiralty Staff, visited him on 20 July. Jagow speculated that Britain might stay neutral and suggested that Germany should threaten London with the occupation of The Netherlands, should they contemplate entering the war. Five days later and soon after the publication of the ultimatum to Serbia, it became clear that Berlin and Vienna's localization strategy had been built on sand. When Sergei Sazonov, the Russian foreign minister, met with the tsar on 25 July he suspected that the aim of the ultimatum, which he believed had the support of the Germans, was to wipe Serbia off the map. The Russian crown council reacted by ordering the preparation of the partial mobilization for the military districts of Odessa, Kiev, Moscow, and Kazan.

This meant that when Moltke returned from his vacation on 26 July it was fairly clear that the localization plan of 5 July had failed. However, as we saw in the previous chapter, this did not lead him to heed the advice of his uncle, who had warned against a "people's war" and counseled the preservation of peace in order to prevent a catastrophe. Instead his nephew began to prepare a short and hard hammer-blow encapsulated in the Schlieffen Plan to which he, as Schlieffen's successor, had made several modifications in recent years. In other words, his response to the Russian partial mobilization was to pull out his full-fledged operations plan against France. There was no other choice because Moltke had shelved an earlier operations plan against Russia and decided to rely exclusively on Schlieffen's concept of a swift defeat of France in the west before turning east against France's ally, the Russians. The western offensive included the invasion of Belgium, which ensured that Britain, the guarantor of neutral Belgium's independence, would also be drawn into the war.

We have also seen that this plan of a massive application of military force had the marks of a preventive war. It was clear that the German army was numerically inferior to its enemies. The element of surprise was to make up for this weakness. But the idea of a sudden strike also came from the conviction that the Russian and French forces would be even stronger by 1915–16. After all, Paris and St. Petersburg had reacted to the two army bills that the Germans had ratified in 1912 and 1913 by enlarging their own armies. After this, the imbalance of forces between the two hostile camps was even greater in favor of the Triple Entente of France, Russia, and Britain.

The army expansions that both sides had introduced in 1912–13 worried both Moltke and Conrad well before July 1914. It was a talking point when the two of them met at Marienbad in the spring of 1914. After his return to Berlin, Moltke had become even more pessimistic. In a conversation with Jagow he described the situation as follows: "The prospects of the future seriously worried him. Russia will have completed her armaments in 2 to 3 years. The military superiority of our enemies would be so great then that he did not know how we might cope with them. Now we would still be more or less a match for them. In his view, there was no alternative to waging a preventive war in order to defeat the enemy as long as we could still more or less pass the test. The chief of the General Staff left it at my discretion to gear our policy to an early unleashing of a war."[6]

This was the strategy that had been put on the back burner in early July 1914 and to which Moltke now returned on 26 July. In Berlin and Vienna it was thenceforth the military who called the shots, pushing aside civilians and taking an even greater risk than Bethmann had done with his localization plan. They knew that this war was militarily justifiable only if it could be won in the west within a few weeks, to be followed by a successful campaign against the slow-moving Russians in the east. Historians have assumed that the decision to trigger a major war by Berlin and Vienna was still based on the calculation, however weak, that victory was attainable. But an even more somber picture emerged from research by the Berne University historian Stig Förster. When Vienna, having announced that Belgrade had failed to fulfill the ultimatum, invaded Serbia, Moltke wrote to Bethmann that a "world war" would result "in the mutual destruction of the European culture states" and that "the culture of all of Europe" would be devastated "for decades to come."[7]

Worse, Förster continued, earlier research had failed to see "that Moltke did have realistic conceptions of the catastrophic character of the impending war. The chief of the General Staff and many of his collaborators did not believe that the troops would be home again by Christmas 1914. That they nevertheless embarked upon a suicidal mission and produced a catastrophe fully conscious of what they were doing can only be defined as criminal irresponsibility." In this sense a small circle of decision makers in Central Europe started a war in Europe that they knew would degenerate into a war of attrition, and about whose outcome they had at this crucial moment no idea. The attack on Belgium, Luxembourg, and France was merely the opening move in a game in which the initial strategy had already lost its direction.

It is only when we contemplate these implications of the Schlieffen-Moltke Plan that we can begin to understand the meaning of a memorable scene that took place in the kaiser's palace in Berlin on 1 August 1914. On the previous day the German government had handed St. Petersburg an ultimatum, limited to twenty-four hours, to withdraw the full mobilization of their army that had just been ordered; otherwise Germany would proclaim its own full mobilization.[8] Since no one expected Russia to accept the ultimatum, Wilhelm II had called his closest advisors together for the signing of the German mobilization order. The atmosphere was very tense. Although waiting for Russia to mobilize first caused the tsar to be seen as the aggressor in the eyes of the German public, those present, Moltke in particular, realized their share in the unleashing of war. They also knew that the masses could not be mobilized unless they could be sold the argument that the Russian steamroller had forced the Reich government into a defensive war.

Explaining this to the German working-class movement and its leadership had become the special task of Bethmann. After the patent failure of his localization strategy, he had entered into negotiations with a number of leading right-wing Social Democrats to persuade them to call off earlier demonstrations to preserve the peace that had taken place in a number of cities and to rally them and their members behind the flag. With the help of Clemens von Delbrück, the state secretary of the interior, the Reich chancellor succeeded at this game. As Admiral Georg Alexander von Müller, the chief of the naval cabinet, noted in his diary on 1 August, the government had done "very well in making us appear as the attacked."[9]

After the mobilization order had been signed and was about to be published, those present at the palace dispersed, only to be called back a moment later. The kaiser reported that a telegram had arrived from the German ambassador to London. It was supposed to contain the news that Britain might remain neutral in the coming conflict. When faced with this glimmer of hope, Wilhelm II proposed postponing the publication of the mobilization order. Moltke protested. The preparations for the invasion of Belgium were now in full swing, he announced, and could not be stopped. The kaiser ordered him to get on the telephone to give orders "that the 16th Division was not to move into Luxembourg." The chief of the General Staff then had something akin to a nervous breakdown, and it was left to Falkenhayn to console him. Shortly afterward, another telegram from London came, revealing that the British foray was much less promising than the circle had been led to expect. The kaiser now ordered that the mobilization be made public. World War I had for all practical purposes begun. Falkenhayn recalled that during the signing ceremony the monarch shook his hand for a long time. Both of them had tears in their eyes. They probably knew—or at least had vague notions of—what they had done.[10]

THE TOTALIZATION OF WARFARE

The war that the decision makers in Berlin and Vienna launched in July 1914 cost some twenty million lives. Over nine million died at the front, often after sustaining terrible wounds and suffering excruciating pain. The magnitude of these losses was a direct consequence of the fact that the war could not be won with a short hammer blow first against France and then against Russia so that victory would be secured by Christmas 1914. Accordingly, the conflict soon developed into the kind of costly war of attrition that devoured millions of people and of which the elder Moltke had warned.

The world war that raged between 1914 and 1918, particularly in Europe, has frequently been called the first total war. Although some argue that the American Civil War deserves this birthright, if we consider how completely all participant nations mobilized their human and material resources to achieve some kind of decisive breakthrough at the front, World War I is more deserving of this title. Many recent studies have moved beyond an analysis of the great battles on the western or eastern front and included the home front: the mobilization of the armaments industries, the regimentation first of raw materials and later of the entire national economy, the restrictions on the free movement of labor, and the censorship of the media. The results of this research have led scholars to stress the gradualism of the whole process and to speak of a totalization of the war. This means that in 1914 government intervention into the life of the participant nations was still relatively mild and not to be compared with the much more total mobilization of all forces two or three years later. However, if we view the world war from the perspective of an unleashing of violence, there is no escaping the conclusion that total war began in the fall of 1914.[11]

This was true, first of all, with respect to the dividing line between combatants and noncombatants, which had been upheld in previous decades at least as far as Europe was concerned. Since Moltke's strategy envisaged the invasion of neutral Belgium as a first step in order to avoid the French fortifications in Lorraine and to attack Paris from the north, the war began with acts of extreme violence. For, instead of capitulating immediately, the Belgians resisted the Germans with a tenacity that caught the invaders by surprise. This resistance in turn threatened to overthrow Moltke's timetable, according to which Paris was supposed to fall some thirty-nine days after mobi-

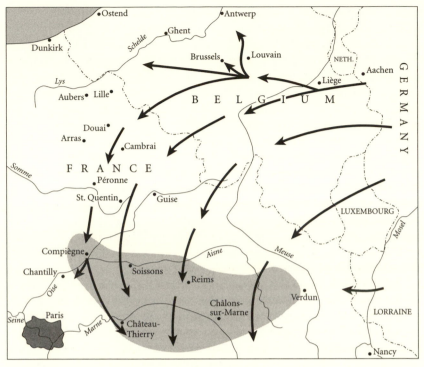

2. German advance toward Paris, 1914 (Shaded area = German retreat to the north in Marne Battle)

lization. It was above all the city of Liège with its surrounding fortifications that proved a mighty obstacle to the German advance. There were 180,000 soldiers who pushed from the east across the border in the first days of August. Some 25,000 railroad cars had transported them across the Rhine River. Between 2 and 18 August over 2,100 trains crossed the Hohenzollern Bridge at Cologne. But Belgian resistance slowed down the German offensive. The fortifications around Liège were armed with some 400 heavy guns. No less important, the civilian populations supported their soldiers in all sorts of ways. In the end a 42-cm gun, "Fat Bertha," had to be brought in to crack the fortifications. It took until the middle of August to do this.

In a desperate attempt to resist the invasion, franc-tireurs began to snipe at the German troops; the latter immediately resorted to shooting hostages and other brutalities. Some 800 inhabitants of the small towns of Andenne and Dinant to the south of Liège were killed, including women and children. In nearby Tamines the number of dead was close to 400 after hostages had been rounded up and executed in the marketplace. Whoever did not die instantly was killed with the bayonet. John Horne and Alan Kramer have recently undertaken a comprehensive study of German atrocities and the attitudes that triggered them.[12]

As the German army advanced toward Brussels, houses were set on fire; basements and lofts were searched by soldiers looking for franc-tireurs; there was looting; and domestic animals wandered aimlessly among the ruins of farmsteads. The ancient city of Louvain with its great architecture and priceless library collections fell victim to German artillery bombardments. Women were raped and over 40,000 were made homeless. It was the novelist Rudolf Binding who, witnessing the destructive rage around him, despaired in the face of what he called "senseless" violence. But following his concept of a war of annihilation, Moltke had proclaimed on 5 August that the conquest of Belgium would be brutal. He added that Germany was fighting for its life. Whoever got in the way of the troops would have to bear the consequences. The result was that the Belgian army suffered some 30,000 casualties.

However, German losses in those first weeks were also enormous, even if they did not reach the level of French casualities; like the Belgians, the French threw themselves against the invaders. Expecting German operations on their eastern border in Lorraine and wedded, like all armies at the time, to the idea of attack, Marshal Joseph Joffre launched an offensive that proved very costly. In the hope of achieving a breakthrough in that region that would no doubt have upset Moltke's plans, France lost some 40,000 men between 20 and 23 August alone. When Joffre finally abandoned the offensive altogether because his troops were called back for the defense of Paris, some 140,000 Frenchmen had been killed or wounded.[13]

Realizing that the Germans were aiming to advance on Paris via Belgium from the north, thousands of civilians took to the roads and fled south. Hundreds of thousands were forced to leave their homes, to which they were not able to return until 1918 once the frontline in the trench war of attrition that was soon to begin in northern France had been established. When they returned parts of the region had been turned into the desolate moon landscapes of modern warfare. The French capital would probably have fallen that autumn if the "miracle of the Marne" had not happened. Although the German troops had gained much of the terrain in Belgium and northern France as envisioned by Moltke, the fierce resistance they encountered had exhausted them and the supply lines had become overstretched. Thanks to the troops that Joffre had moved back to Paris but also to the British Expeditionary Force (BEF) that had meanwhile landed on the French and Belgian channel coast, the Allies succeeded in stopping the German advance. At this point the Germans, led by Moltke, made a fateful decision. Fearing that resistance might be too strong, they ordered a retreat by about twenty kilometers toward hilly terrain that they thought was more favorable for a brief period of recuperation before the final assault on Paris.[14]

Historians have wondered about the reasons for this decision, which effectively transformed the offensive war of movement of the previous weeks into one of fixed positions and attrition. Whatever the immediate reasons for the German retreat in a situation that was confusing and marred by contradictory intelligence about the enemy, the very high risk that Moltke knew he had taken on 1 August and the state of psychic tension it left him in also have to be put into the equation. He sensed at the time that the war could not really be won and, consequently, he had time and again almost expected to find himself in a stalemate, which was tantamount to a failure of his strategy. And now he himself contributed to this self-fulfilling prophecy by withdrawing the German troops and thus handing the Allies their "miracle of the Marne." At the end of his tether, Moltke was soon replaced by Falkenhayn.

By this time the fighting itself had assumed the dimensions of total war; thenceforth the process of totalization would slowly encroach upon the societies of the participant countries as a whole. Now the task was to mobilize all human and economic resources, while it became even more uncertain how this war might end. Perhaps de Bloch was right: there would be no victors. In pursuit of the perspective that we have adopted in this book—to trace the unleashing and escalation of violence in Europe during the first half of the twentieth century—we will first turn to an account of some of the major battles in the west to explain why so many millions of soldiers were killed or mutilated in the trenches until 1918.

The high casualty rate in northern France beginning in the fall of 1914 along a line of trenches some 750 kilometers long was due, on the one hand, to the massive deployment of the new weapons of industrialized warfare and, on the other, new tactics of attack across no-man's-land. Both, the two sides hoped, would bring the decisive breakthrough and final victory. The first of the horrendously costly battles took place at the end of 1914 in the northern sector near the Belgian town of Ypres after the Germans decided to storm the positions of the BEF. When the British succeeded in repelling the first wave, they went on the counteroffensive but similarly failed to achieve a breakthrough or even a significant gain of territory. When the battle was finally abandoned on 2 November, less than half of the 160,000 BEF soldiers were still fit to fight. There were some 41,000 dead on the German side, most of whom were very young soldiers whose death became mythologized by the political Right during the interwar years. Meanwhile, to the south of Ypres, along the Franco-German front, some 80,000 Frenchmen lost their lives, were wounded, or went missing in October 1914. In the month of November another 70,000 were added. By the end of the year the Germans had lost some 241,000 men.[15]

Although losses continued to mount in the following year in the wake of relentless attacks by both sides, soldiers also learned to protect themselves through an extensive system of trenches and dugouts. Even more incredible losses occurred in 1915–16 during major attacks that were preceded by days of artillery bombardments of the enemy lines. What happened along the front near the French town of Verdun in northeastern France in January and February 1916 is illustrative of this type of warfare. Falkenhayn had come to the conclusion that Verdun was important to France not only strategically but also symbolically. He believed that they would defend its fortifications to the hilt and, if lost, try to reconquer them at any cost. This, he calculated, would in turn result in a situation in which the French army would literally be bled white.[16]

His calculations proved correct in the sense that the Germans were able to conquer some key fortifications, which the French then tried to regain. At the end of the battle, the total dead and wounded amounted to just under one million on the French side. But when Falkenhayn added up his own losses, he found that they were about as high as those of France. In other words, both sides suffered gigantic losses in a fashion that had become the hallmark of total war. It was also reflected in the fact that some forty million shells had been rained on the enemy on both sides. Parts of the region around Verdun looked like the proverbial moon landscapes.

The bloodletting in the battle along the Somme River to the west a few months later was even greater than the one at Verdun. Here it was the British field marshal Douglas Haig who was determined to crack the German lines. Accordingly he prepared the attack with an artillery bombardment that lasted six days. In its course, some three million shells landed on a twenty-kilometer-long section of German trenches. After this purgatory, Haig expected the Germans to be totally paralyzed or decimated in their dugouts. When the guns fell silent, the British shock troops went over the top of their trenches and rushed across the barbed wire of no-man's-land to take the German positions. But not all the Germans had been killed in their underground caves. They rushed into what was left of their trenches, put up their machine-guns and flamethrowers, and fought for their lives. By the end of that fateful day, 1 July 1916, the British casualties stood at 60,000. The British Fourth Division lost 5,100 of 12,000 men. Meanwhile the German 180th Regiment of 3,000 men counted a mere 180 casualities. In the course of the long battle of the Somme there were many more such attacks and counterattacks. When it all ended, some 1.3 million had been killed or wounded. Another major battle raged from 31 July to 10 November 1917 near the Belgian town of Paaschendaele. The British, who initiated the attack, succeeded at first in making impressive territorial gains. But after long rains the operation literally got stuck on the mud of the devastated countryside. Total losses in the end: 470,000.[17]

Between battles the soldiers lived a mole-like existence in the trenches and shelters, surrounded by body parts, rats, and lice. During the rainy season, the trenches turned into mud holes. During the often long intervals between battles, sharpshooters would scan the enemy trenches for soldiers moving along all too carelessly. Meanwhile, their comrades would try to kill their boredom by playing cards and other games. This was a universe, made up of men of very different backgrounds, that had never existed before. After weeks of inaction that were punctuated at most by the whistling of a shell or sniper fire, the artillery might suddenly unleash a hellish noise and shells would rain down around a dugout. Occasionally a soldier had a hysterical fit and rushed out, screaming, into no-man's-land, only to be shot by an enemy sniper. If he ran to the rear, he would be picked up by military police. Because the phenomenon of shell shock was unknown, these soldiers in the early years of war were court-martialed. The British film *King and Country* with Tom Courtney portrays the fate of a shell-shocked soldier who ended up before a firing squad. Doctors eventually diagnosed this behavior as a medical condition and patients were sent to special hospitals for treatment.[18]

As we have seen, the artillery bombardments were followed by shock-troop attacks that defenders tried to repulse with machine-guns and flame-throwers. Other new weapons of industrialized warfare were poison gas and tanks, the monstrous armored vehicles that crept across no-man's-land. Given that millions had already been sacrificed, a human life had become very cheap, and even if during an attack one encountered an unarmed enemy, he would be bayoneted without pity. Conditions like these led one soldier to write, "This is not war, it is the ending of the world."[19]

Although the war in the east did not degenerate into trench warfare, it was not more merciful than the fighting on the western front. Looking at the casualty figures, the orgy of violence was probably even greater there than in France. To the dead and wounded must be added millions of prisoners of war who fell into enemy hands on both sides. The civilian population time and again found itself caught between the advancing and retreating armies. It also suffered higher casualties than the Belgians in 1914 as a result of disease and malnutrition. Contrary to Moltke's calculations, the first major battle in the east was fought as early as September 1914 at Tannenberg in East Prussia. The Russians were vastly superior to the German forces in numbers, but they could not take advantage of their superiority because of the incompetence of their military leaders and poor coordination. Their defeat at Tannenberg saved East Prussia and stopped Russian attempts to rout the Germans in the east.

They were more successful against the Austro-Hungarian armies further south in Galicia, again with losses that are still difficult to grasp. Up to December 1914, the Habsburg armies had lost some 1.2 million of the 3.35 million men they had mobilized. On the Russian side 2 million soldiers of a total of 3.5 million were killed. In March 1915 the Austrian commander of the fortress at Przemyl surrendered with 2,500 officers and 117,000 men, and during the first three months of 1915 the Austrians lost another 800,000 men, primarily prisoners of war. By the end of the war in the east POW figures had reached a total of 5–5.5 million, most of whom were not exchanged but kept in camps to prevent their remobilization.

While the military fortunes remained changeable in Galicia, the Germans had succeeded in defeating the Russians in the battle of the Masurian Lakes and were able to push them back to a line that ran from Riga on the Baltic Sea via Pinsk and Baranowice all the way to Czernowitz in the Carpathian Mountains. During these battles some 300,000 Russian POWs fell into German hands. Germany's dominant position in these regions was challenged one more time in March 1916 when the tsar launched the Brusilov offensive. When the attack ended a month later, the Russians mourned the loss of 12,000 men and 85,000 POWs. The Germans lost some 20,000 but were able to regain the territories initially ceded to Brusilov. If we include the casualty figures for the Habsburg armies against whom the Russians had been more successful, losses on both sides ran to around one million if we also count the 400,000 Austro-Hungarian POWs that the tsarist armies made.

In the course of these operations, the extent of the misery that the war of movement inflicted on the civilian population also became more visible. In the territories occupied by the Germans, known later as *OberOst*, an estimated 4.2 million people left their homes. The Courland region lost 54 percent of its population; in Vilnius-Suwalki it was 46 percent, followed by 37.3 percent for Bialystok-Grodno, and 26 percent for Lithuania.[20] In the face of these huge numbers and the poor supply situation in the armies, epidemics time and again took their toll. There were times when there were four soldiers for every wounded comrade who had been infected by cholera, typhus, or other contagious diseases. To this day we have no reliable statistics on diseases among the civilian population and its fate more generally. What we can say is that for many regions it was no less than disastrous. Indeed, it does not require much imagination to visualize the predicament of those who did not have to flee but continued to live in a combat area. For much of the time the armies lived on what they could find in the occupied territories. This meant that beyond the losses in human lives, the losses in wealth and irreplaceable cultural artifacts were also incalculable. Peaceful villages and towns were flattened, just as in Belgium; their inhabitants, if not killed or driven out, faced starvation.

In the spring of 1915, total war reached a climax in the east in the rear of the Turkish front. In connection with the crisis unleashed by the British attempt to conquer the Gallipoli peninsula en route to Constantinople and the Black Sea, the Turks decided to move against the Armenian minority in their midst. It began with shootings of Armenian priests, journalists, businessmen, and other elite groups. During the following two years some two million Armenians were driven into Mesopotamia, in the course of which according to various estimates up to one million men, women, and children were either murdered or died from diseases or as a result of the harsh climatic conditions.[21]

The unleashing of violence that had begun in Belgium in the summer of 1914 thus brought mass death at the front. Some nine million soldiers and officers died in action, often from terrible injuries, helpless and alone in no-man's-land or in the trenches. Most of them were young, which meant that many parents never really overcame the death of their children. Among the mourners were also some three million war widows and ten million orphans.[22] It is still not possible to gauge the full extent of the trauma that World War I inflicted upon Europeans. There were several million who, though alive, had their future ruined by serious injuries. Those who had lost an arm or a leg or both were plagued by phantom pains, reminding them of the ordeal they had experienced at the front. There were also those who had horribly disfiguring facial wounds. With plastic surgery still in its infancy, many veterans did not even dare look in a mirror. Some of these men "with a broken face," as they were called in France, had papier-mâché masks made for them to hide their scars.[23]

Furthermore, there were those who had not been physically injured but had been severely damaged psychically. We have already mentioned the phenomenon of shell shock. Many would never be cured, even after receiving appropriate treatment. Time and again they had fits of heavy trembling and lived as physical and mental wrecks. Finally, there were those—and they may well have been the largest group—who showed no visible symptoms of their trauma but suffered from nightmares, easily lost their temper, and were prone to violence. If they had families, their wife and children would often become the first victims of their mental anguish. For this reason, but also because spouses had become estranged from each other after years of separation, divorce rates shot up after 1918 in all European countries.[24] Here, too, the historian finds it difficult to reconstruct the misery the war produced in addition to the violent death of millions.

Returning to the question of totalization, recent research has seen it primarily as a process that unfolded more slowly. The Israeli historian Alon Rachamimov, who studied the fate of Habsburg soldiers and officers captured by the Russians, has demonstrated that the tsarist regime initially attempted honestly and earnestly to abide by the rules of international law governing the treatment of POWs, even though many of the camps were set up in faraway Siberia.[25] But the more total the war became and the higher the human costs, the more difficult it proved to adhere to those rules. The chaos increased, and established norms began to break down. The proliferation of propaganda that spread hatred of the enemy everywhere contributed to an attitude that no longer viewed the opponent as a human being. A pro-

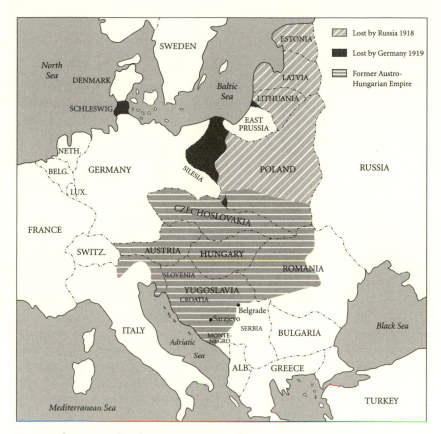

Legend:
- Lost by Russia 1918
- Lost by Germany 1919
- Former Austro-Hungarian Empire

3. Central Europe after the Paris Peace Conference

cess of dehumanization set in. It was no less disastrous that, when the guns finally fell silent, another war began that did not pit soldier against soldier but citizen against citizen within a particular country. It is to these wars after the war that we turn in the next section.

The Wars after the Great War

The conflicts that broke out after the end of World War I with its millions of casualties can be traced to dramatic events in Russia in 1917. In February of that year the tsarist monarchy collapsed and was replaced by a provisional government formed by reformist politicians fearful of revolutionary chaos and of workers' and soldiers' councils (soviets) that had sprung up spontaneously in the factories of the major cities and in the armed forces.[26] But the new government, in which Alexander Kerensky eventually took the reins as prime minister, could not resolve the innumerable problems of an army, economy, and society that were all disintegrating. The left-radical Bolsheviks under Vladimir Lenin were increasingly successful in exploiting the chaos in the country and the anger and bitterness of the masses of peasants, soldiers, and workers. Gradually they gained the upper hand among the delegates in the Soviet movement. By October Kerensky's government was so weak that Lenin decided the time had come to remove it in a violent coup. The Bolsheviks seized power and began to establish a dictatorial regime.

Lenin's methods of stabilizing his regime soon met with resistance, to which he responded with repression. Russia now experienced a process of escalation in which his opponents began to organize a counterrevolution. The Allies who had been worried about the radicalism of the Bolshevik regime from the start were even more alarmed when it decided to take the country out of the war and to initiate peace negotiations with the Germans. Supporting the counterrevolutionaries seemed to offer a chance of overthrowing the new regime, and so Britain, France, and the United States found themselves drawn into a cruel civil war that quickly spread throughout the former tsarist empire. The Bolsheviks had promised peace, bread, and land reform to the masses. But powerful and well-equipped forces were arraigned against them. There were also many nationalities and ethnic groups demanding independence or autonomy. As early as September 1917 a "federal republic" was proclaimed in the North Caucasus. Nationalist unrest also broke out in other parts of Russia. But Lenin formally recognized the independence of just one region, Finland. Meanwhile, his close collaborator, Leon Trotsky, had successfully organized the "Red Army" into an effective force that moved against the "White" counterrevolutionary armies that had been reinforced by French, British, and American contingents. In a bitter struggle, the "Reds" slowly gained the upper hand over the "Whites." But it took until 1921 before the Bolsheviks finally defeated the counterrevolution at enormous human and material costs to an already exhausted and devastated country.

From the start, Lenin believed he had to govern by dictatorial means. In the fall of 1917 he had still given the green light for elections to a constitutional assembly. His hope was that his Bolshevik party would gain a clear majority. However, it gained no more than 175 seats out of a total of 707. After this setback, Lenin did his best to impede the work of the assembly. When the citizens of St. Petersburg took to the streets, they were dispersed by machine-gun fire. Some 100 demonstrators were either killed or wounded, many of them seriously. Thenceforth the Bolsheviks stepped up their repression and surveillance of real or suspected opponents. Lenin's secret police, the Cheka, whose number of civilian and military members rose from 37,000 in January 1919 to 137,000 by the middle of 1921, did not shrink from murder and torture. But it is important to see the dialectics of violence that propelled the unfolding civil war.

In the older literature, the war in which the "Reds" and "Whites" deployed several hundreds of thousands of fighters has been portrayed as a clash between two more or less poorly led armies. What radicalized the conflict were the opposing extreme ideologies that motivated the two sides. But in focusing on the conflict between two armies, one of which was supported by the Allies, it is easy to overlook the costs among civilians who once again found themselves in the middle of military operations and fronts that were moving back and forth. Raging over a much larger territory than World War I, which had been largely confined to the western parts of the country, troops supplied themselves from the land. But both sides also moved ruthlessly against civilians in the cities who were suspected of collaborating with the enemy. Allegedly "Bolshevik" workers were hanged by the dozens in the Ukraine with the support of the Allies. In early July 1918 Boris Savinko established a terror regime in the city of Yaroslav during which he herded some 200 hostages on a "death barge" on the Volga River where they were left to perish. When the Bolsheviks reconquered the city at the end of the month, they executed 400 prisoners within two days. They were also responsible for the murder of the tsarist family at Yekatarinburg during the night of 16–17 July 1918.

After an abortive attempt on Lenin's life, the shooting of hostages increased on the Bolshevik side. At the beginning of September 1918, some 500 civilians went before firing squads in Petrograd. In Kronstadt another 400 lost their lives in nighttime massacres. Meanwhile the "Whites" matched "Red" atrocities in the regions they dominated. We are particularly well informed about conditions in the Baltics through the memoirs of so-called Free Corps fighters who had been recruited in postwar Germany by the Allies with promises of land and money.[27] (We will revisit these men later.) They were the desperados who, after the end of the Russian civil war, returned to Germany, and continued to commit the brutalities, including the raping and killing of "Red" women, that they had practiced in the Russian civil war. Penniless and without a future, they joined a variety of underground organizations in the Weimar Republic devoted to assassinations and acts of terror against civilians.

That by the end of this war Russia was devastated is evidenced above all by the millions who died. An estimated 143 million people lived in the Soviet-dominated regions of the former tsarist empire in 1918. When the civil war ended, but before the beginning of mass starvation (which cost around five million lives), the total population was 134 million. The Cheka is thought to have killed 280,000 people. This human catastrophe is also reflected in the collapse of the country's industrial output. By the end of 1920, manufacturing had dropped to 20 percent and agriculture to 64 percent of their 1913 levels.

The production of coal was no more than one quarter of what it had been before World War I. Before the beginning of the revolution the stock of locomotives was around 20,000. By the end of 1919, some 8,900 were left, of which only half were still operational. During the harsh Russian winters people literally froze to death in their apartments for lack of heat. Petrograd lost two-thirds of its population through hunger, cold, and disease. About half the population perished in Moscow. The overall human losses in the Russian civil war are estimated at 800,000, of whom 350,000 died either in battle or from their injuries. The other 450,000 are assumed to have met their death as a result of illness or other war-related causes.[28]

If fear of the aims and policies of the Bolsheviks fueled the resistance of the counterrevolutionaries inside Russia, rumors about Lenin and his program unleashed tremendous anxiety in the rest of Europe, all the way to the British Isles. This explains why the Allies tried to throttle the new regime with military means in its infancy. The fear of socialism had been strong even before 1914, but now the Bolsheviks presented their radical program not merely in speeches and in leaflets but by implementing their ideas with great determination. What if Bolshevism spread westward? Had soldiers' and workers' councils not also cropped up in Germany, Austria, and Hungary after the collapse of the two Central European monarchies in November 1918? Thus, when strike movements broke out in Newcastle, the cabinet in London at one point in 1919 seriously discussed the creation of a bourgeois militia to be mobilized against radical miners and other industrial workers in the English northeast. Indeed, the fighting that broke out in Central Europe and Italy and the resistance that radical workers encountered cannot be understood without the rallying call that Lenin and Trotsky had issued for the proletariat of those countries to trigger the much vaunted world revolution.

However, the level of violence in western Europe differed markedly from that in Russia. After the proclamation of the end of the fighting, demobilized soldiers caused a good deal of physical damage to the trains that took them home from the trenches. It was damage done in fits of exuberance, not from ideological fervor. It was a different matter for the Allied troops that had been sent east to fight in the Russian civil war. If they were brought home, leaving the "White" counterrevolutionaries to fight for themselves and finally lose, the soldiers, many of whom came from the working-class districts of the big cities, might be infected by Bolshevik propaganda and carry the violence they had participated in into their communities back home.

The developments in postwar Italy took a more radical turn than they did in Britain or France. After Italy had entered the war on the Allied side in 1915, its armies were involved in some very bloody battles against Austro-Hungarian forces in the Alps in which they ultimately gained the upper hand. In return for the Italian entry into the war against its erstwhile German and Habsburg allies, Britain and France had promised Rome territorial and other gains in the event of victory. When these promises were not kept during the peace negotiations in Paris in 1919, many nationalists felt betrayed and mobilized in paramilitary associations ready to take by force what was being denied them at Paris.[29] No less important, the stresses and strains of total war had increased social tensions in Italy to the breaking point. Especially in the north of the country both land laborers on the estates in the Po River valley and industrial workers in the big cities were in a radical mood. The slogan "Viva Lenin!" found a popular echo. Time and again the socialists won hands-down at the polls. Factories were occupied. Terrified by the possibility of a Bolshevik-style revolution, the landowners and businessmen provided trucks to ferry hastily raised nationalist counterforces to the neuralgic points of protest. Faced with embittered proletarians, fear among the large-scale farmers and the urban bourgeoisie grew so strong that scholars have spoken of a "preventive counterrevolution." The result was widespread fighting and civil war.

Among the right-wing ruffians were many veterans who, disillusioned with the liberal government in Rome that had allegedly betrayed the country both at the Paris peace conference and at home, were signed up by the counterrevolutionaries to use the kind of shock-troop tactics they had practiced at the front during World War I. Soon so-called *squadristi d'azione* appeared in the streets of northern Italy's industrial cities to beat up left-wing politicians and ransack workers' clubs and other working-class establishments. Since they did not encounter any well-organized resistance, they felt emboldened to be even more aggressive and launched their attacks in broad daylight. In many places so-called *fasci di combattimento* began to form and to roam the countryside, looking for "Reds" among the land laborers. That the members of the early Fascist contingents were men of violence who transferred their front-line experiences to the growing civil war at home is confirmed by the biographies of their leaders, among them, for example, Italo Balbo. Typical of the younger generation, he had returned from the war convinced of the Italian government's "betrayal" and proclaimed the uncompromising struggle not only against the leftist revolutionaries but also against the liberal-parliamentary republic. As Robert Wohl has put it: "No Fascist leader had a greater reputation for ruthlessness or personal heroism, *'Tutto osare'* (dare everything) was his motto. Destruction and intimidation were his favorite methods. Action for action's sake was his only code."[30]

But there were also many other veterans whose personal lives had been uprooted by the war. They had witnessed how a human life was literally worth nothing. Often without any previous training or experience in a civilian career, they saw little prospect of being integrated into peacetime society and simply transferred the brutal methods they had learned to use against the "external enemy" against the new "internal" one. Society was divided into friends and foes who tried to achieve "final victory" over each other with words but above all with physical force. Accordingly, the seizure of power by Benito Mussolini, who had emerged as the leader of the Fascists, occurred, at least publicly, as a coup against the politicians in Rome. In the ensuing much vaunted "March on Rome," Balbo lived up to his reputation as a man of brute force.

Mussolini worried that the march might have to face the Italian army and fail, exploited the confusion in the government in Rome and negotiated with the king, who on 29 October 1922 finally offered him the post of minister president. In other words, the handing over of power occurred by telephone in advance, enabling Mussolini to arrive in Rome from Milan by train without encountering resistance. His motley contingent was kept outside the capital until 31 October, when they all marched into the city for a splendid demonstration. The March on Rome never took place, but a powerful myth that the Fascists had seized the government by revolutionary means had been created. Thenceforth *Il Duce* (The Leader) and the men of violence around him applied the power of the state that had now fallen into their hands to deal with the opposition and to establish, step-by-step, a dictatorship. Some elements of the working-class movement went underground; others were lured into collaboration. Its leaders, like Antonio Gramsci, and intellectuals of various political stripes were put in prison or in camps. Italy ceased to be the parliamentary-constitutional monarchy it had been; the king had become a pawn in the hands of an authoritarian regime.

In Central Europe the imbalance of power at the end of the war was not as favorable to the Right as it was in Italy. The initial strength of the Social Democrats certainly helped ensure that the major constitutional change in October 1918 unfolded as a "revolution from above" in the course of which Kaiser Wilhelm II and the military High Command under Paul von Hindenburg and Erich Ludendorff ceded their political power to a new government under Prince Max von Baden, who received his legitimation from the majority parties in the Reichstag, the national parliament, elected on the basis of universal manhood suffrage. It was a major shift that effectively turned Germany into a constitutional monarchy with the kaiser as its figurehead, and it happened without physical force and bodies lying in the streets of Berlin.

However, while the army generals, knowing that Germany had lost the war, collaborated in this effort of constitutional change and of negotiating an armistice, the men of violence in the admiralty devised another plan. They were worried that the prestige of the navy would evaporate completely after the war. After all, because of its inferiority compared to the British Royal Navy, it had been sent out into the North Sea only once, for the Battle of Jutland in 1916 (which resulted in a strategic defeat for the Germans), and spent the rest of the war in the harbors at Kiel and Wilhelmshaven. To counter the possibility that in light of this failure postwar German public opinion would deem a rebuilding of a navy unnecessary, Admiral Reinhard Scheer and his comrades in Berlin gave orders for a final do-or-die battle against the British in the North Sea. When rumors about this suicide mission began to circulate among the rank-and-file sailors, they refused to weigh anchor. The station chief then found another solution: instead of steaming northwest into a futile battle against the Royal Navy, the fleet at Wilhelmshaven was ordered to proceed to Kiel on the Baltic Sea through the Kiel Canal. When they arrived there, the sailors mingled with their comrades and local shipyard workers, all demanding an end to the great slaughter. Thenceforth the demonstrations spread like wildfire to other cities.[31]

The masses now demanded the abdication of Wilhelm II and the proclamation of a republic. Following the Russian model, workers' and soldiers' councils were formed all over the country. Hearing of these events, the kaiser at the imperial headquarters in Spa on the German-Belgian border wanted to march to Berlin at the head of his army to quell the unrest. His entourage told him that his army was in the process of total disintegration; there were no soldiers to follow him. Then they put him in a car and gently shoved him across the Dutch border into exile where he died in 1941. Having announced the monarch's abdication, Prince Max resigned after he had called Friedrich Ebert, the leader of the majority Social Democrats, to his office to declare him his successor. While this was, constitutionally speaking, an irrelevant act because Prince Max did not have the power to appoint his successor, the semblance of a legitimate handing over of power was politically significant in that it provided the bureaucracy with a justification to continue to run the administration under the new government.

Meanwhile, another Social Democrat, Philipp Scheidemann, announced from a balcony in the Reichstag building that the constitutional monarchy of October 1918 had been replaced by a republic. For a brief moment, power was now lying in the streets of Berlin and the other capitals of the federation where the princes had also abdicated.[32] It was picked up by the workers and soldiers of the German soviet movement that had been spontaneously created, though not to follow the Leninist example and to bring about a Bolshevik seizure of power. Rather they offered the reins to Ebert, the Social Democrat, and Hugo Haase, the leader of the more left-wing Independent Socialists, in the hope that this provisional government would not only conclude an early peace with the Allies, demobilize the armed forces, and restore stability at home, but also initiate social and political reforms.[33] Ebert and Haase accepted. They had before their eyes the example of Russia of the previous year and wanted to avoid a rise of the Bolsheviks within the German soviet movement at all costs.

Having no troops at his disposal to use against attempts by the extreme Left to stage a Lenin-style coup, Ebert accepted an offer that General Wilhelm Groener made by telephone on 10 November 1918 on behalf of the officer corps. He promised to raise well-armed contingents for the protection of the provisional government and the republic. The idea was to sign up young officers and demobilized soldiers as volunteers, equip them from the army's arsenals, and pay them out of funds that apprehensive industrialists were prepared to put up. Ebert's reliance on the old elites in the military and bureaucracy to restore stability, to weaken the suspect workers' and soldiers' soviets, and to prepare the country for elections to a national assembly for the ratification of a parliamentary-representative republican constitution radicalized the extreme Left. In January the Spartacists, as they called themselves, staged an uprising, more out of desperation than with the hope of seizing power. They were brutally suppressed by those volunteer units— the Free Corps. Equipped with heavy weapons and under the command of army officers, they gave the insurgents short shrift.

Just as under the Italian *fasci*, the Free Corps also resorted to excesses that showed how far the experience of total war in the trenches had lowered the threshold of human inhibition to perpetrate atrocities. The most notorious example is the murder of Rosa Luxemburg, the prominent leader of the Spartacists. She had counseled against the uprising, believing that this was the wrong moment to stage it. Having disagreed with Lenin, who had been prepared to seize power with a small cadre of determined revolutionaries and without democratic backing, she recognized that the mass of the German proletariat was not in a revolutionary mood. Consequently, she expected the Spartacist revolt to be defeated, but nevertheless committed herself to it in the hope of being able to control its more radical elements. After the failure of the uprising, she did not resist her arrest in January 1919. Her captors beat her and then murdered her. Days later, her body was found floating in the Landwehr Canal in Berlin.[34]

This is not meant to downplay the fact that the insurgents also committed many brutalities on the other side of the barricades in the big industrial cities. One of the culmination points of leftist extremism occurred in April 1919 when the Bolsheviks succeeded in establishing a short-lived Soviet Republic in the Bavarian city of Munich.[35] The measures taken by the four-man executive council under the leadership of Eugen Leviné were improvised and very unpopular. When the Munich Soviet began to expropriate the local bourgeoisie, its policies mobilized the latter to resist the regime passively. Wild rumors spread about a "Red terror" with which the regime tried to enforce its decisions; but most of the atrocities occurred only toward the end of April when the Bavarian government of Johannes Hoffmann called in the Free Corps to end the German experiment in Bolshevism.

When reports reached Munich that these troops, while encircling the city, had been executing unarmed communist workers as they reached nearby Starnberg in the south and later Dachau in the northwest, commanders of the local Bolshevik militia ordered the shooting of ten hostages. Retaliation was swift. As in Italy, the "White terror" that began after the conquest of Munich by the Free Corps was much worse than anything the Bolsheviks had perpetrated. Some 140 people who were suspected of having been involved in the Soviet Republic were shot without trial, among them 58 Russian prisoners of war who were unlucky enough to get caught in the dragnet. Another 158 suspects were put before hastily established courts and executed without delay. Some Free Corps units killed suspects, many of whom were denounced, on the spot. According to some police reports the total number of dead was estimated at 557. Other estimates were as high as 1,200. It seems that the number of 600 or 625 that appeared in later studies of the Munich Bolshevik republic are closest to the truth.

In other places, too, the Free Corps used much more excessive force than their leftist opponents. They were also responsible for eliminating the taboo against killing women. Klaus Theweleit has examined this development using the reports and memoirs of former Free Corps fighters.[36] Whether they fought against Russian Bolsheviks in the Baltic states or against German communist workers in the industrial centers of central and western Germany, their anti-communism and ideological fervor had become so vicious that any politically motivated murder seemed justified. This applied not only to male industrial workers who were suspected of Bolshevik sympathies but also to "Red" female aides and even nurses, who were deemed to be prostitutes in disguise. No doubt the connection between violence and sexuality that Theweleit made in his book with often controversial hypotheses deserves further exploration, especially for the period of World War I and the civil wars that followed it. Nevertheless it is difficult even today to explain scenes of the kind described in the memoirs of Adolf Schulz in his battle with insurgent workers: "Behind the hedge lay a woman of this sort in tenderest embrace with her lover. A hand grenade surprised her in the practice of her actual profession."[37] What—this is the disturbing question—was the state of mind of a person who perpetrated this act of violence and later bragged about it?

According to the stipulations of the peace treaty Germany signed at Versailles in June 1919, the new Republican government that had emerged from the national elections a few months earlier was obliged to dissolve the Free Corps. By that time the leftist revolts of the spring had been quelled and the Weimar Republic had a vital interest in ridding itself of the volunteer army. The threat of dissolution now turned the Free Corps against the government. Their resistance culminated in the so-called Kapp Putsch of March 1920 when rebellious units occupied Berlin and proclaimed the overthrow of the republic. The coup collapsed after a few days when the ministerial bureaucracy refused to collaborate with the rebels and the trade unions called a general strike. But the revolt in turn triggered left-wing uprisings by radical industrial workers still longing for the victory of Bolshevism. They were swiftly dealt with by the new army, the 100,000-man *Reichswehr*, that had been formed under the terms of the Versailles Treaty. Although its commander, General Hans von Seeckt, had refused to defend the legitimate Republican government against the Kapp putschists, insisting that "*Reichswehr* does not shoot upon *Reichswehr*," he was perfectly happy to move against the radical Left whenever there was an opportunity.[38]

After the fighting in the Ruhr industrial region and central Germany in 1920 had led to further casualties, domestic politics entered a less violent phase. What had happened until then in one industrial city, Halle, was reported in *Freiheit*, the Berlin newspaper of the Independent Social Democrats, in the following way:

> After laborious negotiations, success came on Monday evening when an agreement between the local garrison command and the fighting troops of the revolutionary workers was made. The military gave in writing an assurance that nothing would happen to the leaders and members of the workers' units, [and so] the workers withdrew from the strong points in the city and the positions outside it. The military . . . soon moved in and established a truly unprecedented terror regime. The parts of the city that had been evacuated were searched by the soldiers and all those who were suspected of having aided the workers in some way were arrested, tied together with wire, taken to the garrison with their hands raised above their heads, and forced to denounce others under various kinds of torture. Yesterday there followed executions under martial law of large numbers in Halle and in different surrounding villages.[39]

In 1921 it was Max Hölz who started another leftist uprising in Halle, which was quickly defeated and resulted in 145 deaths. Over 34,000 workers were temporarily arrested.[40]

In the meantime some of the Free Corps fighters who had not been offered a position in the new army had gone underground to specialize in political murder. Prominent Weimar politicians, such as Finance Minister Matthias Erzberger and Foreign Minister Walther Rathenau, fell victim to assassinations in 1921 and 1922.[41] The deaths of these two men shows how far the use of violence had gone beyond the fight against communism. Now the radical Right included politicians of the center in their practices of physical annihilation. Declared "November criminals" and "traitors to the fatherland," these politicians were blamed for the defeat of the monarchy, the revolution of November 1918, and the humiliating peace of Versailles. They were alleged to have subverted the home front in 1917–18 and to have stabbed the "undefeated German army" in the back.

This distortion of the events of 1918 that many right-of-center Germans believed as they were looking for scapegoats to explain the catastrophe that had befallen the country was made worse by Hindenburg and Ludendorff. Instead of telling the nation what had happened in the summer of 1918 (that is, that they had told the kaiser that the war was lost militarily), they remained silent. They and other officers also knew that Germany had no choice but to sign the Versailles peace. Before the treaty was signed, some of them had been seriously thinking about resuming the war against the Allies but were firmly told that resistance would result in even greater disaster. None of this put a stop to the proliferation of a web of lies about the war and the subsequent harsh peace. It acted instead as a rallying point for the anti-Republican Right and badly undermined the stability of the postwar settlement.[42]

The notion of betrayal became so widespread and obsessive among the radicals on the Right that traitors were being hunted even within their own ranks. Men suspected of having informed the police of weapons caches or more generally of collaboration with the authorities were murdered. These radical nationalists were also increasingly motivated by a racist anti-Semitism and, in typical scapegoating fashion, blamed "the Jews" for the defeat and the widespread postwar misery. Rathenau was assassinated not just because he was branded a politician who was prepared to fulfill the terms of the Versailles Treaty, but also because he was Jewish.[43]

The unleashing of numerous civil wars after the Great War, which also shook Austria, Hungary, and other states of Central Europe, reached its height but also its terminus in November 1923 in Germany when, following the occupation of the Ruhr industrial region by French and Belgian troops, the country and its currency began to collapse. Hoping to exploit the situation, various right-wing radical paramilitary groups prepared for the March on Berlin—taking Mussolini's March on Rome a year earlier as their model. On 8 November 1923, Adolf Hitler and Ludendorff bullied the Bavarian government into supporting such a march, which was to begin the following morning. But when the two men appeared at the appointed time with their paramilitaries in the center of Munich they found that, for various reasons, the government had changed its mind. They were confronted by police units. Suddenly shots rang through the air. There was pandemonium and when it all ended, several Nazis lay dead in the plaza, and Hitler went into hiding until he was arrested a few days later.[44]

After this, there was a relatively brief period of stabilization and recivilization in most of Europe, including Germany, until an even more violent era set in with the collapse of the world economy in 1929. It is to the mid-1920s that we must now turn.

CHAPTER THREE

Recivilization and Its Failure, 1924–1935

The Short Dream of Prosperity for All

The years of relative stability that, from 1924 onward, followed the world war and subsequent civil wars indicate that twentieth-century European history was not a one-way street of escalating violence. As before 1914, there were two avenues along which the region might develop. The first one led to a society geared toward the production of the weapons of industrialized warfare and the creation of a warrior regime whose campaigns devoured millions of human beings; at the end of the second road lay a society which, within a civilian constitutional framework, peacefully consumed the goods that its industries mass produced.

There were times between 1914 and 1923 when it looked as if the former type had overwhelmed the latter and as if the men of violence would be dominant for years to come. However, the mid-1920s revealed that civilianism and democratic civil society had not been obliterated on the battlefields of the previous decade. In fact, they were alive and for a number of years began to develop an impressive dynamism. However, it is doubtful that they would have evolved as far as they did had it not been for the stimuli that the economies of Europe, worn out by World War I and the early postwar crisis, received from the United States. As we saw in the first chapter, the idea of a mass-production and mass-consumption society had taken root across the Atlantic even before 1914. After 1918 the United States made a determined effort to build on those advances and the further factory rationalization that the war had brought to the country's industries.[1]

In the immediate postwar years there was a strong impulse to retreat from Europe, whose war the Americans had reluctantly entered in 1917. Their late entry had decisively contributed to the defeat of the Central European monarchies, but when it was all over the popular mood in large parts of the United States and especially in the Midwest became isolationist. This was reinforced by the experience of the peace negotiations at Paris where traditional power politics seemed to have reasserted itself. When U.S. president Wilson submitted the peace treaty he had helped forge to Congress, it failed to find a ratifying majority, resulting in Washington's political retreat from Europe. This retreat also prevented, at least for the time being, the flow of economic aid and investments that would have helped revive the exhausted national economies of Europe.

However, the rise of political isolationism and disengagement from international politics should not lead us to overlook another powerful urge that swept through postwar America: the rise of a liberal-capitalist economy of the kind that had emerged before 1914. As in Europe, the war had inevitably strengthened the hand of the government that vigorously tried to increase the output of war materials. Now, in 1918, business pushed for a dismantling of the centralizing instruments that had been created to allow business to organize the transition to a civilian economy free from the regimentation that total war had, inevitably perhaps, brought with it. American business wanted to mass produce goods for peaceful consumption for which it knew there was a demand after several years of scarcity due to wartime military priorities.[2]

In these circumstances, Henry Ford became, even more so than before, the embodiment and propagandist of an economic order that produced goods for civilian mass consumption as cheaply as factory rationalization allowed, and then, instead of pocketing the profits, passed some of them on to the consumers through price reductions. Consequently, goods that had hitherto been beyond the budget of an average household suddenly became affordable and contributed to a gradual rise in living standards. More than a select few from the wealthy classes would be able to participate in the prosperity that new technologies and better work organization had facilitated. In this vision of the future American society, living standards were to be raised to such a level that even houses, cars, radios, and appliances would become available to all. Not surprisingly, Ford's memoirs, in which he mapped out this vision, was an immediate best-seller that was quickly translated into several languages.

The evolution of the American automotive industry offers a good illustration of what happened in the United States after World War I once the transition to a peace economy had been achieved. Even a relatively small manufacturer such as Dodge succeeded in modernizing its factory at Hamtramck to churn out some 1,100 cars in a nine-hour shift. Ford's assembly lines at River Rouge extended over several miles. The company produced 420,000 units per year in 1921; two years later the figure had risen to 1.8 million. In 1920 total U.S. output reached 1.9 million. After a brief recession the following year, the figure for 1923 was 3.6 million and roughly continued at this level during subsequent years. There was a brief reduction to 2.9 million in 1927 before a new record was achieved in 1928. Ford's success enabled him, as he had promised, to reduce prices. Similarly, other consumer durables became affordable for a growing number of Americans. The electrical engineering industry underwent a dramatic change, as did the new branches of the chemical industry. Finally, the film industry saw a massive expansion, offering inexpensive entertainment to millions of Americans. In

1922, 40 million people went to the movies; by 1930 this number had risen to 100 million.[3]

To be sure, a widespread fascination with technological innovations like the radio, the record player, and the cinema contributed to the rapid expansion of mass entertainment. It was also considerably cheaper than a car or an electric oven. But there was a link between the two. The studios in Hollywood mass produced not only love stories with happy endings but also dreams of a better life that the actors lived on the screen. Although many families still could only window shop, during the boom of the 1920s, many more found the goods they saw on screen and in department stores were within the reach of their family budgets. This was also the time when companies developed hire-purchase plans by which goods could be paid for in monthly installments. Special sales, advertised in the local newspapers, were similarly designed to stimulate consumption. The boom created jobs and bonus systems. Consequently, people had more money in their pockets not only because of price reductions but also because their employers offered productivity incentives. By 1923 the unemployment rate had decreased to 2.3 percent.

Highlighting these improvements in the daily lives of millions of Americans is not meant to downplay the fact that many others continued to live in great poverty.[4] African-Americans and other minorities in particular saw little change in their material condition, not to mention the discrimination they continued to be exposed to, especially in the South, that often made their lives even more miserable. If many could afford a car or a house, others were forced to live on the poverty line and in the "rental barracks" of the big cities. However, there can be little doubt that the lot of blue-collar workers in the new growth industries and of the middle classes improved. The index of industrial production, which had stood at 67 points in 1921, rose to 100 points two years later and reached 110 points in 1928.

The favorable economic conditions of the mid-1920s are also reflected in the balance sheets of the large corporations. For example, in 1921 NCR, the office machines manufacturer, posted profits of $2.8 million on a turnover of $29 million. Four years later, turnover had grown to $40 million, yielding profits of $7.8 million. At a time when Europe still grappled with the human and material consequences of World War I and the economic dislocations that occurred in its wake, America experienced a growing prosperity. In 1909, as we have seen, the German liberal economist Moritz Bonn had warned against the dangers of colonialism. Two decades later he compared the American economy to the European one and offered the following retrospective on developments in the mid-1920s: "Ford's significance does not lie in [his] assembly-line [production] and a well-thought-out division of labor which the grown-up German children who visit America for the first time see as a *raison d'être* of American life. Rather it lies in the sober fact which is propagated under the slogan of 'social service,' but hence somewhat removed from rational analysis, that American entrepreneurs like Ford know that the masses will only tolerate the accumulation of great wealth in the hands of a few, if they themselves derive a corresponding advantage from it. In a wealthy country like America one permits the entrepreneur to earn as much as he likes, provided that those through whom he makes his money also benefit from it."[5]

The stimulation of mass consumption and the impressive profits of the car manufacturing, electrical engineering, chemical, and entertainment industries attracted investors as well as speculators who hoped to increase their wealth quickly in the stock market. Their hopes and expectations drove up share prices. However, in their growing exuberance many, especially those who had little experience in stock market speculation, forgot that their purchases carried considerable risks. There was also the problem that bankers aided and abetted those in search of making a fortune on the fly, providing them with easy loans with which their inexperienced clients plunged into the stock market. This was fine as long as stock prices kept rising and investors were able to repay their loans on time. In search of higher profits, however, they soon began to invest in shares that were issued by less than solid enterprises. There was also a rise in property speculation. Plots of land were offered that were allegedly ready for lucrative industrial or housing development but upon closer inspection often turned out to be swamps in the middle of nowhere.[6]

The boom of the mid-1920s was also stimulated by the development of investment firms, which not only advised their clients where to put their money but also established their own funds. Their diversified portfolios, they claimed, allowed clients to spread their risk. The result of all these temptations in a largely unregulated market was, at first, that prices went through the roof. Initially they were still more or less aligned with the value and potential of a particular company, but they soon came to be traded at prices that no longer bore any relationship to economic reality. This had certainly become true by the summer of 1929 when it seemed that only the sky was the stock market's limit. The *New York Times* stock index, which had gained 86.5 points during 1928, added no less than 77 points in the months of June and July 1929. In August it jumped another 33 points, almost 25 percent above the level of May of that year. The increase was reflected in individual industrial shares: United Steel rose from 165 to 258 between June and August; Westinghouse from 151 to 286; and General Electric from 268 to 391.

The optimism that drove up prices in the American stock market led many investors to look for promising opportunities in Europe. But here the lack of information on the health of particular firms was even greater than in the domestic market, and the risks increased accordingly. Nor were provincial bankers in, say, Iowa or Virginia any better informed about economic conditions in Europe than their local clients. By contrast, American companies that were planning to invest in Europe had access to sounder information about the state of different branches of European industry. By the mid-1920s it had also become clear that the American government was prepared to commit itself more strongly to European affairs.[7] While parts of the population remained isolationist and continued to oppose commitments abroad, the political and economic elites along the East Coast had recognized soon after World War I that standing apart was not in America's national interest.

If public opinion prevented Washington from reentering Europe through the political front door, by 1924 the business community was prepared to try the economic back door. American bankers helped negotiate a settlement of the thorny reparations question that was acceptable to both the French and the Germans. Against formidable opposition, politicians in Paris and Berlin succeeded in getting the American-mediated Dawes Plan through their parliaments. This plan, named after one of the American negotiators, provided for staggered payments of German reparations, with the regular installments adjusted to the expected growth of the German economy and hence the growing capacity of the country to pay. It was a capacity that had been in doubt in previous years and had resulted in bitter conflict, in the French occupation of the Ruhr region, and in the collapse of the German currency. The crisis ultimately also hit France, which had to devalue the franc. After all this, all sides were prepared to make a fresh start with American help and to design a viable reparations agreement. As a result international relations also became more calculable for the first time since 1914.[8]

These agreements, forged by bankers and signed by politicians, encouraged American entrepreneurs. Once the solution to the reparations question had created greater political and economic stability, the big corporations seized the initiative and began to invest in Europe. Ford built production facilities in Britain and Germany. General Motors took participations in Vauxhall Cars Ltd. in the British Midlands and in Opel Cars at Rüsselsheim near Frankfurt. The chemicals giant Dupont found European partners in I.G. Farben in Germany. All of them cherished the hope that it would be possible, through the introduction of Fordist production methods and modern marketing, to broaden the circle of customers in the same way this had already been achieved in the United States.

Other industries were guided by similar considerations. For example, the Coca-Cola Corporation opened a bottling plant in Essen, in the heart of the Ruhr industrial region. They may not have hoped to replace the local beer breweries with their fizzy drinks, but they certainly expected to compete well with indigenous producers of sodas. The American entertainment industry also saw considerable business opportunities. Even if the purchasing power of European consumers was still lagging behind that of the United States and cars and other consumer durables continued to be a dream rather than an affordable reality, seeing a movie at the local cinema was within reach of the "masses." In 1934, Britain and Germany had some 5,000 movie theaters each, followed by France (3,900), and Italy and Spain (2,500 each). As early as the mid-1920s some 70–80 percent of the films screened had been produced in Hollywood. These years also saw the rise of the radio. In 1927 Britain had just under 2.2 million of them, with Germany trailing behind at 1.3 million. The spread of the record player (Germany had 429,000 in 1929) increased sales of records—no less than 30 million were sold at this time in Germany alone.[9]

Intrigued by the news of the modernity and productivity of American companies as they had been before 1914, Europe's entrepreneurs and trade unionists traveled across the Atlantic to study American management methods, labor relations, and industrial installations. They wanted to know how the United States had succeeded in spreading prosperity more widely and to see to what extent American experiences were transferable to Europe. Thus Carl Bosch, the head of Germany's I.G. Farben chemicals trust, sent Wichard von Moellendorff to undertake a comparison between several European countries and to see what could be learned from the Americans.[10] The visitors were also looking for enterprises that might be prepared to invest in their firms and help them achieve similar levels of productivity. And indeed, there was much room for improvement. The German Automobile Manufacturers Association found in 1926 that at Ford Motors in Detroit an average of 5.75 workers were needed to produce a car; at Daimler-Benz in Stuttgart it was 450. Ford's assembly lines were so efficient that cars came off the line at one-minute intervals. At Opel Cars in Rüsselsheim, which had gone farthest in introducing Fordist production methods, the interval was 4.5 minutes. Still, the benefits were tangible and in some cases prices declined by 50 percent between 1924 and 1929.

Individual investors also went to Europe. There can be no doubt that their search for profit in foreign markets likewise stimulated economic growth in the wake of the reparations settlement.[11] For the moment, the magnetic power of civilian production and consumption within the framework of parliamentary-representative political systems proved strong enough to push into the background the visions of an authoritarian warrior state to which many had adhered in the early 1920s when they joined the Free Corps, paramilitary associations, and veterans' leagues in search of a new front soldiers' state. The idea of negotiation and political compromise replaced the violent attempts of the previous years to gain victory through the use of superior force. Instead of trying to annihilate the opponent, the nations of Europe began to look for the peaceful resolution of conflicts.[12]

This is also the period when Germany, as the power in the heart of Europe, and her former enemies in the west began to settle not only their financial disputes over reparations but also their political ones. In 1925 the Locarno

Pact was signed, which secured the territorial status quo along Germany's western frontier with France and Belgium. In the following year Germany was admitted to the League of Nations, the organization set up in 1919 to provide mechanisms for the peaceful resolution of conflicts and for preventing difficult disputes from escalating into another disastrous war. It was in this improved political climate that the foreign ministers of France and Germany, Aristide Briand and Gustav Stresemann, met in a spirit of reconciliation to tackle the many unresolved legacies of the Great War. Parliamentary politics, while far from completely stable, also worked satisfactorily even in Germany, where the democratic Weimar Republic had almost disappeared in 1923.

Finally, there was also the sociocultural sphere, and although counterfactuals should be handled with caution, it is worthwhile in this case to conjecture how European history would have evolved if the economic upturn of the mid-1920s and the increase in prosperity had continued. The quality of life of many American families had improved, but quite a few average European ones also lived better, even if the acquisition of an automobile was still out of reach. Department stores offered off-the-peg clothes and inexpensive household items. On the weekend city dwellers and young people in the provinces changed their work clothes for something fashionable. Cinemas and dance halls proliferated in their neighborhoods. Next to indigenous tunes there was the charleston, imported from America, that allowed freer and more improvised movement of the dance partners and thus challenged the formal rules of the traditional ballroom. Other young people became jazz fans and collected records of well-known musicians to play endlessly on their wind-up gramophones. These civilians had little interest in wearing uniforms or listening to march music, and the last thing they wanted was another war.[13]

Still, there were rumblings even in the more prosperous and relatively stable mid-1920s of bad times to come. Unemployment rates remained high and, above all, saw fluctuations that indicated that the economies of Europe were skating on thin ice. In Germany, for example, where the unemployment rate had dropped to a favorable 3.4 percent in 1925, it leapt to 10 percent a year later and hovered around 6.2 percent in 1927 and 1928 before rising to 8.5 percent in 1929. There were also the continuing burdens on Europe's economies stemming from the war: the payments to veterans, widows, and orphans, as well as the need for medical provisions to deal with war-related illnesses and the effects of malnutrition. To be sure, these expenditures were necessary not only for humanitarian reasons to prevent people from falling into abject poverty but also because economic stabilization helped contain political radicalization that in the age of universal suffrage would have driven embittered voters into the arms of the extreme Right or Left. In this sense there was a direct connection between economic conditions and political behavior, between prosperity and a functioning parliamentary system.

These problems remained below the surface as long as American corporations and investors were looking for opportunities in Europe. Apart from foreign direct investments, Americans also became interested in the loan business, and big New York investment firms and banks got involved in a thriving bond market. Beginning in 1924, hundreds of millions of U.S. dollars flowed across the Atlantic into private companies and public utilities. Anxious to modernize their infrastructure, many cities issued bonds with which to finance the building of roads and public transport systems. Politicians who also had their reelection in mind tried to increase their popularity with voters by adding parks and recreational facilities. Just as in the United States, ordinary people hoped to see not only a rise in their material well-being but also improved facilities for their leisure activities. It is understandable that American investors took up such loan issues. The interest rates were favorable and acquiring public bonds issued by a big European city seemed a safer investment than putting one's money into a private company whose financial health was either not fully transparent or looked uncertain. Parker Gilbert, the American reparations agent who also closely monitored the economic situation in Weimar Germany, was among the first to be dismayed by this development. He was interested in the modernization of private industry, not in the building of public swimming pools and playgrounds. He observed how funds that industry desperately needed for the acquisition of modern machines flowed into city bonds. But he was powerless to change the pattern. There were few regulatory instruments both in Europe and the United States to channel the flow of money. People still put their trust into the allegedly superior forces of the market, and it was only in the wake of the Great Depression that laws were introduced that allowed governments to intervene in a market that had become unhinged. Whatever Gilbert's nightmares of a looming crisis, the average investor saw the dangers only when it was too late.

The shaky foundation on which the prosperity of the mid-1920s had been built broke in the autumn of 1929. Economic historians continue to debate the causes of the Great Slump. Some see the roots of the catastrophe that hit both Europe and the United States and then the world economy as a whole in the weaknesses of the financial and stock market systems, especially in liberal-capitalist America.[14] Others believe the depression was unleashed by an underlying crisis of the industrial system that was part of the fallout of the Great War and that had continued to smolder in Europe even during the years of recovery after 1924. It is worth considering both arguments briefly.

As far as the financial crisis interpretation and America's role are concerned, there can be no doubt that the stocks of many domestic companies had become grotesquely overvalued as a result of rampant speculation. A downward correction of the market was bound to come sooner or later. Here lies the significance of the Wall Street crash of October 1929, when prices went into a steep decline very quickly. Speculators who, going through their portfolios, thought they had come into wealth, found that many of their shares had become worthless pieces of paper almost overnight. If, in addition to their own savings, they had used loans from their bank to buy shares, the once friendly and encouraging bankers now called in what they had so generously lent. If the customer, having lost a lot of money in the stock market, became insolvent, a chain reaction set in, as his bank in turn ran into liquidity problems. Suddenly, those who had savings accounts but had not joined the stock market scramble of the previous years rushed to their bank to withdraw their savings before it was too late. Those who came early got their money out; others who came a little later found the counters closed. In short, the house of cards began to collapse as private individuals, investment firms, and banks went out of business.

The panic soon reached Europe. Here the chain reaction was partly related to the fact that Americans began to recall their loans. The factories and municipalities that had relied on the steady stream of funds from the United States for their modernization programs had no choice but to drop projects and cut back. First they canceled the repayment of American loans, exacerbating the crisis across the Atlantic. Next, they began to dismiss workers. Civil servants who legally could not be dismissed had their salaries reduced. A period of mass unemployment began, inevitably causing a drastic reduction in consumption as people had to tighten their belts. In short, this was the snowball effect that some economic historians saw as originating in the financial system before it spilled over into the rest of the economy. But this link also indicates that the process could have been triggered from the other end. Indeed, some experts argued that the roots of the crisis must be sought not in the financial sector but in the sphere of production and living standards and that one has to begin the analysis on the European side.

We have already mentioned a number of signs that indicate, on closer inspection, that the industrial economies of Europe in the wake of wartime and postwar dislocations were far from healthy. The stabilization and growth had been precarious. Behind the facade of increased consumption loomed serious structural problems. The ups and downs in the unemployment rate were one indicator of trouble. Strikes called by powerful trade unions were another. In 1926 Britain was hit by a strike that began in the mining industry but soon drew in hundreds of thousands of fellow workers in other branches. In Germany the so-called *Ruhreisenstreit* (dispute in the Ruhr iron industry) broke out in 1928, which resulted in massive lockouts of workers by employers.[15] France also experienced labor unrest.[15] They all fought for an improvement of their living standards at a time when people were talking about an economic boom. Even if the inflation rates were relatively low, they all expected to see a rise in real wages in order to participate in the prosperity they saw around them. If there had been a more wide-ranging increase in productivity and a reduction in prices stemming from the gains in Fordist mass production, Europe's trade unions might have exerted less pressure on the wages front. But as the above comparison with output per worker in the American car industry showed, Europe continued to lag behind in industrial modernization. There was also the misperception of Fordism that Bonn had pinpointed when he spoke of the "grown-up German children [in business] who visit America for the first time."

Many firms just did not find it possible to introduce tangible price reductions of the kind seen in the United States because they were too weak to cut their prices. Faced with continuing market instabilities, entrepreneurs adopted conservative strategies. They may have been fascinated by the idea of rationalized production that Henry Ford practiced at River Rouge and recommended to his European visitors. Their own rationalization measures enabled them to reduce their costs by making some of their workers redundant who, in turn, increased the army of unemployed. But this was clearly not how Fordism was supposed to work. No less distressing, many felt that their profit situation, even after rationalization, did not allow them to pass part of the gains on to the consumer. One major factor that impeded a more competitive pricing policy was the widespread existence of cartels and syndicates, which were more concerned with market stability than market competition.[16]

Cartels were legally binding horizontal agreements between independent companies in a particular branch of industry through which the members fixed prices and laid down production quotas, thus undermining competition. The power of cartels was often also strong enough to ostracize firms that broke ranks or non-members who tried to undercut agreed price levels. These cartels were particularly common in German industry, but they also existed in other European countries. It was a tradition that was different from the American system where, beginning with the Sherman Act of 1890, so-called anti-trust legislation had in essence banned and indeed criminalized anticompetitive behavior via cartels. The same applied to syndicates, that is, sales organizations through which cartel members in Europe marketed their products at agreed prices. The overall effect of the system in the United States was to push industry in the direction of oligopolistic competition, or concentration in a number of large corporations that encouraged price reductions in order to attract new consumers. In Europe, by contrast, cartels impeded price cuts for the benefit of the consumer, if only because prices had to be pegged at the level that secured the profitability of the least efficient cartel member.

Finally, there were many entrepreneurs and managers who, even if they could reduce prices, had ideological reservations about creating an American-style mass-consumption society. Educated middle-class professionals and intellectuals, as well as the business elites, feared that the rise of a mass-production and mass-consumption economy would promote the unfolding of a "mass society," subverting traditional hierarchies and class differences.[17] In this respect they were deeply suspicious of the American model where, it seemed to them, mass production and mass consumption had reinforced mass democratic politics and mass culture. The overall impact of these perceptions of the society that had grown up across the Atlantic was an anti-Americanism whose dynamics have been the subject of a good deal of recent historical research.[18] Not surprisingly, there were powerful elite groups in Europe who resisted "Americanization," and this opposition in turn put the brakes on the advance of a civilian society devoted to the peaceful consumption of its mass-produced goods.

Economic historians have pointed to yet another factor to explain the instabilities of the industrial systems of Europe in the mid-1920s. Focusing on the German case in the heart of Europe, which contemporaries on both sides of the Atlantic viewed as key in their quest to overcome the devastations of the war and to generate "prosperity for all," the Munich University economic historian Knud Borchardt has advanced the hypothesis that the Weimar economy was also weakened by high welfare state expenditures.[19] Although the origins of this welfare state went back to the pre-1914 period, its growth had been accelerated by the need to cope with the claims of war veterans, widows, and orphans, as well as by the desire of the early postwar elected governments to prevent a further political radicalization of the "masses." This is why they conceded not only higher wages despite galloping inflation but also additional social security benefits. The effect of these policies, Borchardt insisted, had been to overburden the national economy. This in turn resulted in an increased resistance by employers to social expenditures, as manifested in the lockouts during the *Ruhreisenstreit*. Their resentment contributed to the blocking of vital investments in the modernization of industry. Whatever gains rationalization may have brought them were eaten up, so they claimed, by their obligations to contribute to Weimar's social security system. Although Borchardt's arguments have been challenged, he certainly pointed to a dilemma resulting from the consequences of World War I in Europe that politicians and businessmen did not know how to resolve and that therefore contributed to the structural problems of the interwar economy.

During the 1920s a number of factors were thus at work that, taken together, have led the protagonists of the industrial crisis theory to consider them more important for triggering the Great Slump than the Wall Street crash of 1929. Ultimately it was probably both. Although the degree of modernization and efficiency of American corporations was, on the whole, greater than that of their counterparts in Europe, the stock market was a barometer signaling that not all was well in the industrial system of the United States. Share prices even of corporations that were deemed solid vacillated in the years before 1929. Uncertainty about the market was often just below the surface. What kept it from breaking through was that the experts disagreed as to the state of the economy and that many investment banks continued to float loans, in 1927–28 even at an accelerated pace.[20]

The first clear signs of the impending stampede came on 29 October 1929, when the *New York Times* index for industrial shares declined by 8 percent to a level that had been reached three months earlier. On the following day, a Thursday, trading on Wall Street became very hectic with some 13 million shares changing hands. To prevent a further decline a number of banks agreed that afternoon to try to bolster confidence in the market. By the end of the day there was a recovery and the index had sunk by only 12 points. The next two days also remained relatively stable, certainly in comparison to the losses that were registered the following Monday. On that day, the *New York Times* index slumped by 49 points. Another 43 points were lost the following day, the infamous "Black Tuesday."[21]

What followed over the next few months and years is well-known: massive bankruptcies and dismissals on both sides of the Atlantic. By 1932 some 12 million people had lost their jobs in the United States—24.1 percent of the working population. In Germany the figure reached 6.1 million in February 1932—over 30 percent of the working population. Britain was also hit hard; the number of unemployed reached 2.5 million by the end of 1930. Coal production declined by one-fifth and in many of the small mining communities all men were without work. Ship building declined to 7 percent of what it had been before 1914. London abandoned the gold standard, thereby increasing the flight of capital. In France the agricultural sector had remained larger than it had in Britain, and this prevented the country from being as badly affected as those with larger urban and industrial populations. Still, the number of unemployed that stood at 191,000 in 1931 climbed to over 300,000 by 1933.[22]

The Great Slump almost inevitably increased social and political tensions everywhere. Violence that had become part of daily life during World War I and the years thereafter returned, and with it reappeared men who had a vision of the future that was different from the civilian one of the mid-1920s. During those years, Europeans had dreamed about a society in which, if not all, certainly many would achieve prosperity. They had glimpsed it and, in a modest and unequal way, even enjoyed it. After 1929 it was gone and the future pointed to another period of conflict that in large parts of Europe would destroy civilianism and civil society.

MILITARISM

The violence that World War I had unleashed was not tamed by the armistice and peace of 1918–19 but continued in numerous civil wars. The boundary between soldier and civilian had largely disappeared and a human life to some people remained as cheap as it had been during the mass slaughter in the trenches or in the battles on the eastern front. At the same time, the short-term stabilization of the mid-1920s had demonstrated that there was an alternative to the martial visions of the Free Corps fighters and "political soldiers" who found it difficult to adapt to postwar society. The economic crisis that began in 1929 exacerbated social and political conflicts and was grist for the mills of the men of violence on the extreme Right and Left.

No less significant, in peculiar ways the foundations of their activities during the 1930s were laid during the years of relative stability. During this period they refined the arsenal of arguments and organizational practices they had developed in wartime and in the civil wars that followed. All European societies had to deal with the consequences of a catastrophic war, but the ways in which they did varied from country to country. After the signing of the Paris peace treaties, the majority of the populations in western Europe were longing for a durable peace. Although the conflict had been psychologically and materially devastating, they believed they had won and that the sacrifices had not been in vain. One mourned the dead, built well-maintained war cemeteries and monuments to commemorate the fallen, and occasionally expressed bitter resentment against the Germans.[23] Many families continued to reel from the shock of mass death and the loss of loved ones. They were reluctant to talk about their emotions and suffered in silence. However, they, too, hoped to return to normalcy as soon as possible; they, too, did not want another war. Finally, the prospect of economic improvement also helped western Europeans to forget and had a restraining, "civilizing" effect.

If we consider the German predicament, it is probably accurate to say that in Central Europe a majority of the population, albeit a smaller one than in Britain or France, also wanted peace. What impeded the transition to peacetime normalcy was that the economy was in an even more desolate state than that of the western Allies. As we have seen, economic and financial crisis led to political crisis, all of which reached a high point in 1923. There was also the psychological situation. Unlike the populations of France or Britain, the Germans had lost the war. There was no consolation in victory. It was difficult to justify the war in terms of a futile but heroic effort that had ended in defeat when even the Italians, officially on the winning side, felt bitter about their "mutilated" victory that had not brought them the territorial gains their allies had promised them. Many Germans therefore simply put their head in the sand and refused to acknowledge defeat. They adhered to the illusion that the army had remained undefeated in the field and believed the patent lie that the brave soldiers had been stabbed in the back by the left-wing radicals who triggered a revolution at home. Accordingly, they continued to fight the war by other means, including the murder of alleged "November criminals" and other "traitors to the fatherland."

Still, in the defeated nations only a small minority of people supported the idea of waging war after the Great War by means of coups, assassinations, and street fights. However, there was a somewhat larger group of veterans who, though not practicing violence, never fully adjusted to civilian life and became members of veterans' associations.[24] Some of them had served in their communities during the revolutionary years of 1918–19 to help restore law and order. Although they subsequently retired from active duty, some two million of them were attracted by associations that upheld the memory of the war, gave financial support to needy members, and organized events at their local branches. Such associations also emerged in the victorious nations where they tended to raise their voice in politics from time to time to support their government's reparations and restitution demands against the defeated powers, occasionally criticizing these policies as feeble. Conversely, the associations that grew up in Germany and Austria tried to pressure their politicians into granting their claims for veterans' pensions and welfare benefits and to form a common front of opposition against Allied demands for reparations. If nothing else, they contributed to the persistent international conflicts and tensions of the early 1920s.

By contrast, the organizations that were formed out of the remnants of the Free Corps after the latter had been dissolved and outlawed attracted a different type of veteran. As early as 1920–21 they had displayed a disturbing proclivity to violence when they assassinated prominent Republican politicians like Erzberger and Rathenau or resorted to *Feme* murders against alleged traitors within their own ranks. During the years of relative stability in the mid-1920s most of them expressed their hatred of the Weimar Republic in words rather than murderous deeds. But with the onset of the Great Depression after 1929 politics once again became polarized and mobilized the activists of the early 1920s. They were supported by a younger generation of men who were even keener to work for radical change.[25] Soon their resentments against the parliamentary-democratic republic that they had burdened with the defeat of 1918 and their desire for action poured out from the beer halls into the streets to engage political opponents in violent struggle. Compromise between the two sides was unthinkable. The foe had to be annihilated. It was in the civil war between these two fronts that the Weimar Republic was ultimately pulverized.

It now also became clear that the more tranquil mid-1920s had been more precarious not only economically but also politically than had met the eye. On closer inspection, even the more moderate nationalist veterans' associations of Central Europe contained plenty of ideological ferment. Their leaders and many of their followers had nothing but disdain for a civilian republic that was trying to modernize its economy to create prosperity and democratic participation for all. They wanted to replace the notion of a society that peacefully consumed its mass-produced goods by a *Frontsoldatenstaat* (state of front soldiers) geared to military conquest and to rectifying the "injustices" of the Versailles peace. It was a state in which people would be consumed by mass-produced military goods in pursuit of a political order organized along military-authoritarian lines. These radical veterans and the youth organizations they founded had learned various lessons from World War I, but they were different from the notion of "No more war" that millions of other Europeans adhered to.

However, the latter were not pacifists. Faced with naked aggression, these nations were prepared to defend themselves and their system of civilian values. This basic position was reflected, for example, in the conclusion of the Kellogg-Briand Pact of 1928. This international agreement outlawed wars of aggression in the hope that a ban would make major wars impossible. What the west Europeans and Scandinavians were also hoping to promote with such extensions of international law was a civilianization of society. These would be societies devoted to the peaceful exchange of goods, social reforms to reduce internal conflicts, and international trade to increase the general standard of living. It was the vision of a free and democratically organized society in which the soldier would assume an increasingly minor role and certainly not occupy a central or even dominant position.

However persuasive this vision of Europe's internal organization may have been, it had one serious flaw: domestic stability and prosperity depended on the continued inequality and exploitation of the colonies and the rest of the non-Western world. After World War I, resistance against these dependencies was felt in all colonial empires. But few people could conceive of a civilian consumption society that existed without the overseas territories that had been conquered in the nineteenth century. Most countries possessing colonies were neither economically nor sociopsychologically prepared for a world without colonies. The British began to look for compromises and a way to transform their empire into a "Commonwealth of Nations."[26] But the nationalist-imperialist and racist dispositions of the pre-1914 period had survived the cataclysm of World War I. And as the experience of that earlier period had also shown, these dispositions were inseparable from the use of violence overseas that came back to haunt the Europeans on their home ground.

If the interconnections between colonialism and violence had not been threatening enough, after 1929 the movements of war veterans proved even more dangerous to the preservation of a civilian society. As we have seen, the more radical elements among them aimed at a remilitarization of society. They labored to prepare a second wave of violence and dreamed of a soldierly

community. Since its spokesmen and intellectual elite openly called themselves "militarists," militarism provides a good way into the utopia they had
in mind. Social scientists have defined militarism in two ways.[27] Some relate
it to societies in which policymaking, foreign relations in particular, is determined by the primacy of military considerations. In a system of "political
militarism" of this kind, the generals have the final authority, as was the case
in Germany at the end of July 1914, if not long before. The other definition
focuses on the question of how far the categories, mentalities, and modes of
operation of the military have percolated into society at large. What, in other
words, is the spread of "social militarism" among the general population.

The ideas and programs that were developed by the radical veterans' associations in the mid-1920s espoused both types of militarism. Its spokesmen
wanted a state whose foreign and domestic policies were guided by military
and soldierly principles, and they visualized a society centered around the
principles of hierarchy and obedience, whose members were forever prepared to make sacrifices, even giving their lives, and, in which the community, often modeled on the "community of the trenches" of World War I,
was more highly valued than the individual and individual liberty. Militarism
found expression in members' appearance: tightly cut uniforms instead of
casually worn ready-to-wear jackets and trousers; short-cropped hair instead
of androgynous long locks; boots instead of loafers or sandals. Such contrasts,
behind which stood very different conceptions of modern living and societal
organization, can best be studied by examining photos taken at the annual
"front soldiers days" organized by the *Stahlhelm*, one of Weimar Germany's
most powerful veterans' associations. Its members met in major cities to
sleep in military tents, carry banners, listen to marching bands, and receive
their food standing in line at mobile field kitchens wheeled in for the occasion. By contrast, other men and their families, rejecting militaristic lifestyles, sought more free-wheeling and leisurely recreation in their garden
allotments or the parks of their city, some of which had been built with the
help of American money.[28]

However, there was also tension between the two types of militarism, both
of which had become visible before 1914 in the elder Moltke's thinking about
the evolution of modern warfare and the advent of the "people's war." Here
the political militarists postulated that the political system must be structured so that a small circle of military professionals would have the final word
when it came to vital decisions such as waging war or keeping the peace.
Their conceptions of conflict were still wedded to the notion of the cabinet
wars of the eighteenth and nineteenth centuries. Sociologically, this elite
hailed from a small stratum in which, with the end of aristocratic predominance, officers of bourgeois origin could rise to top command positions.[29]

Social militarists by contrast were oriented toward building a popular consensus from below, although their concepts should not be confused with the
idea of democratic participation in a modern liberal-parliamentary sense.

The much discussed *Frontsoldatenstaat* rested on the voluntary acceptance of hierarchy and subordination that had become part of the mental makeup of the member. Their concept of war was the "people's war" that the aristocratic Moltke had always feared because it was based on a principle of equality that was anathema to nineteenth-century military thought and action. As the myth of the "community of the trenches" postulated, if all men were equal in the face of death, why should they be rigidly divided into classes in a future warrior society? The experience of World War I had also shown that it could not be conducted without modern technology and industrial mass production. Accordingly, these elements were now also integrated into the vision of a twentieth-century militaristic society.

The difficulties arising for the idea of a new warrior society from the tension between an aristocratic militarism and a populist one, as well as from the problematic dynamic of modern military technology, barely affected the rank-and-file member of veterans' organizations in Weimar Germany and even less so in the countries of western Europe.[30] Many of them continued to believe above all in the allegedly classless "community of the trenches" that was said to have existed at the front during World War I. The task of the future, as they saw it, was to create this community in peacetime and to anchor it firmly in society. However, there were a number of intellectuals on the militaristic Right who believed that this vision had to be given a more solid ideological grounding to overcome civilianism.

One of the most influential among these intellectuals in Central Europe was Ernst Jünger. After writing extensively about his war experience on the Western front, in the mid-1920s he became a major voice as editor of *Die Standarte*, a journal financed by the *Stahlhelm* veterans' association with the explicit mission to design a program for a future *Frontsoldatenstaat*. The ideas Jünger developed in those years finally appeared in book form in 1932 under the title *Der Arbeiter* (The worker).[31] It was published at a moment when, at the height of the economic crisis, Germany stood at a crossroads, with one path pointing to a dictatorship pledged to producing war materials and unleashing a new world conflict that would devour human beings by the millions; the other one leading back to a parliamentary-democratic society that was wedded to the generation of civilian prosperity for all.

Jünger's *Der Arbeiter* envisioned a laboring industrial society that was very different from the latter model. In it he tried to dissolve the tension that existed between the aristocratic and populist militarism and the technological tools developed and refined by industry since the late nineteenth century. According to him, soldiers and factory workers were similar. One produced lethal weapons on sophisticated machines; the other used these weapons on the battlefield, the factory of death of the twentieth century. In the next chapter we will see how Jünger's writings before 1933 tallied with the policies of total mobilization in peacetime and with war under European fascism and the National Socialist dictatorship in particular. What is important at this point is that the ideological formulas of men like Jünger contributed to a politicization of the veterans' movement, especially in Central Europe. They also reinforced mentalities among the members that saw the use of violence as a continuation of politics by other means. These men were prepared to accept a total mobilization of resources for war even before it had begun. The *Stahlhelm* and other associations, like the Italian *fasci di combattimento* before them, armed themselves with sticks and knives and added paramilitary units to their main movement. They mobilized their members not only politically as voters, but also sent them out into the streets of the towns and cities to resume the civil wars of the early 1920s against their leftist and Republican opponents. The practice of trying to settle disputes by negotiation and compromise was rejected and replaced by physical struggle until an unconditional victory had been won.

To be sure, the escalation of conflict did not go to such extremes in all countries of Europe during the crisis of the 1930s. Britain was spared the bloodshed that occurred in Germany and Austria. There the hope of salvaging the policies of the mid-1920s against the men of violence remained stronger among the general population, even if some organizations, such as the Union of British Fascists, wanted to erect autocratic rule. By contrast, the victims of violence could be found in the streets of the Weimar Republic almost daily. On 17 July 1932 the town of Altona to the west of Hamburg in northern Germany mourned eighteen dead after a fight between local Nazis and communists. It was also on these occasions that the methods of killing that had been developed in the civil wars after 1918 and would soon be practiced in Hitler's concentration camps were sharpened. The infamous Potempa murders where Nazis literally trampled a communist to death is another example of how far civilianism had collapsed in 1932.[32]

In short, the fighting leagues, as they now tended to be called, contributed greatly to the renewed escalation of violence and the militarization of entire societies. The parliamentary governments of Europe tried their best to contain or tame the paramilitaries; where authoritarian regimes won the day, the associations were deliberately deployed as propellants of violence. The dream of a civilian mass-production and mass-consumption society faded. The total mobilization for another world war had begun.

THE STALINIST EXPERIMENT IN VIOLENCE

As the militaristic tendencies that reappeared in the heart of Europe in the wake of the economic crisis gave rise to fears about the future, the Soviet Union underwent an evolution that is no less relevant for understanding the direction of interwar history. Under Stalin's dictatorship, Russia experienced its own total mobilization, though of a somewhat different kind than what Jünger envisioned. Ultimately, though, it was no less bloody. As with the Russian civil war of 1917–21, Stalin's policies of violence must be seen in a dialectical relationship with developments further to the west.[33] In the Soviet Union, the Bolsheviks had introduced a model of society that inspired not only fear among the European middle classes but also hope among millions of industrial workers. They supported the introduction of the Leninist experiment in their own countries.

The dialectic was set in motion in the clash between the opponents and protagonists of the Bolshevik vision of the future. For the radicals among the anti-communists, Lenin's regime was not only a living nightmare but needed to be destroyed by any means. Accordingly, the fascists, the Nazis in particular, rationalized the preparation of another world war in terms of an inevitable struggle for survival against the "Jewish-Bolshevik" foe in the east.

We also saw above how the Russian civil war had ended with Lenin's victory over the "White" counterrevolutionaries. After the Bolsheviks had secured their power over the huge Euro-Asian territories of the former tsarist empire, they faced the task of rebuilding a country and economy devastated by close to a decade of war and civil war with hitherto unimaginable human and material losses. Although Lenin had staged his revolution in an agrarian society with but a tiny industrial proletariat and capitalist bourgeoisie, he remained enough of a Marxist to want to establish a classless *industrial* society, except that he proposed to skip the bourgeois stage that Marx and, following him, Lenin's Menshevik opponents had postulated all societies would have to pass through. The question was how to reach the final goal most safely. Lenin was pragmatic enough to recognize that the reconstruction of the country had to be the first step on the way toward a modern industrial Russia. He also knew that the rebuilding and the subsequent transformation of society could not be undertaken without the support of agriculture and above all the *kulaks*, the wealthy peasants, nor without foreign investments.[34]

In line with these calculations, Lenin pursued a double strategy after the end of the Russian civil war. On the one hand, he initiated the New Economic Policy (NEP), which slowly dismantled the strict regimentation of the economy during the previous period of "war communism."[35] The mechanisms of the market were restored. The right to private property was affirmed with certain restrictions. Peasants were allowed to sell their produce in the open market for profit. The nationalization of enterprises was halted in industry and competition between private and nationalized companies was encouraged. The country thus developed something like a mixed economy. In the name of reconstruction and greater productivity, the entrepreneur was given permission to pay higher wages for more specialized labor. The success of this strategy soon became clear when output rose markedly.

At the same time, the Soviet regime that in 1917 had predicted the destruction of capitalism and the outbreak of a proletarian world revolution under NEP proved very open to foreign investment now that the regime had survived the counterrevolutionary challenge and the prospect of a world revolution had evaporated. Western firms were invited to return to the Russian market. Entrepreneurs for whom the risk of trading with the Bolsheviks had been too great now became interested. The British government did its bit by formally reestablishing its trading links, while the Americans, still firmly opposed to Bolshevism on ideological grounds, stayed away from a deal with Lenin. Furthermore, London responded to the change in Bolshevik economic policy by designing a plan to form an international consortium. With its help capitalist investments were to be channeled into communist Russia.

However, these plans, which British prime minister David Lloyd George put forward, came to naught in June 1922 at the Genoa Conference, at which prospective consortium members gathered to formulate a program. The Russians did not want to subscribe to a program that would have resulted in "capitalists" from various European countries being drawn into the country. Instead they preferred to deal with only one industrial power: Germany.[36] In a secret move, the two sides met at Rapallo near Genoa to seal a German-Soviet agreement. What no doubt facilitated the deal was that prior to it the two outsiders of the international system had begun to work together in secret in the military field and for reasons that will become clear in the next chapter. Not surprisingly, Lloyd George was very angry. The Russo-German connection continued after Lenin's death in 1924. There was a fierce struggle for Lenin's mantle among the key members of the Politburo. It was eventually won by Joseph Stalin, who had a different vision than that of Lenin's NEP. He wanted to industrialize the Soviet Union with the help of the country's own resources and without Western investments.[37]

Stalin's concept of building "socialism in one country" was initially directed against his arch rival in the Politburo, Leon Trotsky. The latter had called for world revolution in 1917 and still hoped to trigger one. Accordingly, he pleaded for a "permanent revolution" and continuing subversion of the capitalist world to prepare its eventual and supposedly inevitable downfall. Lenin, while not completely abandoning belief in this revolution, did not consider it a top priority, and, as early as January 1918, had focused on the consolidation of the Bolshevik regime and later the rebuilding of Russia, in his case with Western help. Stalin's position in the post-Lenin power struggle aimed to not only obliterate Trotskyism, but also retreat from the NEP. The Soviet Union was to pursue its industrialization and modernization policy without a major participation of foreign capitalists. He was an isolationist, fearing that foreign investments and contact with Western ideas would warp the building of socialism.

The struggle over the future direction of Soviet domestic and foreign policy lasted until 1927. At the end of the process, Stalin had also removed a
number of other rivals who had initially sided with him against Trotsky. He
now was in the undisputed position to implement his concept of "socialism
in one country." In 1928 he advanced a program for the rapid industrialization of the Soviet Union that no longer counted on Western help. There was
henceforth only one source from which he could marshal the financial means
for his plans, especially in the absence of a developed industrial or commercial sector: agriculture. Stalin aimed to extract the resources from the
wealthy *kulaks*. Since he did not expect these peasants to volunteer their
assets, he decreed the forced collectivization of their properties. When the
kulaks resisted this policy, Stalin retaliated with great brutality. Large-scale
expropriations were accompanied by deportations and murders by the secret
police. The regime established "special settlement camps" for some of these
victims, and by 1940 some nine million of them had gone through this system. Others were pressed into collective farms. In desperation, the *kulaks*
slaughtered their animals and destroyed their grain reserves. Between 1929
and 1933 the stock of domestic animals slumped by 17 million horses, 30
million cattle, and 100 million sheep and goats, a decrease of 50–65 percent.
Although it might be argued that the slaughter of so many draught animals
benefited the mechanization of Russian agriculture and also opened professional opportunities to trained agronomists, technicians, and veterinarians,
there is no denying that Stalin's program amounted to a human and economic
catastrophe, about whose extent we are still incompletely informed.[38]

The dislocations that Stalin's collectivization caused in the country in turn
impeded his ambitious five-year plan of industrialization. As difficulties
mounted and real wages dropped by about half between 1927–28 and 1936,
protests rose among the workers in the urban centers, which were met with
repression. Factories were forced to increase their productivity under often
impossible terms and conditions. Soon the Stalinist camp system filled up
with industrial workers. These policies were accompanied by a growing militarization of Soviet life. The principle of strict discipline had been enshrined
from the start of Bolshevism at the turn of the century in Lenin's concept of
a cadre-party of committed fighters. The revolution and the years of "war
communism" had strengthened this principle when the Bolsheviks fought
for their survival against the "Whites" and the Western Allies. These military
pressures were bound to have profound repercussions on the regime and
Russian society as a whole that had only known tsarist autocracy before then.
In enforcing his program Stalin could therefore rely on the traditions of a
police state. Moreover, it was a program that focused on the expansion of
heavy industry as the foundation of a successful industrialization. This im-
plied that both peasants and workers were to make sacrifices. The notion of

their benefiting from forced industrialization as consumers was, if it existed at all, pushed into the distant future.[39]

Recent research has shown that the process of militarization was also promoted by the fact that a considerable part of heavy industrial production was geared toward the manufacture of armaments.[40] And yet it is probably misleading to make too close a comparison between Stalinism and the militaristic visions of Ernst Jünger or—as will be discussed in a moment—of Adolf Hitler.[41] As indicated by the slogan "socialism in one country," Soviet policy was defensive. Industrial production was not designed to facilitate a racist war of conquest and extermination of the kind the Nazis spoke about. Stalin wanted to revolutionize the internal structures of Soviet society. His concept of building socialism in isolation from the rest of the world was, at least for the duration of this process, not concerned with conquering the world with military force. If urban workers were increasingly added to the exiled *kulaks* in the Siberian camps, this was due to the paranoia with which Stalin and his clique reacted to the resistance against their dictatorship in the towns and cities. Given the proliferation of this resistance, seeing conspirators everywhere who were then suspected of being Western spies and capitalist stooges was almost inevitable in the obsessive atmosphere of this engineered upheaval.

Soon Stalin's "revolution" began to devour its own progenitors. After the peasants and workers came the arrest and execution of assorted party leaders and other elite groups. The assassination of Sergei Kirov, the head of the Leningrad party organization, on 1 December 1934 was an important turning point. Tens of thousands of Leningrad citizens were arrested in its wake and sent to Siberia. Hundreds of thousands had their party membership revoked and became victims of the secret police.[42]

As Stalin tightened his grip, even children were caught in the police dragnet. A law was passed in April 1935 that declared minors to be adults and henceforth exposed them to the full range of sanctions in the criminal code, including the death penalty. Meanwhile the torture of men and women of all ages continued in the expectation that forced confessions would reveal the full extent of the opposition that allegedly threatened the existence of the Soviet state. The country became infected with fear and hysteria. While the purges created opportunities for upward mobility among younger professionals and technicians, ultimately everyone had to expect the early morning knock on the door as the police arrested millions of mostly innocent people. In this political climate of persecution it is not surprising that the witch-hunters finally began to suspect and arrest each other. Nor was the Red Army protected against this terror regime. By the late 1930s, leading officers, falsely accused of collaborating with Hitler, were tortured and liquidated.

In the end, the chiefs of the secret police were also given show trials and put before the firing squads.

It is not difficult to see that these mass murders had serious consequences for Stalin's industrialization program and his capacity to resist Hitler's invasion of the Soviet Union.[43] The Red Army was weakened in an almost suicidal fashion. Even if heavy industry was churning out tanks and guns in impressive quantities, at the time of the Nazi invasion in 1941 five years after the purges the Red Army continued to have a shortage of experienced and senior officers. The arrest of countless managers and workers undermined the aims of the industrialization program. The vast but inefficient system of camps that tried to exploit the slave labor of its inmates could not make up for the losses in production in the industrial centers in the western parts of the Soviet Union. Even with the information we now have on many aspects of the camp system, it is still difficult to grasp the extent of Stalin's murderous regime that ravaged the country in the 1930s.

It was a program of the total mobilization of society for aims that nevertheless differed from those of the men of violence who, during the same period, geared their fascist dictatorships toward wars of conquest and the creation of a new "racial" order. No doubt comparable in its methods and practices of militaristic repression, Stalin's utopia nevertheless differed from Hitler's.[44] If historians insist on maintaining a dividing line between the two dictators, this does not imply an underestimation of the horrendous human and material costs of Stalin's experiment in violence. In the meantime we have at least retrieved from the archives a few more figures relating to the sacrifices that Russian society was forced to make to the Bolshevik collectivization of agriculture and the forced expansion of industry. According to these estimates, the authorities killed between five and ten million people. Further millions were sent to the camps, where many of them also perished as a consequence of the inhuman conditions there.[45]

In conclusion, we must come back to the dialectic that Stalin's violent experiment imported into European politics. The rumors and vague details about the mass murders and deportations roused the opposition outside Stalinist Russia. More important, the radicalism of his policies was grist for the mills of those who believed that Bolshevism required the most radical countermeasures. The relative strength of communist movements in Europe outside the Soviet Union provided an additional justification for the argument that the "civilized" world faced a deadly enemy. Its promoters knew how powerful an argument it was for mobilizing the European Right.

Just as the Great Slump with its seemingly insoluble problems of mass unemployment slowly increased the misery and despair of millions, the polarization of political opinions and ideologies proceeded apace. The most radical elements came to believe that the struggle could only be won by the ruthless annihilation of the internal enemy. In this sense there was a direct link between the policies of violence that Stalin pursued against his own population and those that became commonly accepted in the rest of Europe under the banner of fighting the deadly contagion of Bolshevism. However, to what extent were these justifications of fascist violence merely a cover? Did the total mobilization the extreme Right that began during the 1930s have deeper causes—causes that lay in the colonialism and racism of the pre-1914 period and in the experiences of World War I and its consequences?

CHAPTER FOUR

Violence without Bounds, 1935–1945

TOTAL MOBILIZATION IN PEACETIME

Ernst Jünger's *Der Arbeiter* of 1932 was preceded two years earlier by his "The Total Mobilization," an essay that anticipated many of the positions underlying the book. In the essay the author first discussed "a few data. . . that differentiate the last war—our war, the greatest and most lasting event of our time—from other wars whose history has been transmitted to us." In that war, he continued, "the relationship which the individual partners had to technology had to play a decisive role." Indeed it is here that "the actual moral factor of this period is to be found, to whose subtle and imponderable radiations not even the strongest armies can stand up which are equipped with the latest weapons of annihilation of the machine age." After all, the "age has long passed in which it sufficed to send hundreds of thousands of recruited subjects onto the battle-field under reliable leadership." Today, Jünger wrote, total mobilization is required in the course of which, "next to the armies that encounter each other on the battle-field, new armies arise of transportation, nutrition, armament—[in short] the army of labor in general." In this way, "the wars of knights, kings, and burghers" would be replaced by "wars of *workers*—wars about whose rationalized structure and pitilessness the first great conflict of the 20th century has given us an inkling."[1]

However, in his view "the technical side of Total Mobilization" was not the decisive aspect. There existed a deeper lying precondition: "the *preparedness* for mobilization" that could not be sufficiently grasped by reference to economic explanations. For this reason, "the school of historical materialism" could touch on no more than the "surface of the process." Germany, Jünger argued, had lost World War I because it had undergone no more than a partial mobilization. "Large areas of its power" had been inaccessible to a total mobilization.

Germany's success had been partial instead of total. The task of this age was to secure all forces to achieve total victory. Jünger saw indications of this wherever "patriotism has been replaced by a new nationalism that is strongly pervaded by elements of consciousness": thus, "in Fascism, in Bolshevism, in Americanism, in Zionism, in the movements of the peoples of color progress has begun to push in ways that were unthinkable until now." In many places "the humanistic mask" had "almost worn off." In its place had appeared "a half grotesque, half barbaric fetishism of the machine, a naive cultivation of technology." This, he added, was particularly true in places "where one lacked an immediate [and] productive relationship to the dynamic energies of whose destructive victorious sweep the long-range guns and the bombs of the armed flight squadrons are the martial expression."

Socialism and nationalism, Jünger concluded, represented the "two big millstones between which progress will grind up the remnants of the old world and finally itself." Today its "identity was becoming ever more clear in all countries, and even the dream of freedom is disintegrating under the iron claps of a pair of pliers." To him it was "a grand and terrifying spectacle to witness the movements of ever more uniformly shaped masses when the world spirit puts out its traps." Each of these movements contributed to "sharper and more pitiless recruitment [Erfassung]." There were "types of compulsion here that were more powerful than torture: so powerful that humans greet them with jubilation." However, "behind every way out that is marked by symbols of good luck" lurked "pain and death. The best to the person who enters these spaces [well] armed."[2]

Later, after his words had become reality, Jünger was reproached that he had been the intellectual father of an age of mass mobilization and inhumanity. He defended himself with the argument that he had done no more than write about inevitable developments that were already encapsulated in the structures of the postwar world. He denied that he had contributed to what happened in Europe in subsequent years. However, this is probably too simple a view of the interaction between ideas and their implementation. As the last sentence quoted from his essay demonstrates, the lesson he proposed to draw from World War I was to prepare for the impending age of pain and death not by partial mobilization but by rallying all forces in peacetime.[3]

This was also the demand of another warrior who has made an appearance in earlier chapters of this book: Erich Ludendorff. Though introduced somewhat belatedly, his policies in the High Command had contributed decisively to the totalization of war in World War I. His lesson was, though, that at a minimum this total mobilization should have started in August 1914 or, better, yet, well beforehand. In 1935 he raised his voice again by publishing a widely read slim volume titled *Der totale Krieg* (The total war). In it he demanded that "the state, i.e., the total politics and the conduct of total war, had to take special measures," such as "the most rigorous censorship of the press, stricter laws against the betrayal of military secrets, a stopping of border traffic with neutral states, bans on [political] gatherings, arrest of, if no-one else, the heads of the 'disgruntled,' surveillance of railroad traffic and the radio." Economic mobilization, he continued, could not be started "soon enough in peacetime." He also attached great significance to equipping the armed forces with the most modern weapons. Last but not least, the supreme commander of the future had to be able to rely on the "uncompromising submission to his orders." This commander would have to concentrate the attack in one place. A war on several fronts was to be avoided at all costs.

Ultimately, Ludendorff was less interested in technology than in the "spiritual" factor. During World War I he had for the first time expressed the opinion that "the spirit secures victory." In his view, the cohesion of the people was key, and this applied to peacetime as well: "The more the nations regain their race consciousness, the more the soul of the people stirs within them, the more widely the folkish conditions of life will be recognized by all; the more will also be sharpened the eye for the nation-destroying activities of supra-state powers of the Jewish people and the Catholic church with their striving for power and for political solutions that walk over the nations." Once all this was recognized, "the more a policy that aims at the preservation of the life of the people and is conscious of the requirements of total war, will come about under its own accord." This, Ludendorff concluded, will simply be "the given folkish policy" that will "willingly put itself into the service of the conduct of war; for both have the same goal: to preserve the folk."[4]

Authors such as Jünger and Ludendorff provided the men of violence of the interwar years with not only the pseudo-justifications but to a considerable degree the recipes for their deeds. Among these practioners of violence, Hitler, Stalin, and Mussolini certainly deserve the front-row seats, with their entourage and activist foot soldiers right behind them who had been the warriors in the early postwar period and had applied their destructive methods in the streets. Nor should we overlook the professional officer corps, whose members followed the writings of the authors of the "front generation" and were asking themselves about the lessons that the *Reichswehr* should learn from the experience of World War I. It was fundamental to their deliberations that they never genuinely accepted Germany's defeat in 1918 and the reduction of the German power position in Europe. Almost all of them wanted a revision of the Versailles Treaty, and if this could not be achieved by peaceful negotiation, they were prepared to support a change of the status quo by force.

In their mind, this was particularly true of the territories Germany had lost in the east and the existence of an independent Poland. As Hans von Seeckt, chief of the *Reichswehr*, wrote as early as 11 September 1922, for him the Polish state was intolerable and incompatible with the vital interests of his country.[5] Poland, he added, would have to fall and with it would crumble one of the pillars of the Versailles system, that is, French hegemony in postwar Europe. The task was therefore to prepare for a future struggle in the east.

At the same time, there were power politicians who wanted to expand the 100,000-man army the Allies had imposed at Versailles. Their aim was not merely to restore Germany's prewar position in Europe but to expand its territory. They were also students of the elder Moltke and other theoreticians of war; however, like their predecessors before 1914, they refused to accept the pessimistic conclusions that Moltke had drawn from the prospect of a "people's war." They did not agree to that, even after the disastrous World War I, wars between industrialized nations were no longer thinkable. Even in the age of mass mobilization, assembly-line production of military hardware, and the increased destructive potential of modern weapons they wanted to uphold the option of war-making. In short, if there had to be a revision of the hated Versailles Treaty by military means, its success had to be made more certain than it had been in July 1914. They did not want to be in the position of the younger Moltke, for whom the invasion of Belgium and Luxembourg had been the opening move in a conflict about whose victorious outcome he himself harbored serious doubts. These learning processes among the professional military help explain why the old idea of total annihilation of the enemy in swift lightning wars continued to hold sway. The new element was that this future was to be thoroughly prepared well in advance during peacetime.

The problem was that a war of aggressive territorial revision and expansion, directed not merely against enemy forces but entire populations, was not feasible with military power of the kind that existed in Germany in the early 1920s, that is, a small professional army that was banned from having modern weapons like tanks and planes, supported by a welter of paramilitary units that were poorly equipped, and had to receive their training in secret in the woods of eastern Germany away from the watchful eye of the Inter-Allied Military Control Commission (IMCC). Militias were useful primarily in the context of domestic militarization against the radical Left and the *Rotfrontkämpferbund,* the paramilitary arm of the Communist Party. They might also be deployed as a temporary stopgap in an emergency, should skirmishes occur in the borderlands with Poland. However, a future major war of annihilation needed a different type of armed forces.[6]

Such a war could not be conducted without the most modern weapons that the opponent would have but that Germany was prohibited from producing and deploying. The lightning war of the future required tanks and troop carriers; fighter planes were needed for aerial warfare of the type that science fiction writers had fantasized about before 1914 and that began to develop for real toward the end of the Great War. That the "Black *Reichswehr,*" the shadow army of weekend volunteers, was not suited for modern warfare became clear during secret maneuvers in remote parts of the country on Sundays when the mobilized units pulled life-size wooden tank models through the terrain.

The weaknesses of the Weimar armed forces were increasingly recognized by a younger generation of officers. They were more technocratically minded and began to abandon Seeckt's idea of training a secret army of reservists. Instead they saw themselves as a professional core that would be equipped to take charge of a large "people's army" of draftees, to be reintroduced in violation of the Versailles Treaty at a politically favorable moment. That moment came in 1935 when Hitler decreed the levy of a universal service Wehrmacht and made both the professionals and the recruits take their oath to him personally. How far the professional officer corps had diverged from the early postwar concept may also be gauged from its involvement in the murder of Ernst Röhm and his entourage and the political emasculation of his Brownshirts, the SA (Sturmabteilung). This paramilitary organization had first become notorious in the Hitler-Ludendorff putsch and the proposed March on Berlin of November 1923.

In subsequent years it had been a thorn in the flesh of the officer corps and the Weimar government when, during the years of renewed civil war in the early 1930s, Röhm challenged not only the law-and-order function of the police but also the arms monopoly of the *Reichswehr*. This challenge became more serious after the Nazi seizure of power in 1933 when the SA had grown to 400,000 men and promoted the idea of mass militia as the appropriate organizational form of the country's military power. After Röhm had also begun to question Hitler as the absolute führer of the "new Germany" and spoke of a "second revolution" to complete the one initiated by Hitler in January 1933, Hitler decided to murder his long-time associate and the rest of the SA leadership. Seeing the benefits of a destruction of the SA for their own position and plans for the future, the top army brass provided the logistical support for the bloodbath that Hitler ordered on 30 June 1934. In this "Night of the Long Knives" they thus became accessories to murder. It is very telling of the mentalities that had taken root among the officer corps that they condoned the simultaneous settling of some other Nazi accounts which included the murder of one of their own, General Kurt von Schleicher, as well as a number of innocent civilians. It is estimated that over one hundred people were brutally killed in a bloodthirsty frenzy during that night in which not only Hitler but also Heinrich Himmler's Blackshirts (SS, Schutzstaffel) took the lead. On 3 July, the Nazi-dominated Reichstag rubber-stamped the murders as an action justified by the need to protect the state (*Staatsnotwehr*).[7]

The new thinking about the war of the future and German strategy is reflected not only in the dissolution of the Black *Reichswehr* and later the paramilitary associations but also in the increased cooperation with the Red Army in the Soviet Union.[8] As far as the Soviets were concerned, cooperating with the Germans enabled them to learn from the latter about General Staff work and operational matters. The Germans in turn were given an opportunity to develop and test, on Russian soil and out of reach of the IMCC, the weapons they were not allowed to have under the terms of the Versailles Treaty and without which a future lightning war could not be conducted. Thus, when Jünger formulated his ideas about total mobilization, a younger generation of *Reichswehr* officers tried to lay the foundation in peacetime for armed forces that were modern and possessed a no less modern and well-prepared leadership.

Against the backdrop of these developments the professional officer corps concluded a pact in January–February 1933 with Hitler, the führer of the Nazi movement whom Hindenburg, the monarchist field marshal of World War I fame and popularly elected president of the Weimar Republic since 1925, had appointed as Reich chancellor on 30 January.[9] On 3 February, the new man not only promised the *Reichswehr* generals a fundamental revision of the hated Versailles Treaty, by force if necessary, but in a session of his cabinet a few days later also announced his intention to begin a program of rapid rearmament. The aim was to put at the disposal of his regime and the officer corps the means for a violent transformation of the territorial status quo in Europe and an expansion in the east. When Hitler ordered the prompt start of this rearmament program and in June 1934 moved to destroy Röhm's militia concept, the deal between the men of violence in the Nazi government and in the armed forces was sealed. The officer corps took a personal oath to Hitler and put their expertise for the preparation and waging of a lightning war at his disposal. Thenceforth a younger generation of officers refined its strategic planning for a future revisionist war and developed and tested in maneuvers the tactical recipes for a lightning war of movement with highly mobile armored units. In breach of the Versailles Treaty, the German air force began to think about how a total war might be waged against civilian populations in the cities.

Since Moltke's alternative of preserving peace in the era of "people's wars" had long been abandoned and Hitler's officer corps could think only in terms of a surprise offensive, the military preparations of the Wehrmacht began to develop, from 1935–36 onward, a dynamic of their own that buttressed the increasingly aggressive revisionist foreign policy of the Hitler dictatorship. For the parliamentary-democratic states of western Europe that were still coping with the Great Depression, it was difficult to obtain popular support for expensive rearmament programs when funds were inadequate to provide unemployment benefits and other welfare assistance to those who continued to suffer from the economic crisis. These voters expected their elected representatives to use the sharply reduced tax income for needy families.[10] A fascist dictatorship, by contrast, enjoyed two advantages. To begin with, it could deploy the most modern methods of propaganda through a media system over which it had gained total control. Its mission was to turn a general support for its economic policies into an allegedly massive acclamation for a revisionist foreign policy and a concomitant strengthening of the country's "defensive capabilities," while ruthlessly suppressing any dissent. Second, it was under no obligation to be truthful about its expenditures. Accordingly, the regime found many covert and bogus ways to finance its arms buildup.

The extent of the system's secret accounts remained so opaque that historians faced a difficult task after 1945 when they tried to calculate the exact amount of money Germany had expended on its war preparations. Estimates of German military investments between 1933 and 1939 range around 100 billion marks. The share of the military budget had been 6.3 percent of the gross national product in 1933; by 1936 it had risen to 19.4 percent and by 1938 to 25.3 percent. The Reich debt mounted from a little over 12 billion marks to 42 billion during the same period. The infamous Four-Year Plan of 1936 accelerated these efforts but also tried to prioritize expenditures. No modern industrial economy was able to sustain such growth in its arms buildup without eventually facing either bankruptcy or the pressure to go to war to recoup military investments through looting its neighbors' assets. In a secret appendix to the Four-Year Plan Hitler decreed in August 1936 that the country's economy be "capable of [waging] war" in four years' time and that the Wehrmacht be "capable of action" at that point.[11] Clearly Jünger's and Ludendorff's admonitions did not go unheeded. Germany was undergoing a mobilization that, if not total, certainly forged the Wehrmacht into a formidable instrument of aggression within a few years.

The officer corps had adopted an attitude toward mobilization in peacetime that virtually obliterated the boundaries between soldiers and civilians. Both were subjected to terroristic warfare from the start. The type of mentalities and principles that had taken root long before Hitler's attack on Poland in September 1939 may be gauged from the handling of the *ius in bello*. To be sure, there were civilian international lawyers who tried to uphold the rules agreed at The Hague before World War I concerning foreign occupation and the treatment of enemy combatants and civilians, and to remind the officer corps of their continued validity. But it is revealing of the thinking about warfare that had gained the upper hand in the Wehrmacht High Command that the chief of the Abwehr, the military intelligence branch, counseled his representative prior to a visit to the High Command not to use humanitarian arguments. Such arguments would merely encounter a sharp rebuke.[12]

That international law would no longer be strictly observed may also be seen in the changes in officer training. In the 1920s, the Germans had begun to develop the subdiscipline of psychology, called *Wehrpsychologie*, that tended to ignore international rules of warfare. Building on discussion that had first taken place before 1914 and had stressed the importance of will-power and iron nerves in the education of a modern officer corps, its protagonists were more interested in strengthening these characteristics than in respecting human life.[13] True, in that earlier period the definition of a modern officer had remained fairly unspecific and was based on the assumption that an aristocratic family background offered the best guarantee for proper soldierly demeanor. Nor should we forget that similar ideas about military education held sway in other European armies, just as the concept of annihilating the enemy was not adopted only by Schlieffen and the younger Moltke. In 1906 Ferdinand Foch, also, believed that willpower and determination were the best guarantees of victory for the French officer corps. World War I changed this, too. What had remained poorly defined before 1914 was systematized after 1918 and transformed in Germany into the pseudoscientific subdiscipline of *Wehrpsychologie*.

In April 1927, at a time when the *Reichswehr*, as we have seen, underwent a major change in its overall organization, shedding its militias with their secret exercises in the Pomeranian forests, the *Reichswehr* ministry decided to create a "Psychological Laboratory" that was to assist it in the selection of officers. Although the suitability tests included physical appearance on their checklists, an important part was devoted to analyzing the applicant's character with regard to self-discipline, determination, inner stability, and willingness to make decisions. From the middle of the 1930s, "race biological" criteria were added to the list, and in 1939 the laboratory was renamed Main Office of the Wehrmacht for Psychology and Race Science. If an applicant passed the tests that the *Wehrpsychologen* had developed, the subsequent military training made certain that "the steel-hard personalities" emerged at the end of the process whose production Colonel General Walther von Brauchitsch demanded in December 1938.[14]

For an understanding of German mobilization in peacetime yet another aspect of military training and war preparation is important. The nightmare of a war on two fronts had troubled German generals long before 1914. They knew after 1918 that they continued to be numerically inferior in relation to their neighbors and potential foreign enemies. Consequently, the idea of a preventive war—striking before the other side was ready—that had moved Moltke in 1914 was still very much alive among his successors in the interwar years. Hitler himself articulated this idea before the generals in an infamous speech in November 1937, recorded by one of his adjutants, Colonel Friedrich Hossbach. The notion of surprise also remained central to German military thinking, even if this meant violating international law. And there was another shift that would repeat itself in World War II. In 1914–15, the German army had confidently relied on its better training, equipment, and leadership. But when it became clear by 1916–17 and especially with the entry of the United States on the side of the Allies that Germany was not only numerically inferior but also with respect to the military hardware, the idea of willpower gained ground. The myth of the fighter who, even in the face of a better equipped enemy, will assert himself against all odds thanks to his superior psychological fiber was born.

When the Wehrmacht confronted American troops in the second half of World War II, the latter tended to rely primarily on their material superiority. If they encountered resistance as they advanced eastward in 1944–45, they halted the infantry, brought in the heavy armor, and shot up the enemy positions before moving forward through the rubble. On the German side, the Nazi regime by then extolled not only the willpower of soldiers and officers but also that of militias of ill-equipped Hitler Youths and elderly men who had been recruited in a last-ditch effort and who had no chance against enemy tanks and guns. In the hour of defeat the generals, like their predecessors in World War I, came to rely on the myth that personal heroism could still turn the tide. Of course, guided by *Wehrpsychologie*, the training of "steel-hard personalities" had been part and parcel of military education long before then, and it could also be found in the curricula of the indoctrination sessions in the Hitler Youth and Nazi student associations. Here the figure of the "heroic fighter" was held up to the young who, faced with a combat situation in the much hailed future war, would remain tough. In 1944 all Germans were learning one of the bitter lessons of World War II: material advantage could not be trumped by the qualities of the hero whom *Wehrpsychologie* and Nazi youth propaganda had been trying to produce.[15]

However, these trends in military thought and training were not confined to Germany, as the case of France illustrates. The French army also had its doctrine of annihilation, and Foch was one of its most ardent advocates.[16] But there were other voices. In particular, he was opposed by Philippe Pétain, who saw the best chance of victory in the defensive and the construction of unconquerable fortresses along the eastern border of France. There, in Pétain's mind, the German invaders would bleed to death. In 1914, the Foch school had temporarily won the day so that Joffre promptly launched his attack along the Alsace-Lorrainean border while Moltke invaded Belgium further north. Meanwhile, the British relied primarily on the navy, but it, too, had prepared itself for a battle of annihilation in the North Sea, even if the all-out clash with the kaiser's navy never took place.

When the war on the western front became one of attrition, many French officers and civilians came to believe that a defensive strategy had not only saved the country from defeat in 1914 during the "Miracle of the Marne" but had also become the key to ultimate victory. And when the Americans entered the war, attrition of the Central Powers seemed to be opening the path to their annihilation. Consequently, it was not Foch but Pétain who became the hero of postwar France.

French defensive thinking continued after 1918, although, given Germany's weaknesses, in a different shape. When the Americans who had once promised to assist France in its quest for security against another German invasion and in its effort to rebuild the devastated northern provinces retreated into isolationism and the British were more concerned with keeping their empire together than remaining engaged on the European continent, Paris and Brussels decided to act on their own.[17] Following the losses of the war, France's population was considerably smaller than Germany's. Worse, the radical revisionism of the German anti-Republican Right sounded very alarming to French ears. It was understandable that the French would not only insist on the payment of German reparations for economic reconstruction, social welfare for its war victims, and the repayment of their war debts to the United States but also try to prolong the greater weakness of a defeated and exhausted enemy to the east of the Rhine River. The occupation of one part of the Rhineland and the demilitarization of another as well as the temporary support for Rhenish separatist movements were elements of a strategy of keeping Germany weak.

French insistence on German reparations payments and German resistance to it finally led to the French occupation of the Ruhr industrial region in January 1923. Taken together, Paris's policies amounted to an offensive strategy, but one that did not aim at annihilating the enemy. The objective was to keep the Germans in chains, the "chains of Versailles," as the Germans saw it. The metaphor is significant. Its introduction into the daily language of the time indicated that German power in Europe had not been obliterated. The Reich was merely temporarily hampered in its capacity to be a major actor on the international stage. If it succeeded in ridding itself of those chains either through diplomacy or violent action, it would be as a result of its industrial and demographic strength, which was potentially still greater than that of its western neighbors.

This larger context of the postwar European balance of power must be remembered to avoid making the mistake of calling France's policy toward Germany aggressive in the way Hitler's policies came to be. Paris enjoyed no more than an artificial hegemony in the early 1920s. This hegemony was not based on French economic and military power but on the ephemeral weakness of its eastern neighbor and traditional archenemy. The demilitarized and occupied Rhineland was not a platform for the launching of an annihilating hammer-blow to Germany but represented a forefield to ensure that a future conflict with Berlin would not from the start once again take place on French (and Belgian) soil.

For reasons that have already been mentioned, France's artificial hegemony ended in 1924.[18] In subsequent years, German foreign minister Gustav Stresemann succeeded in negotiating a French retreat from the Ruhr and later from the Rhineland. The IMCC ended its surveillance of the restrictions to which the *Reichswehr* was subjected under the terms of the Versailles Treaty. It is therefore no accident that on the German side these developments coincided with the dismantling of the Black *Reichswehr* and the rise of a younger generation of revisionist German officers. They now began to reorganize the 100,000-man army into a modern professional force to serve as the core of a universal service Wehrmacht under Hitler when the draft was reintroduced in 1935.

This leads to yet another difference in German and French military thinking that is relevant in this context: While the *Reichswehr* continued to nourish the idea of a violent revision of the Versailles Treaty, which it then proceeded to pursue under the more favorable conditions of the Hitler regime, France's defensive posture firmly reasserted itself after 1924. The decision to build the so-called Maginot Line of fortresses in the Vosges Mountains and along the eastern border of reconquered Alsace-Lorraine became the tangible expression of this shift. Once again Pétain had won the day. Consistent with this strategy, he supported a law that proclaimed to protect France's frontiers and colonial possessions.[19] It should be added that the Maginot mentality was in tune with the basic principles of a civilian-parliamentary political culture that had deep roots in France. By contrast, the strength of a similar political culture was undermined in Weimar Germany, constitutionally a civilian-parliamentary democracy without deep roots in German history, by a variety of adverse factors even before 1929. Hit by economic crisis thereafter, Weimar democracy collapsed in 1933 and was replaced by a dictatorship in which the men of violence inside and outside the officer corps increasingly set the tone by reference to Jüngerian and Ludendorffian notions of total mobilization in peacetime.

The construction plan of the Maginot Line envisioned that the belt of fortresses would be completed within ten years. But it is indicative of how military thought in Europe continued to take Germany as its reference point that the Maginot mentality never swept the French officer corps completely. With the rise of Hitler, a countermovement was gaining strength by the mid-1930s that showed that the debate about the future of warfare had not been settled in favor of a Maginot-type defensive response to the growing German threat. Not surprisingly, Foch, the veteran of the offensive, raised his voice once more. He was joined by a younger officer named Charles de Gaulle. Although originally a protégé of Pétain, de Gaulle very eloquently began to spread his contrarian views in lectures and essays. No less important, his criticism of Pétain's strategy was not rooted in a dogmatic belief in the offensive and the battle of annihilation that was so widespread in the Wehrmacht. It was based on lessons that he argued he had learned from his own observations as a young officer on the western front. One of these was that beyond a few basic axioms, there were only circumstances and personalities that counted, and if circumstances changed, military strategy had to be adjusted.[20]

With this constantly in mind, de Gaulle never stopped looking east across the Rhine where a parliamentary republic, whose foreign minister had pursued a policy of reconciliation with France and peaceful revision of the Versailles Treaty, had given way to a Hitler dictatorship and its rearmament program. For de Gaulle this change raised the worrying question as to whether the Maginot Line was still the correct response to French security needs. As early as 1928 he had become convinced that France's occupation of the Rhineland would come to an end, and a year later Stresemann did indeed negotiate the retreat of French and Belgian troops, though the region remained demilitarized. A few years later, Hitler marched into the Rhineland, thus remilitarizing the German west right up to the French and Belgian borders. But long before this reckless breach of the Versailles Treaty, de Gaulle had lost confidence in the protective walls that had been drawn in Europe during the 1920s by international agreements. He feared the Germans would first insist on the return of the territories they had lost to France's ally Poland in 1919. Alsace-Lorraine would be next on their radical revisionist agenda.

Not unlike the American political scientist Harold Lasswell, who a few years later spoke of the rise of a modern "garrison state," de Gaulle came to hold the view that a military organization of society that he witnessed in Nazi Germany embodied the spirit of the age.[21] He believed that the French republic that was still civilian, but in the crisis of the 1930s was increasingly beleaguered by militaristic and fascistic associations, would have to learn the lessons from those changed circumstances. With Germany rearming, this meant that he decided, as a professional officer, to work through the implications of this change for the future of warfare.

It is against this backdrop that he took an early interest in the tank, whose appearance he had witnessed in World War I on the western front, and which came to see as the decisive weapon of the future. For years de Gaulle followed German publications on this subject very closely. Soon his interest expanded to armored personnel carriers with which troops could be transported quickly and under the cover of darkness deep into enemy territory. In 1933, the German army placed its orders for military vehicles with Krupp and other companies under the guise of commercial trucks. De Gaulle noted how Hitler, again in breach of international treaties, began to assemble the first panzer units. The following year de Gaulle published his first book on the future of armored warfare in which he urged a reorganization of the French armed forces. France's security, he wrote, could no longer be guaranteed by fortifications. A future war required machines and mobility of the kind that these weapons alone could provide. Tanks would give the army speed and punch.[22]

However, de Gaulle and his group of younger fellow officers, who observed Heinz Guderian and other panzer warfare specialists in Nazi Germany so sharply, were not influential enough to get their ideas accepted by their superiors. In March 1935, Pétain once again praised the existing French system of defenses and cautioned the reformers. De Gaulle did not give up. His thoughts continued to revolve around the highly dynamic political and military developments beyond France's eastern frontier. France, he insisted, must be capable of retaliating with the same speed and toughness with which he expected the Germans to attack. Otherwise Hitler would move the Wehrmacht around Europe as he pleased. In the end, the demand of a younger generation of French officers for armored units did not go completely unheeded. In 1940, France had more tanks at their disposal than did the Germans. But neither these machines nor the fortifications along the Maginot Line were able to prevent a German breakthrough, and, unlike in 1914, the French army quickly collapsed after these early defeats. This time the Wehrmacht had prepared itself better for the invasion. France had no choice but to capitulate to a triumphant Hitler and his generals on 22 June 1940.

The rearmament policies of the Red Army must also be seen as a defensive response to events in Germany before and even more so after the Nazi seizure of power. Stalin and his marshals also worried about the aggressiveness of the Japanese in Manchuria. After 1933, Stalin steadily increased investments in war materials. Up to 1936, the Soviets produced some 2,000–3,000 military aircraft per annum, as well as more than 3,000 tanks and 30,000 machine guns. The years 1937 and 1938 saw further increases; by 1940 Stalin had some 20,000 tanks. This meant that the losses the Red Army suffered immediately after the German invasion in the summer of 1941 were never so high that the gaps could not be filled, and soon American materials also reached the Russians via Archangel in the north. If there was a militarization of the Stalin dictatorship in the 1930s, it should be compared with the French or British response to the Wehrmacht. Britain, above all, made a considerable effort to strengthen its air force. Given Stalin's "socialism-in-one-country" strategy, his policies did not represent an aggressive militarism of the kind that Jünger and Ludendorff had theorized about and that the German officer corps practiced.

The Wehrmacht under Hitler did not just prepare itself psychologically for a war of aggression and annihilation. The production of military equipment proceeded at great speed. German industry expanded its methods of mass production, but it was the production of weapons. Historians have debated how far the Nazi rearmament program was impeded by the "butter question," that is, the desire of the regime to gain and retain the support of the masses through economic concessions at a time when the country had virtually returned to full employment but was hit by growing inflation due to the excesses of military production. The British historian Tim Mason has argued that Hitler tried to provide guns *and* butter and then failed to provide both in sufficient quantities. According to his colleague Richard Overy, the führer and his generals were guided much less by social and economic considerations than Mason assumed. Rearmament was their first priority.[23]

The total mobilization of Germany's material resources thus pursued the deliberate depletion of the national economy. Although it was a disastrous policy, Hitler was not too concerned about the economic consequences of rapid rearmament and the huge hole it opened up in state finances. As he put it in retrospect in March 1942 in the course of one of his "Table Talks," the long monologues he liked to engage in after dinner at his military headquarters and were faithfully recorded for posterity: "Since the reintroduction of universal military service [in 1935] our armaments have swallowed up gigantic sums that are completely uncovered until now. There are only two paths: either these tax debts are in the course of time put on the shoulders of the German population or they will be paid from the potential gains of the occupied territories. It should be self-evident that the latter" policy would be applied.[24] It was this policy of a delayed balancing of the budget that spoke volumes about the basic character of the Nazi regime. What followed was a most brutal practice of looting, resettlement, and extermination.

However strikingly unsophisticated Hitler's economic calculations may have been, they did not lack an inner logic if they are put into the larger context of his *Weltanschauung*. That he was serious when he pontificated about his plans in World War II may be deduced from the practices of exploitation and expropriation that he had already applied to Germany's Jews during the 1930s. Soon after coming to power the regime not only organized anti-Semitic boycotts of shops but also began to "Aryanize" Jewish property. One result of this practice was massive corruption and self-enrichment by those who organized this program and who acquired Jewish assets, as will be seen below. No less important, "Aryanization" put millions of marks into the regime's coffers, which helped finance the public deficit and the country's rearmament effort.[25]

The role of party bosses and ministerial bureaucrats who were involved in "Aryanization" leads us to a type of men of violence that was somewhat different from the "steel-hard" professional officers who prepared a future war in the Wehrmacht. The latter continued to operate primarily in more traditional power-political and military categories. The Nazi leadership, on the other hand, viewed the world in social Darwinist and racist terms that had been circulating since before 1914. After World War I their ideas evolved into a radical ethnonationalism and imperialism. Among this group, Hitler, who saw himself as a veteran and "political soldier," must be mentioned first. In the mid-1920s he published *Mein Kampf* (My Struggle), in which he gave an undiluted summary of his ideas. In January 1933 he became Reich chancellor of Germany and in August 1934, shortly after Hindenburg's death, he was officially confirmed as the führer of a nation that despite the ravages of the Great Slump continued to be potentially the strongest economic and military power on the European continent.

What *Mein Kampf* contained was nothing less than the visions of a man of violence par excellence who was prepared to "reorder" Europe over the death of millions of people. His ideology consisted of a lethal mix of biological racism, anti-Semitism, and anti-communism that formed the foundation of a "New Order" based on conquest. Here from among hundreds of statements is a telling digest of his attitude toward violence, which also captures well the contrast between the two models of society that have been at the center of this book: "The ultimate decision on how the struggle for the world market will come out will lie with violence and not with economics. It has been our curse that in peacetime a large section, especially of the patriotic bourgeoisie, had become convinced of the idea that economic policy would make it possible to refrain from violence. And even today their main representatives are to be found in those more or less pacifist circles who, as the opponents and enemies of all heroic, folkish virtues, like to see in economic activity a state-preserving, even a state-forming force. . . . [However,] the sword must come before the plough and before the economy [comes] the army."[26]

Since the beginning of the Nazi movement Hitler had been surrounded by "old fighters" with a similar mindset. Many of them also had a record of violence as Free Corps volunteers and paramilitaries of the swash-buckling type that Italo Balbo represented in the Italian Fascist movement, straining for action. Many of them had no more than a primary school education and especially during the economic crisis in the early 1930s found a home (and pay) in the Nazi Party or its associations such as the Brownshirt SA. Those who had risen in the ranks led their units into the street brawls that occurred almost daily in the towns and cities of Weimar Germany. After the Nazi seizure of power they took charge of the police apparatus of the German state, unleashing their criminal potential on their political opponents, arbitrarily arresting and beating them up in the streets in broad daylight. If their families or friends went to the local police station to protest, their complaints were basically ignored and a bunch of SA men might turn up on their doorstep the next morning to "teach them a lesson."

Soon the violence became more systematic. The first Nazi concentration camps were established in March 1933. A month later, the camps were overflowing with some 50,000 inmates who were maltreated, humiliated, and sometimes murdered. By the end of 1934 the number of inmates had fallen to around 3,000 before another wave of arrests in the mid-1930s. In October 1938 the total number of concentration camp inmates reached 24,000. Many of the prisoners were never indicted, and the judiciary's sentencing powers were expanded by a number of special measures that radicalized existing criminal codes to support the Nazi system of terrorizing the population. Thus political opponents could be punished more severely with the help of the 4 April 1933 Law for the Prevention of Political Acts of Violence. It enabled the robed men of violence who presided over the local courts to impose arbitrary and draconian penalties.

In addition to long prison sentences, these "ordinary" courts issued 16,650 death sentences, most of them after 1939. To this figure must be added some 11,000 death sentences that were meted out by special courts. The People's Court, established to deal with defendants accused of treason, condemned a total of 5,279 Germans to die, mostly by hanging or guillotine. The notes of the chaplain at Wolfenbüttel prison near Brunswick give an idea of how quickly death came for opponents of the Nazi regime who had been hauled through the ordinary system of justice. Two days before Christmas 1943 he recorded in the death register: "Execution by guillotine—6.35 P.M., 6.38 P.M., 6.40 P.M., 6.42 P.M., 6.44 P.M."[27] It should be added that the above figures pertain to civilians and exclude soldiers sentenced to death in military courts or by special courts introduced, for example, in Poland in an attempt to bring the populations of the occupied territories to heel. Nor do they include the millions of Europeans, Jews and non-Jews, who were caught in the brutal warfare adopted by the Wehrmacht and the war of extermination against certain minorities, which will be examined in the next chapter.

It did not take long for the policies of violence to regain their visibility, policies that had been very public in the first weeks after January 1933 and had subsequently been pushed behind the prison walls and barbed-wire compounds of the concentration camps. The murder of Ernst Röhm and his entourage in the "Night of the Long Knives" at the end of June 1934 has already been mentioned. Apart from the involvement of the Wehrmacht in these crimes, there was also the SS, whose units did most of the killing and replaced the politically obliterated Brownshirts as the main organ of Nazi terror. It was led by Heinrich Himmler, whose predilection for violence was enhanced by his racist visions of a future "Aryan" society. These visions in turn guided his obsession with research and pseudoscientific experimentation designed to prove an assortment of racist "theories."

But he was also a cunning policeman and organizer who by 1936 had succeeded in combining his SS, which had originally been founded as Hitler's personal security force, with the entire law enforcement apparatus of the traditional German state, making him Reichsführer SS and chief of the German police. This new police force attracted men of violence who were not driven by fantastic utopias; nor were they "old fighters" with their mostly primitive notions of wielding power who had moved into elevated positions in the Nazi Party just before or after the seizure of power. These were coolly calculating technicians of power who had gone to university and in many cases had even earned a doctorate, usually of law. They all were anti-Semitic and attuned to the ideology and language of the Hitler dictatorship. But favored by Reinhard Heydrich, perhaps the truest embodiment of this type, they used the power that Himmler's police empire or their position, usually as Himmler's representatives in the ministerial bureaucracy, gave them with a clear sense of purpose.

What fascinated them were the unlimited possibilities and their power over the life and death of millions of people. They used the latest technologies of criminal investigation and torture and, while manipulating and brainwashing the rank and file, they persecuted the real and imagined opponents of the regime so pitilessly at home that the anti-Nazi resistance had by 1936 lost what little effectiveness it may have had three years earlier. The methods of the SS technocrats also proved superior in their internal struggle against the "old fighters." Whatever their ideological commitment to Nazism and its policies may have been, ultimately all leaders accepted the notion that the only way to deal with opponents, whether internal or external, was to annihilate them. In their eyes, a human being was worth little or nothing.[28]

In this respect there was a point of close contact between the Nazi technicians of power and the attitudes of *Reichswehr* officers who had concluded their alliance with Hitler in January 1933. Of course, both sides initially eyed each other with suspicion. The alliance was strengthened by the Röhm murders in June 1934, and eight months later the generals were given the universal service army they had prepared for ever since their modernizing push of the late 1920s. Divided into sixteen divisions, the 100,000-man army of the Weimar period was to be brought up to a total strength of 580,000. In return, the Wehrmacht took its military oath to Hitler. There were, it is true, a few generals who feared that their alliance might turn into a pact with the devil. They distrusted the radical aims of Nazism and worried about another world war before the total mobilization that they had begun would be completed. Up to 1938, Hitler succeeded in getting rid of these wayward officers through a number of moves that can only be called Machiavellian. They were replaced by their comrades who were not only absolutely loyal to the führer, but also shared the view of modern, highly mobile terroristic warfare against foreign armies and civilian populations that German strategists had meanwhile developed and refined.

Hitler and the Wehrmacht staged a dress rehearsal of this type of warfare during the Spanish Civil War in 1936–37. This conflict had demonstrated even before the Germans appeared on the scene that the use of the most brutal methods had advanced in other European societies since World War I and its violent aftermath. But it was the Nazis who, beyond the basic ideological motivation behind the civil war as a struggle against socialism and communism, saw Spain as a testing and training ground for their latest weapons and tactics. It offered a particularly good opportunity for the air force after the development of planes had made considerable strides since 1918. These considerations explain why it was the specially constituted "Condor Legion" that was moved to the Iberian peninsula with 5,600 men and 150 planes to support General Francisco Franco's rebellion against the Spanish republic. Later the figure was increased to 16,000.

One of the driving forces behind this unit was Wolfram von Richthofen, whom the British historian Piers Brendon described in the following words:

> The Colonel was . . . a prototypical Prussian officer. He had gimlet blue eyes, cropped blond hair, chiseled Aryan features and a ramrod Junker bearing. But he was a technocrat as well as an aristocrat. He loved engineering and he worshiped efficiency. He treated his brown-uniformed men (who wore Spanish insignia of

stars and bars) like cogs in a military machine. Austere, impatient and demanding, von Richthofen was a strict disciplinarian. He detested small talk, confining conversation to professional matters. Driving his fliers hard, he drove himself harder, in more senses than one: he handled his 3.7-litre Mercedes like a Messerschmitt [fighter plane]. He was a flute-playing fitness fanatic who did physical jerks every morning, yet he had only one lung and smoked 40 cigarettes a day.[29]

At the end of April 1937, it was this man who pushed for a bombardment of the small Basque town of Guernica. The attack was pure terrorism. Although the Germans did not yet deploy dive bombers, their planes came in several waves of forty to release their lethal payload. It was the first "carpet bombing" in the history of air warfare. The entire town went up in flames. Those who tried to flee were machine-gunned by low-flying fighter aircraft. Of the 7,000 inhabitants, several thousand lost their lives in a bloodbath that did not take more than three hours. Hitler and Air Force Chief Hermann Göring were satisfied when the news of the destruction of Guernica reached them. They had gained valuable experience that was applied at the beginning of World War II in raids on Warsaw, later on Rotterdam, and finally on Coventry and other British cities.

Even if the mobilization of German society at the outbreak of World War II was not as total as Jünger and Ludendorff had postulated, the course of the lightning wars that Nazi Germany unleashed in 1939–40 cannot be understood without examining the psychological and material preparations of the previous years.

Terroristic Warfare

Following the "liquidation of rump Czechoslovakia" in the spring of 1939, the Wehrmacht resorted to another act of naked aggression by invading its eastern neighbor Poland on 1 September 1939. The officer corps thus not only became an accessory to the imperialist and exterminationist aims of the Nazi regime but also implemented the principles of total warfare that it had prepared in previous years intellectually and—for example, in Guernica— had put into practice. Ludendorff had sketched these principles in his book. Men like Guderian and Richthofen had refined them.

The attack on Poland amounted to nothing less than a huge hammer-blow that hit not only the poorly equipped Polish armed forces but also the largely unprotected civilian population. As the German troops advanced, they encountered Polish regulars whom they quickly defeated. In all, they captured some 700,000 soldiers. But there were also many scenes that were reminiscent of those experienced by the Belgians in August 1914: civilians were summarily executed; houses were razed; and terrified women and children were rounded up. Still, in comparison to World War I, there was an important difference from the start. Moltke adopted his reprisals against the Belgian civilian population in 1914 in order to secure the strategic objective of his operations plan—the defeat of the French army—as quickly as possible. By 1939, measures against civilians had become an integral part of the German way of warfare. Hitler and his generals wanted to annihilate both the Polish armed forces and the civilian population, or at least to enslave it. To achieve these objectives, they bombed Warsaw, this time deploying dive bombers whose howls and deadly payloads wreaked havoc and terrorized hundreds of thousands of innocent citizens. The crucial point is, though, that this type of terroristic warfare was explicitly covered by orders concerning the treatment of the civilian population that had been issued, with the approval of the Armed Forces High Command (OKW), to the SS liquidation squads that followed the advancing troops and became active in the rear areas.[30]

Their task was to murder the Polish elites and the local Jewish populations. Accordingly, the shooting of priests, intellectuals, professionals, landowners, and other elite groups began without delay in the occupied territories. Their extermination was calculated to leave the mass of the Polish people without leaders and to transport them in a major "resettlement" operation to the so-called *Generalgouvernement* in the south of the country. By March 1941 some 365,000 men, women, and children were expelled from their houses and farmsteads in western Poland. The *Generalgouvernement* in effect became a huge concentration camp of destitute people from which the Germans began to recruit slave laborers to be shipped to Germany to work in industry and agriculture. The expellees were allowed to take along no more than a few personal belongings. The farmsteads that they left behind were, as part of the Nazis' racist Germanization policy, to be occupied by ethnic Germans from the Baltic states, Transylvania, and other parts of eastern Europe. Consequently, the wholesale murder of Poland's elites was accompanied by racist population policies and the uprooting of civilians that cost further innumerable lives. Some 20 percent of the Polish population did not survive World War II, half of whom were Jews who fell victim to the Nazi Final Solution.

These policies had one weakness, though: the commanders of the front-line troops had internalized the need to deal harshly with the enemy (combatants as well as civilians), in pursuit of Germany's total war aims. However, their training had not included the stone-cold liquidation of innocent civilians without legal proceedings.[31] When the news of the shootings reached the front-line commanders, some of them protested against what clearly were war crimes. The murderous activities of the SS units in the rear areas for which the military had overall responsibility also violated these officers' honor code, which had not been completely cast aside. They were also demoralizing to their ordinary soldiers, or so they claimed. By October 1939 the protests had become so loud that Johannes Blaskowitz, the general responsible for the rear areas, finally composed a memorandum to Hitler at the beginning of November. In it he warned against the negative impact that the executions and mass arrests were having on the rank and file. He added that if these activities were inevitable, they should at least be based on formal legal proceedings. Hitler was enraged and demanded the dismissal of the general. The war, he added cynically, could not be conducted with the methods of the Salvation Army.

If Blaskowitz's protest remained unheard, it was not just due to the pitilessness of the führer but also to the attitude of his military superiors at the Wehrmacht High Command. They had been in touch with Reinhard Heydrich of the SS Reich Security Main Office (RSHA) at the start of the campaign. They agreed on this occasion that the military would retain formal authority over the rear areas but that the SS would take over certain police functions. As Canaris also learned, it was understood that certain groups of Poles—aristocrats, priests, and Jews—would be shot on the spot. The leaders at the top thus knew quite well what would happen after the invasion of Poland, and they were in a weak position vis-à-vis Hitler and Heydrich when the protests from the front-line commanders arrived. They had already sold the pass. In the end, the Wehrmacht was relieved of their responsibility for the rear areas. Later such legal subtleties were also dropped.

The lightning war strategy with which Germany destroyed Poland within a few weeks and which was accompanied by an occupation policy that devoured hundreds of thousands of human beings was no more than the beginning of a type of warfare that treated combatants and civilians with great harshness and, unlike in 1914, was total from the beginning. The swift victories may have left the German population back home under the illusion that the Wehrmacht conducted its operations in the style of nineteenth-century warfare with a minimum of civilian casualties, but the actual experience of the occupied countries not only in the east but also in western and northern Europe was different, even if the reprisals and killings did not assume the same proportions there as in Poland. Nor were France, Belgium, Holland, Denmark, and Norway subjected to massive resettlement practices. Yet, the rupture in the daily peaceful routine in the villages and towns was traumatic everywhere. In the west and north a measure of normalcy did return after the respective armies had been defeated by the Wehrmacht's powerful strokes. Only after 1942–43 did these countries experience a renewed escalation of violence as the tide turned against Hitler and Mussolini and resistance against the occupation forces increased.[32]

Historians continue to speculate as to what was on the minds of German soldiers when their tanks and trucks rumbled through peaceful villages; when they searched houses, demolished furniture, and terrified women and children; when they participated in the shooting of hostages or, after the armistice, sat in local bars and cafés. Meanwhile the air force continued its lethal work by bombing the Dutch port of Rotterdam and later Coventry and Birmingham in England. The number of civilian casualties quickly surpassed those of the ordinary soldiers, who had often been mobilized in a great hurry. If the campaigns in western and northern Europe have been called *Normalkriege* (normal wars), this was no doubt true in comparison to the fighting in the Balkans or the east. However, this was no longer a normal war in the traditional sense but one that was in tune with the notions of terroristic warfare that the German military had developed before 1939 and that were perfectly compatible with the social Darwinist concept of struggle held by Hitler and the Nazi movement. For the Wehrmacht this was the *Normalkrieg* of the twentieth century.[33]

This by now also applied to the "race-biological" elements that were not only at the core of Nazi ideology but had also become absorbed into the army's psychological testing and training program. In the east, racism formed the basis of the extermination of the Jewish populations and—though perhaps less systematically—the Slavs; in western Europe this racism appeared, initially at least, in a curiously positive guise. Eastern populations were immediately subjected to mass murder or demoted to the status of helots within a system of exploitation that can only be called colonial in the worst pre-1914 sense. In the west only certain minorities, Jews in particular, were earmarked for liquidation whereas those whose genetic heritage was "Aryan" were deemed capable of being integrated into the future folk community. As in Nazi Germany in the 1930s, "blood" became the most important criterion by which the conquered populations were classified.

There were men and women in western and northern Europe who were taken in by the racist utopia of Hitler's Thousand-Year Reich of all Germanic nations; the majority, however, kept their distance from a collaboration that was grounded in biological theories. Instead, many ordinary citizens of France, Belgium, Holland, Denmark, and Norway accommodated themselves to the occupiers, at least in the early years when it looked as if the Germans were going to win the war. Since any resistance and the hiding of Jews and other men and women sought by the Nazis incurred severe punishment, the number of courageous hearts began to rise again only when the defeat of Germany appeared more clearly on the horizon. But even now, it is safe to say, occupation policy in these countries never assumed the forms that were first practiced in Poland and that reached a new stage, quantitatively and to some extent also qualitatively, when Hitler invaded the Soviet Union on 22 June 1941.[34]

When analyzing this gigantic campaign it has to be borne in mind that the practices of total warfare had been tested several times before, first in Poland and subsequently in the Balkans when Hitler was forced to come to Mussolini's rescue after the latter, without informing his ally, invaded Greece at the end of October 1940, only to suffer a severe setback. The Fascist dictator had entered World War II reluctantly, but after witnessing Hitler's rapid successes he became anxious to acquire territory in pursuit of his dream of turning the Mediterranean into an Italian lake. Once the campaigns against Yugoslavia and Greece had been concluded and Hitler decided to move against Stalin, with whom he had formed a purely utilitarian and temporary alliance in August 1939, it was above all the dimensions of the war that changed dramatically. This became a campaign that cost the lives of millions of Red Army soldiers and civilians. Entire villages disappeared and requisitioning by the advancing troops was so extensive that the local populations were left without food or heat. The brutality of the war in the Soviet Union may also be gauged from the fact that the casualties on the German side soon also ran into the millions.

Historians by and large agree on the reasons for Hitler's attack on Stalin. It is inseparably linked to the ideology of Nazism and its führer. In *Mein Kampf* and in innumerable speeches he had spoken of the German need for *Lebensraum* (living space). Without an expansion to the east, the future of the Reich and the "Aryan race" could not be secured. Accordingly, Hitler, following his defeat of France in June 1940, did not concentrate his planning on an invasion of the British Isles, even if this is what many contemporaries expected. Instead he prepared for the annihilation of the Soviet Union.[35] This vast region was to be not only the agricultural base to solve Germany's food problem, it would also provide the raw materials needed by German industry. On both counts the memory of what had happened to the country in World War I with regard to the provision of food and raw materials was the warning example of what Hitler wanted to avoid at all costs. But there was, as always, also a race-biological angle to the invasion: the expected victory over Stalin in another lightning war was to facilitate the extinction of the "Jewish-Bolshevik" archenemy of the "Germanic race" with its alleged headquarters in Moscow. This was the double coup with which the führer hoped to lay the foundations of a radical reordering not only of the societies of the European continent but of international politics and the global economy more generally.

Hitler and his political and military advisors were not completely naive about the size of the task involved in the destruction of the Soviet Union. This is reflected in the fact that the planning for the campaign and for the treatment of the indigenous populations was more systematic than it had been against Poland in 1939. The notion of what was to be done found a particularly clear expression in the discussions surrounding the so-called Commissar Order that was issued before the invasion. In blatant violation of international law, this order decreed the murder of all political functionaries, the *politruks* and commissars, that were attached to the Red Army. The fact that the OKW was actively involved in the formulation of this order indicates that the military, unlike in Poland, was not just passively drawn into the crimes that began with the invasion. It was an integral part of it. Another plan, drafted on 2 May 1941, proposed the systematic starvation of the Russian population. In the weeks before 22 June, a number of other guidelines were issued regarding the behavior of the troops and martial law that were taken from peacetime Wehrmacht thinking about the nature of total war. A few experts with detailed knowledge of international law raised concerns about the orders but were, not surprisingly perhaps, ignored.[36]

If there were any uncertainties remaining among the officer corps about the character of the impending war in the east, Hitler removed them as early as 30 March 1941 in a speech before the assembled top brass. The campaign, he said, would not be a conventional war but an ideological struggle against a deadly "Jewish-Bolshevik" enemy. Germany's future depended on the extermination of this enemy and the simultaneous acquisition of territory, of *Lebensraum*. For these reasons, he continued, it would be necessary to break the resistance of the Red Army also from within by liquidating its *politruks* and commissars.

When, accordingly, the Wehrmacht set out to attack the Soviet Union, the method of a brutal surprise attack that had served it so well in the past was successful insofar as the Red Army was unprepared for the onslaught. Still recovering from the Stalinist purges of its leaders in the late 1930s, the rapid and sweeping pincer movements of the German armored units overwhelmed the Soviets. Hundreds of thousands of Red Army soldiers were lost during the first weeks. Although the number of the fallen was high, most Soviet combatants were captured. In the fighting around Bialystok and Minsk, for example, the number of POWs was around 320,000. Those who were identified as *politruks* and commissars were immediately executed by the Wehrmacht or the security services of the SS.

In the meantime, regular Russian soldiers could hardly be said to have fared much better. If they collapsed from exhaustion or illness on the long treks to the rear areas, they were shot.[37] Once the survivors arrived in hastily built camps, they were forced to live in holes without adequate shelter, food, or medical support. Statistics that the Wehrmacht kept with typical meticulousness recorded that some 5.7 million Soviet POWs fell into German hands during the war. Of these, at least 2.5 million died; some estimates are as high as 3.3 million. Some camp commanders protested against the intolerable conditions under which their prisoners had to live, but their complaints were ignored. This explains why of the three million POWs that the Germans had captured by the end of 1941 only half were still alive in the spring of 1942 after an unusually harsh winter. At the beginning of World War I, as will be recalled, both sides had tried hard to observe international conventions regarding the treatment of POWs. The millions of Soviet POWs who per-

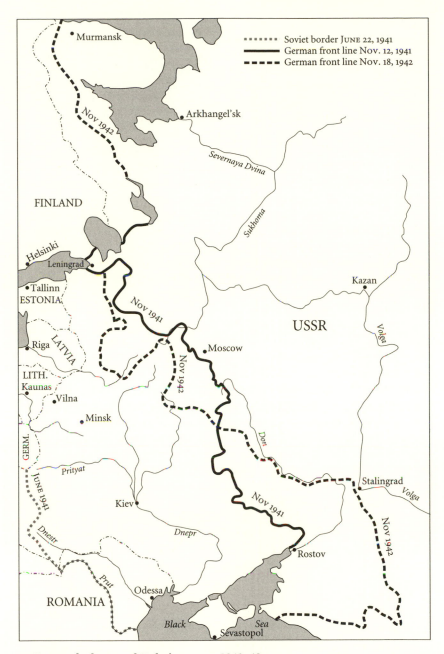

4. Eastward advance of Hitler's armies, 1941–42

ished were victims of a deliberate policy of extermination by starvation, a policy the Wehrmacht also began to practice toward the civilian population. Classified as *Untermenschen* (subhumans), millions of people thus withered away if they were not caught by the dragnet of the liquidation squads.

Civilians who had not fled eastward before the German advance, leaving behind all their belongings, faced a similarly terrible fate. To begin with, Wehrmacht logistics were based on the assumption that the troops would live off the conquered territories, which would incur the resistance of the local populations. Some of them joined the partisans in the woods and swamps of western Russia, to which the Wehrmacht responded with reprisals. Innocent villagers were taken hostage and shot. Many who survived such sweeps were driven into the arms of the partisans. The result was an escalation of the war in the rear of the German army. The partisans tried to disrupt the supply lines, causing the Germans to stage large-scale anti-partisan operations. Time and again large stretches of Belarus and other regions were subjected to operations in which tens of thousands of ordinary civilians got caught. At the end of March 1943, Hitler ordered another radicalization of this type of warfare, if radicalization was still possible. What was true of the occupied Soviet Union also became a widespread pattern in the Balkans and in Greece where the *Bandenkrieg* was also waged without mercy.[38] The men of violence whose policies had mass produced counterviolence tried to assert their domination so crudely that Nazi occupation policy became completely arbitrary.

The chaos that this policy generated in the rear inevitably had a negative effect not only on the operations of the front-line troops but also on the systematic exploitation of agriculture and raw materials. But from the point of view of those responsible for all this, there was one advantage: it established a screen behind which another key element of Hitler's war could be initiated—the genocide of Europe's Jewish populations. In this context it cannot be stressed too strongly that the Holocaust first began in the villages and not in the camps that were built from 1942 onward. In continuation of the policies adopted in Poland in the fall of 1939, police and other special units began to lead Jewish villagers—men, women, and children—into the surrounding forests. There they were killed with a pistol shot in the neck, often after they had been forced to dig their own grave before the eyes of their murderers. Christopher Browning and other historians have made an effort to describe what happened to innumerable victims.[39]

It is difficult to comprehend that men who were often themselves husbands and fathers were prepared to commit such crimes. We know of cases where the commanding officer gave them the opportunity to absent themselves from these bloodbaths. Some did, but most stepped forward and participated. Others watched the mass hangings of alleged partisans silently or with sheepish grins. As a result, the infamous liquidation squads alone killed some 550,000 civilians between June 1941 and April 1942. Among the most notorious of these massacres was the shooting of 33,771 Jews in the ravine of Babi Yar near Kiev in the Ukraine at the end of September 1941. We have similar records from Lithuania and the Latvian capital of Riga, where some 15,000 Jews were murdered at the beginning of December 1941.

These practices cost the lives of hundreds of thousands in the relatively thinly populated western parts of the Soviet Union; the Wehrmacht soon threatened the big cities. The Army Group North advanced toward Leningrad in the summer of 1941—the place from which the hated "Bolshevik bacillus" had spread in 1917. Expecting an early collapse of the Soviet Union, Hitler remarked in July 1941 that not much would be left of the city. He expected it to be razed. The führer used even more drastic words when he met Otto Abetz, the German envoy to occupied Paris. He saw in Leningrad the source of an "Asiatic poison" that had been poured into the Baltic Sea for too long; it had to disappear from the face of the earth.[40]

However, the Red Army knew how vital it was for the survival of the Soviet Union that the realization of such plans was thwarted. Its resistance to the German advance was stubborn and ultimately successful. As late as September 1941 the OKW, certain of victory, contemplated three solutions for Leningrad. The first one was to allow the city to capitulate; the second was to pulverize it with an artillery bombardment; the third to besiege it until all of its inhabitants had been starved to death. The Soviets denied the German army the triumph of capitulation. Furthermore, they succeeded in stopping the advance outside the range of Hitler's guns. The Germans proved too weak and overstretched to cut the supply lines of the city across Lake Lagoda completely. For the next two years Leningrad remained under siege, suffering incredible human losses until it was liberated in 1943. The proposed murder of its inhabitants did not take place. As this atrocity was being contemplated by the Germans, Field Marshal Wilhelm von Leeb spent some time worrying about the impact this slaughter might have on the morale of his troops. There was no need for him to worry. Leningrad was never conquered, but some 600,000 Leningraders died of hunger and illness or froze to death.

Frustrated by their lack of success, some General Staff officers seriously toyed with the idea of a massive gas attack that would kill the population of Leningrad. The project had to be abandoned because this kind of total warfare would have required several hundred thousand poison shells, which were lacking, as were a sufficient number of guns. Hitler did not give up, however. In September 1942 he ordered another offensive to be followed by mass murder. This plan, too, had to be shelved—another sign that by then the tide was beginning to turn against the Axis Powers.

First indications of this had come a year earlier during the advance against the other citadel of the "Jewish-Bolshevik" enemy: Moscow. The huge losses the Red Army had sustained in the first weeks of the war reinforced Hitler and his generals in the belief, held before the invasion, that the Soviet Union would collapse as quickly as Poland and the western and northern European countries had done in 1939–40. In August Hitler had self-confidently predicted the total annihilation of Moscow. The city was then to be flooded and turned into a lake. The rest of the conquered territory was to be put—as he had envisioned all along—under a colonial-style administration. Its human and material resources were to be ruthlessly exploited. The Jews, the führer added on 27 July, were to be wiped out like vermin from the occupied eastern regions and from Europe as a whole.

By early autumn 1941, however, there were increasing signs that not only Hitler but also his generals had grossly underestimated the Red Army and the civilian population.[41] Notwithstanding the horrendous losses, Stalin succeeded in mobilizing the enormous potential in human resources for the "Great Fatherland War." By transferring key industries and their machines to the Ural Mountains, he maintained the production of war materials and even increased it. Deliveries of tanks and guns also arrived from the United States. By June 1941 some 140 divisions with 10,000–15,000 tanks and 8,000 fighter planes were stationed along the country's western borders. According to German calculations, some three million Red Army soldiers had been captured and countless tanks and planes had been destroyed. But the Soviets continued to resist the invaders ferociously, causing the Germans, whose reserves to replace their casualties were much smaller, a loss of almost one million soldiers. Among the armored units these losses were so great that the Sixteenth Panzer Division had no more than 140 tanks that were still deployable.[42]

For the Wehrmacht it proved no less catastrophic that its leaders had completely underestimated the logistical problems arising from the vast distances they had to cover from the original border to Moscow and the regions further south. As far as size was concerned, the Soviet Union was a very different category from Germany, France, or Holland, where one could move one's armored vehicles from one end of the country to the other over well-maintained roads within a few hours. In Russia and the Ukraine, the same armored units had to cover hundreds of miles. This meant that logistical planning also assumed different proportions. In addition, few roads were paved, and the rainy season turned dirt roads into impassable mud tracks. With the rise of the partisan movement, the overextended supply lines were increasingly vulnerable to disruptions. By the summer of 1944, these attacks had become so ubiquitous that all railroad lines of the Army Group Center at one point had been dynamited in innumerable places.

These were conditions that the planners had not anticipated as they had contemplated the nature of total war in the 1930s. They also overestimated their own power and expertise. The lightning war victories had made officers and soldiers overly confident. They thought that with their tanks and dive bombers and under the leadership of a "genius," Hitler, they had become invincible. Their megalomania now cost them dearly.

The impressive initial successes of the hammer-blow they had delivered to the Soviets in June 1941 had made them certain of an early victory in the east. But by the fall it became increasingly clear that the movement of the Army Group Center toward Moscow was slowly running into the ground. The resistance of the Red Army was aided by the onset of the rainy season, followed by an extremely harsh winter. To be sure, the Wehrmacht had expected Stalin to capitulate before a weather change would come to his rescue. But their underestimation of the Soviet capacity to fight was also due to the fact that they viewed the Slavs as *Untermenschen* who were too "primitive" to know how to conduct a modern war. Consequently, it would be wrong to attach as much importance to the changes in the weather as German generals have done in their postwar memoirs. The German offensive ground to a halt because of the effectiveness of the Soviet officer corps and the unexpectedly fierce resistance of regular troops—a resistance that was disorienting to the ordinary German soldier who had been told by incessant racist Nazi and Wehrmacht propaganda that the Russians were hopelessly inferior.

Time and again the Red Army was able to throw freshly raised troops into battle. The civilian population was also effectively mobilized under the banner of defending the fatherland against the German invaders who were behaving like barbarians. Industrial workers mass produced weapons in factories that had successfully been relocated to the east, and American arms arrived in ever larger numbers. As a result, the Red Army not only stopped the Wehrmacht outside Moscow but in fact rolled it back by some seventy miles. German losses during this reversal were exacerbated by orders to defend positions to the last bullet. To retreat in orderly fashion to positions further back in more favorable terrain was viewed by Hitler as treachery. It was a concept of war that increasingly stressed the importance of willpower over technological superiority. When defeat finally came, this last-ditch mentality had caused additional millions of casualties.

While Army Group Center was on the defensive during the winter of 1941–42, Army Group South continued to make slow progress in the Ukraine.[43] That the latter was ordered to resume the offensive with renewed vigor in the spring of 1942 must, paradoxically perhaps, be taken as a further sign that the prospect of a German victory in the Soviet Union was diminishing. Abandoning the conquest of both Leningrad and Moscow was determined above all by the necessity to get hold of the raw materials and the oil fields to the southeast in order to supply a war whose end was nowhere in sight. By the middle of August 1942 the Caucasus had been reached, but the occupation lasted only until December of that year.

There were other indications that the lightning war of the summer of 1941 had failed as early as the winter of 1941–42 and that the Axis would therefore lose the world war sooner or later. By the fall, the entry of the United States on the side of the Allies was regarded as inevitable. Thereafter the superiority of this coalition in terms of manpower and industrial capacity vis-à-vis Germany, Italy, and Japan would become glaring. One set of figures makes this indisputably clear: in 1943, the Allies produced weapons valued at $62.5 billion versus $18.3 billion on the German and Japanese side.[44]

German propaganda now increasingly promoted the notion, well-worn in Germany since World War I, that determination to win was all that counted. Commanding generals now issued racist orders to their troops, emphasizing the ethnic struggle between Slavs and Germans. Positions were defended tooth and nail at the cost of ever higher German losses. If the lightning wars had so far resulted in the death of millions primarily in the conquered countries, the Nazis' disdain for human life now included their own soldiers. The orders to hold untenable positions to the last man were reinforced by an ever more draconian prosecution of violations of the military code. The total number of dead and missing soldiers by the end of the war ran to an estimated 5.5 million; Wehrmacht judges condemned some 30,000 officers and soldiers to death for desertion, "cowardice in the face of the enemy," and other offenses. Those who survived and were captured were sent to one of the Siberian camps where the death rate was high. According to Western estimates over 3 million fell into Soviet hands as POWs, of whom 1.2 million perished. Stalingrad, where in November 1942 the Red Army succeeded in encircling 270,000 members of the Sixth Army, became the symbol of these developments. Until they finally capitulated the city three months later, over 90,000 had died there. Some 150,000 were carted to Siberia from where the last POWs returned in 1955.[45]

The German civilian population similarly came to believe that the war was being lost. Between 1939 and 1941 ordinary people on the home front had largely been spared from military action. By 1942, total war had also reached the Reich. The economy that had prepared itself for a return to peacetime in the summer of 1941 was now geared to full war production. In February 1943, propaganda minister Joseph Goebbels made his infamous speech at the Berlin *Sportpalast*. Before a carefully selected audience, who cheered his words enthusiastically, he proclaimed the onset of total war. Food rationing was decreed and successively extended. Goods became scarcer and scarcer. Allied bombing raids began to disrupt industrial production, and armaments factories were relocated to mine shafts and tunnels in the mountainous parts of central Germany. Due to strategic decisions made in London and Washington, the civilian population soon became the main target of air warfare on the assumption that the destruction of the residential neighborhoods of the big cities would demoralize the home front and accelerate the end of the war. Hamburg was badly hit by raids at the end of July 1943, in which some 30,000 people died; Berlin saw a particularly heavy attack in February 1945 with 22,000 casualties. Two weeks later the bombing of Dresden resulted in 38,000 dead. The total number of civilians who lost their lives in the cities with their firestorms, as refugees trekking west ahead of the advancing Red Army, or in the chaos of the fighting in the final weeks of the war has been estimated at 2.3 million.

It might be surmised that the prospect of defeat would prod the Nazis and their military associates to mobilize all available labor in the Reich and the occupied territories. To an extent this was what happened with regard to the latter from where slave laborers were recruited in ever larger numbers. Toward the end of 1944, they numbered around 7.5 million. On the other hand, the number of women working in the armaments factories increased only marginally. Nazi ideology had put "Aryan" women on a pedestal and had encouraged them in the 1930s to become homemakers and mothers, and this now stood in the way of wartime recruitment. In May 1939 some 14.6 million women, most of whom were working class, were employed in the Nazi economy. After a small but telling decline in 1940–42, the figure reached 14.8 million in May 1943 and 14.9 million in September 1944. It was primarily foreign slave laborers who replaced the countless men in the factories, offices, and farms who had been drafted into the Wehrmacht in the face of growing losses.[46]

Meanwhile, thousands of German men were busy in the occupied territories, together with indigenous collaborators, pursuing a program that seemed to have no relation to a coolly calculated assessment of military priorities that might have been advisable in the face looming defeat. It was a program that was an outgrowth of the racist doctrines of Nazism and the anti-Semitic obsessions of Hitler and his entourage: the "Final Solution of the Jewish Question" in Europe.[47]

We have seen that many Polish Jews became victims of the SS liquidation squads in the fall of 1939. Those who survived were put into ghettos, where they were forced to produce war-related materials and live under the most inhumane conditions. At the same time Hitler began to speak of the impending extermination of Europe's Jews. Next came an escalation of what had first begun in Poland in 1939 and now continued on an even larger scale in the villages and towns of the Soviet Union after the Nazi invasion: the shooting of Jewish men, women, and children by the SS with the assistance of the Wehrmacht. Gradually this program was expanded to Jews all over Europe after Göring had authorized mass arrests on 31 July 1941.

Most of the estimated 2.8 million murdered Jews in the Soviet Union were shot or hanged, but with the geographic expansion of the occupation the number of Jews who fell under German authority became so large that existing killing practices became complemented by another method, namely

Legend:
◆ Pre-WWII Camps
■ Other Major Concentration Camps
■ Extermination Camps

North Sea

Baltic Sea

STUTTHOF ■

NEUENGAMME ◆
Hamburg

RAVENSBRÜCK ◆
ORANIENBURG ◆
SACHSENHAUSEN
● Berlin

Vistula

■ TREKLINKA

Warsaw ●

■ WESTERBORK

BERGEN-BELSEN ■

COLUMBIA HAUS

■ CHELMNO

SOBIBOR ■

DORA-MITTELBAU ◆

Elbe

Weser

MAJDANEK ■

LICHTENBURG ◆

GROSS-ROSEN ■

Rhine

BUCHENWALD ◆
SACHSENBURG ◆

BELZEC ■

● Frankfurt

THERESIENSTADT ◆
● Prague

◆ AUSCHWITZ-BIRKENAU

FLOSSENBÜRG ◆

Danube

■ NATZWEILER

MAUTHAUSEN ●

DACHAU ◆
● Munich

Vienna ●

● Budapest

5. Nazi concentration and extermination camps

the construction of camps in which the victims were asphyxiated in specially
built gas chambers using carbon monoxide and Zyklon B poison. The first
experiments with poison gas were conducted at the beginning of September
1941 on hundreds of Soviet POWs at Auschwitz in southern Poland.

In 1942 the Jews who had been herded into the ghettos of the major
cities in Poland were deported to installations that had been erected for their
genocide. When the so-called Reinhard Action ended, some 1.6 million men,
women, and children had met their death in those places of horror at
Treblinka, Belzec, and Sobibor. To Hitler and his associates this program
had become inseparable from his conduct of the war as a whole. By 1942
Jews arrived in the extermination camps from all over Europe. Some of them
survived as forced laborers; most of them were selected at the ramps of the
rail terminals and sent into the gas chambers. How fanatically the regime
pursued this policy is evidenced by the fact that in the months after May
1944 some 440,000 Hungarian Jews, mainly from outside Budapest, were
sent to their death in Auschwitz. Another group that was caught in the racist
dragnet that extended all over Europe were the Sinti and Roma (Gypsies).
Many of them were likewise rounded up and deported. Scholars disagree
on how many of them were murdered, but a likely number is 200,000.

Although there is probably no other field of modern European history
that has been researched as carefully and comprehensively as the Jewish

Holocaust, we are confronted here with a reality that has lost nothing of its enormity even some sixty years later. The years 1942–45 represent the high point in a process in which violence saw fewer and fewer bounds and which in many ways still seems incomprehensible. If the various elements of this program of annihilation are added together, the Nazi racists decreed that some six million Jews were to be denied the most elementary human right, that is, to live. The problems of explaining all this to posterity are truly daunting. Perhaps it is still possible to comprehend the fears and anxieties of millions of those who were tortured and killed. We can also listen to the stories of those who survived the hell of the ghettos and camps, forever traumatized. What poses a much greater challenge to the researcher is to penetrate the mind of the perpetrators or those who looked on as thousands were hanged and shot. They heard the wailing of mothers and saw the whimpering children as they stood by or actively participated in their murder.

It is also true that non-Germans were among the perpetrators and bystanders: soldiers, policemen, and auxiliaries from all over Europe. In Croatia and Romania anti-Semitic outrages were initiated by the indigenous population. In October 1941 the Romanians slaughtered close to 20,000 Jews from Odessa. The number of those murdered in camps by Ukrainian and Romanian policemen in the winter of 1941–42 was even higher: 70,000. But terroristic warfare had not only been prepared and perfected intellectually in Germany before 1939; tens of thousands of Germans participated in atrocities once the war had begun. Whatever purges other European regimes and their collaborators launched against minorities in their midst, Jews in particular, they would hardly have been possible on this scale without the German occupation. However much the war was a European and later a world war, there can be no doubt that the unleashing of violence and its subsequent delimitation radiated from the center of the continent.

VISIONS OF A NEW EUROPEAN ORDER

The resettlement and killing of millions of people in the context of the total warfare that Germany practiced between 1939 and 1945 had a flip side about which we continue to know much less than we do about the orgies of violence.[48] The main reason for this gap in our knowledge is that the course of the war prevented the full realization of Hitler's plans for a reordering of Europe's economies and societies. It is nevertheless revealing to examine these plans not as purely speculative counterfactual history of the kind that has again become fashionable in recent years. The point with the Nazi New Order ideas is that they did not remain air castles or blueprints that were filed away by some bureaucrat. Instead, a number of projects were begun with a stubbornness that also characterized the pursuit of the Final Solution and, more significantly still, continued even at a time when the defeat of the Hitler regime was imminent. It is also relevant that Germany came very close to victory in the summer of 1941. If the Soviet Union had collapsed at that point, there can be little doubt that Hitler would have completed many of the programs that were initiated at the moment of greatest triumph in 1940–41.

At the most general level, Nazi reordering concepts consisted of two elements. On the one hand, they wanted to secure the material base for the future prosperity of a national community that was defined in racist terms. On the other hand, there was the concern for the continual improvement of the "racial qualities" of this community as a way of fostering the "Aryans'" dominance over the subjugated societies. As to the first element, Hitler and his circle never had the slightest doubt that prosperity could not be achieved through peaceful exchange of goods with other countries. It would have to be secured by force. This conviction was rooted not only in the social Darwinist worldview of the Nazis, at the center of which was the notion of a struggle for survival among "races." It was also clear from the start that the costs of a more broadly distributed higher living standard of the "Aryans" could not be financed except by the conquest and looting of the resources of other nations. In Hitler's view, Germany's own industrial and agricultural base was too narrow to achieve prosperity. However efficient German factories were, domestic raw materials, while not completely absent, were insufficient to sustain an adequate supply of goods for the Reich population. Nor was the Central European space large enough to accommodate and feed the expected growth of the population. Additional space had to be acquired and this could only be found in the east and in the wide open spaces of the "Jewish-Bolshevik" Soviet Union.[49] In the 1930s, Hitler created the military means to gain *Lebensraum* at a huge cost that had deepened the public deficit. But we have also already quoted him on how he proposed to cover these expenditures and to improve the living standards of the Germans; not through new taxes but by exploiting the conquered countries.

That the regime seriously contemplated a radical reordering of the economies of Europe is reflected, for example, in the architectural and manufacturing plans the Nazis started before 1939. The first project to be mentioned in this connection is the decision to develop the *Volkswagen* (people's car) and to enhance the motorization of German society.[50] Although the social utopia Hitler had in mind was that of an authoritarian police state and warrior society, he appreciated that Fordist mass production was not only useful for the manufacture of tanks and planes to win his war but also benefited the masses once victory had been won and some of the industrial capacities could again be devoted to the provision of cheap civilian goods. In this sense the *Volkswagen* project was motivated by the insight that the Third Reich's long-term future could not be secured merely by propaganda, police-state methods, and militarism. Ordinary Germans were also to be kept at bay and happy by facilitating the realization of their dreams of a better life. Accordingly, elaborate plans were made to build the Volkswagen Works at Wolfsburg near Braunschweig, with Ferdinand Porsche, the designer and developer of the famous rear-mounted boxer engine, visiting Ford's assembly plants in Michigan to learn from the Americans. Other experts drew up programs that would enable ordinary Germans to sign up for a savings plan, at the end of which they would be able to take delivery of their family car.

Although the highway system that the regime began to construct soon after 1933 was laid out in line with military-strategic calculations to facilitate the swift movement of troops and armor to Germany's eastern and western borders, it would in peacetime of course be used by a motorized mass-consumption society. The Strength-through-Joy recreational programs of the German Labor Front (DAF), the Nazi pseudo-trade union, must also be seen as attempts to satisfy the hopes of people who had never before been in a position to go to the mountains or take a cruise to the fjords of Norway. Now the DAF's summer camps and steamers made this possible. Companies were encouraged to brighten up the workshops, build sports facilities, and offer other benefits calculated to convince the workforce of the superiority of Nazism as a socioeconomic model.

But whatever the schemes that were being invented well before World War II, it would be misleading to equate them with the ideas of a mass-production and mass-consumption society that had been developed in the United States even before 1914 and that came, albeit ephemerally and all too incompletely, to Europe in the mid-1920s. Indeed, the blueprints of a future Nazi society differed in two fundamental respects. They were not inclusive in the sense that all citizens would be allowed to participate in them. Just as Jews and other minorities were being denied political and social rights, slowly marginalized, and ultimately murdered, they were also to be deprived of the benefits of an "Aryan" mass consumer society.

The other point never to be forgotten when discussing the *Volkswagen* project and other Nazi policies is that the enjoyment of consumer goods and leisure was to take place within the framework of a brutal regime and police state, founded on social Darwinist and racist principles, that demanded strict ideological conformity and did not grant freedom of expression and civil rights. What it permitted and constantly organized on a large scale was participation at mass rallies, ideological pep talks, and political training sessions. This, as the German cultural critic Walter Benjamin argued many years ago, gave the masses a sense of involvement, though in effect they had been disenfranchised. What they saw and cheered was a facade of "democracy" behind which lurked a führer state that was geared toward repression, perpetual war, and genocide.

In light of this, a related aspect of Nazi policies on leisure and the material well-being of "Aryan" Germans is particularly incongruous; the attempt to create something like a new European "high culture." Financed by the Goebbels ministry, German intellectuals and journalists began to write about and discuss, in the 1930s, the contours of a cultural order. Like-minded colleagues from Italy and later from other western and southern European countries were invited to "poets' meetings." Cynically exploiting a shrine of Central European culture, the town of Weimar where Johann Wolfgang von Goethe had lived and worked for many years, such meetings were held as late as 1942. But, as with the debates over Europe's economic future, the gatherings never left any doubt that the Germans would call the shots within this fascist "high culture" and that it was window dressing for the entertainment of delusionary cultural producers eager to work under a brutal dictatorship.

The harsh political realities behind the lure of improvements in material and "cultural" conditions for all Germans at the expense of the conquered and persecuted nations of the rest of Europe become particularly tangible when, next to the *Volkswagen* project, the DAF facilities, and "poets' meetings," we look at Hitler's plans for the rebuilding of the country's major cities. The German historian Jochen Thies has analyzed in some detail the ambitious plans Hitler and his architect Albert Speer developed from the late 1930s onward. There are photos that show the two men inspecting scale models of assembly halls, ministerial buildings, railroad stations, bridges, sports stadiums, and monuments.[51] Many of them were again conceived in deliberate competition with feats of American architecture and civil engineering, such as the suspension bridge across the Elbe River in Hamburg for which the Golden Gate Bridge in San Francisco provided the incentive. The size of Speer's railroad station designs took their cue from Grand Central Station in New York, and Berlin was to have the largest assembly hall in the world, seating 180,000 people. Most of these projects remained on the drawing board. But that Hitler was very serious about completing them is evidenced by the fact that work on the expansion of the postwar grounds at Nuremberg where the Nazi Party would rally once a year to celebrate its "achievements" continued as late as 1943.

Social and political historians have been arguing for a long time that large public buildings are not merely erected to accommodate bureaucrats or transportation terminals. They are also symbols of power cast in stone, intended to express the prestige and might of rulers, be they kings, emperors, tyrants, or presidents. Those who view these buildings from afar or enter them are supposed to be in awe of and overwhelmed by their massiveness and splendor. Hitler was aware of this function of monumental architecture and on one occasion during his "Table Talks" at the führer headquarters during the war he put his approach to his architectural program as follows: "Once a year a contingent of Khirgizes will be taken through the capital of the Reich [Berlin] in order to fill their imaginations with the force and size of its monuments in stone."[52] For German visitors the sight of these buildings was to be both inspiring and intimidating. They were to look upon them with pride, admiring what they had achieved under the far-sighted leadership of their führer and ignoring the concentration camps that were also waiting for them if they opposed the regime. In the latter case, Himmler, as Reichsführer SS and chief of the German police, was always ready to deal with them.

Nazi armaments, prosperity, "culture," and buildings were to be financed from the reckless looting of the societies Hitler intended to invade. Again, experts had begun to work on schemes of exploitation and appropriation well before 1939. They wrote articles and secret memoranda on the structures and institutions with the help of which a Nazi *Grossraumwirtschaft* was to be run. This was first of all an economy, encompassing large spaces in western and eastern Europe, that would be largely detached from the world economy. While some industrialists envisioned a resumption of international trading links after the war was over, some radicals in the Nazi Party and bureaucracy hoped to establish a self-sufficient bloc detached from the rest of the world.[53] For the latter group this bloc included the Soviet Union, the space that Hitler had long identified as part of Germany's *Lebensraum*.

This bloc, whose features resembled in many ways those of the "Greater East Asia Co-Prosperity Sphere" that the Japanese conquered in China, Korea, and Southeast Asia at the same time as Germany expanded in Europe, would compete, power-politically and commercially, with the British Empire and the American-dominated hemisphere. We will examine in a moment how Hitler saw the struggle for supremacy developing between these blocs. The question to be investigated here is how the Germanic empire was to be organized internally. On this score, there seems to have been little disagreement between the planners in the ministries and their academic consultants that the Reich would be the undisputed financial, industrial, and commercial center of the new *Grossraum*. Whether it was the currency or the ownership of commercial property, all would be geared toward the Reich as the unquestioned hegemon, even where companies were not expropriated and taken over by German managers or the technocrats of the sprawling economic enterprises of the SS. There was no question of the occupied nations having any measure of equality.

After 1945, some former Nazis liked to compare "their" New Europe with the European Economic Community that the West Europeans created in the 1950s with American help. Nothing could be more misleading. If a comparison is to be drawn, it might be with the "Comecon" that the Soviets organized between themselves and the East European countries they dominated after World War II. This holds true not only with respect to the location of the center of gravity of the two arrangements (Berlin and Moscow) where guidelines were set and policies coordinated, but also to the division of labor between the member regions. According to the concepts of the German planners and administrators in World War II, the Reich would constitute the industrial heart, linked to the other sites of industrial production and trade in western Europe; the east would provide agricultural produce, raw materials, and cheap labor.

When in 1941 Germany's final victory against Stalin seemed to be around the corner, a fuller debate set in in the Reich Economics Ministry and in the industrial associations. Following the occupations of France, Belgium, Holland, Denmark, and Norway, representatives from German enterprises were sent around in search of acquisitions. Many of them appeared in the suites of the top executives to demand that the company in question be handed over to them. Others were less brutal and, respecting prevailing property rights, offered participation and cooperation. But then Göring appeared on the scene in his position of plenipotentiary of the Four-Year Plan and patron of the *Reichswerke* at Salzgitter near Hanover. He announced that the Nazi state had not only a direct interest in the New Economic Order but also predominant rights. Hitler, on the other hand, was at this point inclined to postpone the question of how both German and European industry, finance, and commerce were to be organized until after the war had been won.

This did not prevent the academics in the institutes and universities from refining on paper the structures under which the closed space economy was to operate. We have already noted that German industry was highly cartelized even before 1933. After Hitler's seizure of power virtually all markets became completely dominated by these horizontal agreements between independent firms that fixed prices and decreed production quotas for cartel members. It was a system that suited the centralizing aspirations and the military production goals of the Hitler dictatorship well because the lack of economic competition and a free market could be more easily controlled and regulated. In short, this was a national economy that was still capitalist in that it upheld the principle of private property, but it was a capitalism that was at the same time authoritarian, militarized, favoring the producer, and inimical to the consumer. This peculiar model of an industrial mass-production economy that had swept the board inside Germany in the 1930s was, in the minds of the experts, to be transposed to the rest of occupied Europe. Its details were probably best summarized in a book that the economist Arno Sölter published in 1940. Its title—*Grossraumkartell* (Closed space cartel)—says it all.[54]

If disputes arose among the Economics Ministry, Göring, assorted businessmen, and researchers such as Sölter over what to do with western Europe's industry, the economic treatment of the east also generated a good deal of heat among the agencies concerned. However, the view prevailed quite early on that this *Grossraum* was not to be industrialized and economically developed. With the large spaces of agricultural land in Russia and the Ukraine before their eyes, the experts wanted to exploit the region more in the style of a crude colonialism that the Europeans had practiced before 1914 in the Congo and other parts of Africa. Beyond the recruitment of slave labor to work in the German heartland and deliveries of raw materials, the agricultural east would send its produce to the urban centers further west at prices that were to be determined and imposed by the bureaucrats in Berlin. It was also to be used for the settlement of Germans who would be enticed with promises of farmland and neat dwellings in the new regional administrative centers. The settlers were to be connected to the "homeland" through highways, one of which was to be built all the way to the Crimea, and through high-speed trains that would thunder through the countryside on special wide-gauge rails.

If we now draw a line between the "resettlement" of Poles to the *Generalgouvernement* that began in 1939 and also the mass killings of the subsequent years to which not only the Jews and Roma but also many Slavs fell victim, it becomes clear that, just as Hitler's plans to build the *Volkswagen* and massive railroad stations, the memoranda for the economic reordering of Europe were not just pipe dreams. Our analysis is not a purely intellectual exercise in counterfactual history. Rather this is what would have been completed after the anticipated end of the successful campaign against the Soviet Union in 1941. With victory in mind, Hitler was dead serious when in mid-September 1941 he outlined the following scenario in another of his "Table Talks": "[In the course of our settlement of the Russian space] the 'Reich farmer' is to be housed in exquisitely attractive settlements. The German [administrative] offices and authorities shall have wonderful buildings, the governors [will live in] palaces. Around these authorities will be established whatever serves the maintenance of [daily] life. And the town will be surrounded, up to 30 to 40 kilometers, by a ring of beautiful villages, connected by the best roads. What lies beyond this, will be a different world, in which we shall let the Russians live as they wish. [All that we have to secure is that] we rule them. If there is a revolution, we shall merely have to drop a few bombs on their towns and the matter will have been settled."[55]

It should be clear then that the mass killings and expulsions that began in the rear areas in 1939 and on an even larger scale in 1941 had another equally racist purpose: to make room for the "Aryan" settlers who were scheduled to arrive from Central Europe. This idea also appeared in the so-called *Generalplan Ost* to which Himmler gave his blessing in June 1942. Five months later a first phase began when tens of thousands of Poles were deported from the area south of Lublin to make land available for German farmers. In the 1930s, the Nazi regime had begun its policy of "ethnic cleansing" when it "Aryanized" German Jewish property and forced its owners to leave the country. This policy now continued in a manner that was typical of Nazi methods and in the expectation that the Wehrmacht would quickly defeat the Red Army. Obviously, after the liquidation of millions of people in the east the projected resettlement and housing program that Hitler mapped out in September 1941 would have encountered fewer obstacles.

Similarly, it would not have been difficult to organize the colonial exploitation of the regions the army had secured. This is why Hitler and the men of violence around him never forgot to consider that the Slavic "subhumans" whom the Germans had already turned into helots could always be disciplined with the help of a few dive bombers and that they could also be cowed into submission by sending their local leaders on a visit to Berlin to view the imposing buildings of the capital of the New Order empire. Of course, most of them would be built in granite to ensure they lasted a thousand years. The mentality with which top Nazis approached the agrarian east is also reflected in a recommendation by Martin Bormann, one of Hitler's closest collaborators and powerful right-hand man, that flogging be introduced. This means that at a time when the colonial empires of other powers were in decline and Britain, for example, was experimenting with new constitutional forms, such as the Commonwealth, the Germans resorted to practices of domination that had been used in Africa forty years earlier.[56]

During the 1960s historians debated whether Hitler's conquests would have remained limited to Europe and Central Asia or whether his ambitions extended to global domination. Although the evidence is incomplete and a definitive answer is impossible because he failed to defeat Stalin, there is enough archival material to show that the Nazi regime and its generals began to work on the steps to be taken after the collapse of the Soviet Union. Thus, in July 1941 both the navy and the air force received orders that they were to be given priority over the army in the allocation of raw materials for armaments production. Around the same time, the Wehrmacht leadership began to develop operations plans for the invasion of Afghanistan, the gateway to India, the "crown jewel" of the British Empire. There were also plans to occupy the Azores in the Atlantic, which would be used as a base for a "world power fleet" that Hitler had ordered the navy to start building in January 1939. This was the so-called Z-Plan under which several aircraft carriers, battle cruisers, and long-range submarines were to be operational by 1944–45.[57]

As early as 1938 Göring's air force and the German aircraft industry had begun to design long-range bombers and reconnaissance planes capable of flying to the American East Coast and back. The African continent also interested Hitler at this time. After keeping his distance from the conservative-nationalist movement that had been agitating after 1919 for a return of the colonies Germany had lost under the Versailles Treaty, he gave orders in 1940 to create a colonial ministry. Soon German experts developed plans for a colonial administration. Civil servants were trained for duty in Africa and linguists worked on a German-Swahili dictionary. In his book on the subject,

Dream of Empire, the American historian W. W. Schmokel rightly doubted that a "non-existent empire" had ever been so circumspectly administered as the Nazi one in Africa.[58] What cannot be doubted, though, is that these schemes were serious and would have been implemented if Hitler had won the war. It is also safe to assume that the treatment of the indigenous populations of this colonial empire would have been as brutal as that meted out to the peoples of eastern Europe from 1939 onward.

Considering that the conflict was by now a world war, it is worthwhile to look beyond the European scope of this book and to ask what the other Axis Powers, the Italians and Japanese, were contemplating and doing at this time. Compared to Hitler's territorial ambitions, those of Mussolini were more modest. If the Fascist dictator had been Hitler's model in the early 1920s, he was now the junior partner in the alliance. This did not prevent him from envisioning an empire that would have the dimensions of the ancient Roman one.[59] He was particularly keen to dominate North Africa to round out his acquisitions after his war against Ethiopia in 1936, with neighboring Eritrea having been an Italian colony since 1889. In this conflict Hitler had played a somewhat peculiar role in that he secretly supplied emperor Haile Selassie with arms, thus prolonging Mussolini's campaign, but in the end supported the latter in establishing an Italian-Ethiopian empire. Mussolini tried to grab another piece of territory when he set out to conquer Greece in October 1940. One and a half months earlier he had attacked British Egypt from his base in Libya.

In both campaigns, the Italian army soon got itself into such deep trouble that the Wehrmacht had to come to its rescue. Yugoslavia and Greece fell at the end of April 1941, Crete on 1 June. Meanwhile the Italians, having been pushed back by the British near Tobruk, began a counterattack that was mightily aided by the German Africa Corps under Erwin Rommel. By mid-April they had reached the Egyptian border. But with American support the British forces rallied and by the summer 1942 Italy and Germany had to retreat in the face of superior Allied troops. Six months later, the last Italian contingents were forced to capitulate around Tunis, thus ending Mussolini's dream of empire. From July 1943, Tunis served as a launching pad for the Allied invasion of Sicily and southern Italy, which succeeded, and in September an (at first secret) armistice was signed. When the new Italian government declared war on Hitler, the Germans took control of the country and organized the resistance against the American army that was slowly moving north. It was only in June 1944 that Rome was taken by the Allies. Meanwhile the Fascist dictator ruled a small enclave on Lake Garda in northern Italy, the "Republic of Salò," after the German paratroopers, in a daring operation, had snatched him from his confinement at Gran Sasso.

In comparison to the Italian adventure in imperialism, the policies adopted by the Japanese for the reordering of Asia are of world-historical

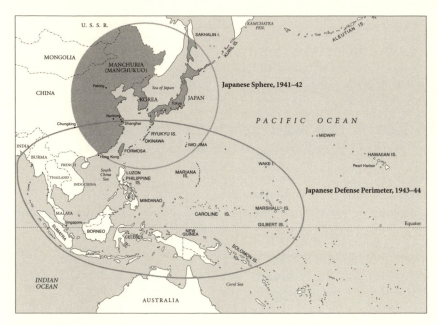

6. Japan's expansionism

significance.[60] The Japanese case is also of interest because it paralleled German development in several respects. Moreover, there were many political connections and intellectual affinities between the two countries. Some of these dated back to the pre-1914 period when the Japanese monarchy took over a number of elements of the Prusso-German constitution when it crafted its own. After World War I, from which it benefited as a neutral power, Japan rose to the position of a major industrial nation that competed successfully within the international trading system, above all during the "golden mid-1920s" when Europe experienced its recovery from the war. The United States became one of Japan's most important markets. Two-thirds of its exports consisted of textiles and silks.

The Great Slump had a profound impact on the country. Exports collapsed, and according to independent estimates, unemployment reached over two million. One of the political consequences of the economic crisis was that the liberal parties that had worked closely with the export industries during the 1920s lost their predominance in the national parliament. A coalition of right-wing forces in which the army had a particularly strong position emerged. The ethos of the officer corps became increasingly suffused with social Darwinist concepts of struggle and a peculiar militaristic ideology that celebrated self-sacrifice and an aggressive spirit. Words such as "retreat" and "capitulation" were not listed in the guiding "Principles of the Imperial Army." Willpower, on the other hand, was given a prominent place in army training. Though aware of the importance of modern military technology, the officer corps also tried to instill a psychology that was not dissimilar from the "steel-hard" personalities trained in the Wehrmacht.

In an age of increased protectionism and nationalism typical of the 1930s, military and agrarian-conservative groups gained the upper hand over the political and commercial circles that had embraced the liberal system of the previous decade. The former had always been skeptical that multilateral trade in industrial goods (through which Japan had also secured access to the raw materials elsewhere that the island monarchy lacked) would be the path to lasting prosperity for all sections of the population, including the poor peasants. Just as in Germany, by the early 1930s the voices who argued that the nation could only survive if it expanded its space and established an empire on the Asian mainland had become louder and more influential. It was also clear that such a space could only be acquired by war.

This is the background to the Japanese occupation of Manchuria in 1931 and the installation of the puppet regime of Manchukuo. From this platform the Japanese, led by the military, began to conquer China and Korea in subsequent years before moving further southeast all the way to Singapore and Burma. Viewed by them as a colonial economic space, it came to be known as the "Greater East Asia Co-Prosperity Sphere." But this was a euphemism that veiled what was in effect a formal empire.[61] In many ways similar to the German Reich in terms of its structural and organizational features, it was something like a *Grossraumwirtschaft* in which Tokyo functioned as the command center and, together with the military, the *zaibatsu* industrial and trading conglomerates played their role as economic exploiters of other nations' resources.

If the two powers that had formed the Anticomintern Pact in 1936 (to which Mussolini acceded a year later) had won World War II, they would have met somewhere in Central Asia. Their structures of political and economic organization may have been compatible, but what might have torn them apart was the racism that their leaders, in their different ways, worshiped. For the moment, however, the Axis Powers found themselves in a deadly struggle against the liberal-capitalist market economies and the parliamentary-democratic constitutional orders of the Anglo-Saxon world. In the Japanese attack on Pearl Harbor on 7 December 1941 and Hitler's declaration of war against Washington four days later the war had assumed global dimensions. The years 1941–42 are therefore the high point in a drama in which nations with two different value systems wrestled with one another and two different models of how to organize a modern industrial society clashed.[62]

Whatever the structural similarities between German and Japanese imperialism and their warrior states, their methods of domination also invite comparison. While German occupation policies have already been described in some detail, the men of violence in Japan gave a foretaste of their approach to exploitation when the army moved into Manchuria in 1931, leaving many dead in its wake. In January 1932, the navy, not wishing to be left behind, staged a horrendous "punitive expedition" against the Chinese port of Shanghai.[63] It began with a bombardment of the densely populated city from the sea and air. Subsequently, naval units advanced through the narrow lanes of the Shapei district, where they unleashed a terrible bloodbath. The atrocities were exacerbated by pillaging and rape. When Chinese contingents finally arrived, they succeeded in putting the sailors under so much pressure that they had to be relieved by the Japanese army, which in turn treated the civilian population even more harshly. In all, some 250,000 people were estimated to have died.

Another low point in the cruel Japanese-Chinese war was reached in December 1937 when the city of Nanking was conquered by Japan. After 1945, the attorney general of the district estimated that 280,000 people were killed during this operation. Between 8,000 and 20,000 women were said to have been raped. During World War II, the Japanese finally penetrated the Southeast Asian islands of the Dutch colonial empire. They built concentration camps in which POWs, but also women and children, were held in great misery under intolerable conditions. Illness was rampant and caused many deaths.[64] In this respect, too, comparisons with German occupation practices offer themselves. Although it is not easy to draw this line between German and Japanese behavior, it must nevertheless be said that the pitilessness of the Nazi system surpassed the Japanese one. True, the Japanese military were responsible for the slaughter of millions of people, but they did not build gas chambers and organize the industrialized mass murder of their victims.

The Japanese also harbored ancient feelings of superiority toward the peoples of the Asian mainland that amounted to racism. However, only in Nazi-occupied Europe did "blood" matter so much. While the Dutch or Danes were seen as genetic "cousins," Jews and Slavs were classified as "racially inferior." They were treated as "subhumans" who could be recruited as slave laborers, while Jews were not even given the right to exist. Exceptions were made in this world of racist fanatics, for example, with a number of children whose blond hair and other exterior characteristics indicated that they supposedly had a high percentage of "Aryan blood" in their veins. They were forcibly transplanted into a German environment. It is estimated that in Poland alone the Nazis seized 20,000 of these children.

The fortunes of war turned against the Axis Powers almost simultaneously. By the summer of 1942, the Red Army began to gain the upper hand in the east. The Italians and Rommel's troops were on the defensive in North Africa. In the Pacific war, the Americans were able to turn the tide in the battle of the "Midway," which has been aptly called Japan's "Stalingrad at sea." Mobilizing their own war potential, the Allies began to reverse the attempts by the three dictatorships to reorder the political and economic map of the world. Resistance also escalated in the occupied territories. The Wehrmacht reacted to this resistance by introducing the same but ever more radical methods against the civilian populations to which the Jews and Slavs had been subjected in the east from the start. From September 1943, the German troops, by now in full retreat on the eastern front, adopted a scorched-earth policy. A year later, Norwegian villages suffered the same fate. In June 1944 SS units murdered the inhabitants of the French village of Oradour before leveling it. In September 1944 the occupiers imposed a food embargo in Holland, which resulted in the death of thousands.

Even if the Nazi New Order—always assuming victory against Stalin—could have established itself and if the number of collaborators and followers among the west and north Europeans had risen, these regions would have remained no less unstable than those in the east with their roaming partisans.[65] And in the final analysis this would also have been true of the life of the German *Volksgenossen*. For however "racially pure" they may have been by their ancestry, their families would potentially have been threatened by an ideology that did not classify people merely by their allegedly superior or inferior "race" but one in which a biological racism had melded with eugenic theory.

Already before 1914, debates on genetically fixed criteria of individuality had spilled over into another one, at the center of which stood an argument over genetic differences *within* a particular "race" and which revolved around inheritable genetic diseases. In addition to the racist arguments of the kind we have examined so far, movements grew up in Europe as well as in North America that did not merely want to prevent passing on physical and mental diseases to the next generation, but also contemplated means by which the genetic quality of a society might be improved through the blending of "healthy genes." In connection with these discussions, some finally raised the question of euthanasia, that is, the ethical admissibility of helping the terminally ill or the very old and infirm to be administered a "gentle death."

It is indicative of the growing significance of eugenics that the transmission of genetic diseases to the next generation had become a focal point of public health discourses in many Western societies long before the Nazi seizure of power.[66] Some countries even began to sterilize men and women who were deemed to be compulsively criminal or "genetically burdened." The official claim was that the respective medical intervention was undertaken with the consent of the individual concerned. But in many cases it seems the consent was given under duress or without full knowledge of its consequences. Many men who were sterilized were mentally too ill to be capable of understanding what was being done to them. But this did not prevent the eugenicists from praising the benefits of sterilization for society and future generations. Since they flatly denied that mentally or physically disabled people were capable of leading a fulfilling life, thousands got caught in the net of the advocates of sterilization, even more so since the behavior of the long-term destitute, "asocials," and prostitutes was increasingly being explained in terms of their gene pool. The assertion was that men and women of a certain family background could be controlled in their procreative drive only if they were made infertile.[67]

The flip side of this kind of public health policy was the promotion of the "normal" family that was genetically healthy and hence in a position to secure the perpetuation of society and "race" if it produced three or four children. After 1933, this became a propaganda slogan of a German government that saw the world in terms of "race" and good and bad genes. Thenceforth whoever came from a family that was not afflicted by genetic diseases was put under a special obligation to secure the future of the folk community. And this future was not to be jeopardized by an "egotistical" limitation of the number of children or even childlessness. "Aryan" women who bore more than four healthy children were awarded the *Mutterkreuz* (mother's cross). In short, although many of these ideas were around before 1933, in that year a government came to power that made eugenics an official part of its policy.

Accordingly and side by side with the introduction of discrimination against entire, allegedly inferior "races," measures were also taken that were directed against "Aryan" families. They were obliged to verify not only that their family tree did not contain "non-Aryans," but also that their forebears had not suffered from genetically transmitted diseases. Whoever criticized the introduction of such documentation could from July 1935 onward be punished for "agitation against the law for the prevention of genetically diseased offspring." The no less telling "law for the protection of German blood and German honor" was introduced to criminalize sexual intercourse between Jews and non-Jews. Finally, euthanasia of the terminally ill and infirm elderly also appeared on the Nazi agenda.

Thanks to the work of scholars such as Gisela Bock and others, much has been revealed about the program of forced sterilization of "asocials" and other marginal groups.[68] Around 400,000 people fell victim to this program. As we have seen, the concentration camps filled up again in the late 1930s; many of these inmates were the homeless, petty criminals, and those who "refused" to find jobs whom the regime had begun to round up more systematically. The first wave of arrests in March 1937 caught people with a prior criminal record. The "work-shy" followed them in June 1938. Several thousand homosexuals were also picked up. During the war, many members of these groups were murdered together with Jews, Sinti, and Roma.

Conversely, the regime introduced programs to improve the genetic quality of the "Aryans." Among them the *Lebensborn e.V.* (Fountain of Life Association) acquired a sinister reputation as the organization that paired, for procreative purposes, selected unmarried women with SS men who conformed to the ideal of the blond, blue-eyed "Aryan."[69] Special homes were opened for the children who were subsequently born out of wedlock.

As far as euthanasia was concerned, it may be assumed that the regime would have handled this question less cautiously after the anticipated victory against Stalin than it did in the 1930s and at the beginning of World War II. Nevertheless, as a harbinger of things to come after the war, it is significant that another "euthanasia" program was initiated in peacetime. By 1939 the biologism of the Nazis had become so radicalized that mentally and physically disabled men and women were no longer just forcibly sterilized but also murdered within the framework of the T-4 initiative, so-called after the number in Berlin's *Tiergartenstrasse* where the office in charge of the project was housed. From August 1939, physicians had to submit the names of physically or mentally disabled children. Two months later, in a number of mental hospitals throughout the Reich and under the supervision of accredited physicians, children and adults of all ages whose further existence had been certified as being "unworthy of life" were killed. In the context of this program in which physicians and nurses administered lethal injections, those responsible began to experiment. Victims were driven around in trucks with hermetically sealed rear compartments connected to the engine. The victims were of course asphyxiated by the exhaust fumes. The corpses were removed upon the truck's return to the hospital and cremated in ovens. The families were informed that their loved ones had died of natural causes.[70]

The stench from the crematoria soon led to rumors among the local populations that eventually also reached the families of the murdered. Their protests came to the attention of the bishop of Münster in Westphalia, Clemens von Galen, who in August 1941 used one of his sermons to castigate the T-4 program. These and other protests led to the temporary cessation of the killings, but they were soon resumed in even greater secrecy. As late as the end of 1944, inmates of the Mauthausen concentration camp were gassed at the Hartheim mental hospital. As with the Final Solution of the Jewish Question, the regime was not easily diverted from its racist and eugenic policies. The total number of victims of the T-4 program was around 100,000.

Herein lies the deeper significance of all these practices: in principle every "Aryan" family was also a potential object of Nazi racism. This was true even before 1939: if a mentally or physically disabled child was born into a such family or a healthy child was crippled by an accident, this child was not merely threatened by forcible sterilization but also by euthanasia. In view of the dogmatism with which Hitler and Himmler held their views on these matters but also in light of the fact that hundreds of thousands of Germans were murdered by this program, envisioning how these policies would have been continued with the Nazi New Order after victory is not just purely counterfactual speculation. While the extermination and enslavement of the "inferior races" in the east was well underway, the life of "Aryan" families in the Reich was determined not merely by increased repression and the war's coming to the homeland, but also by the eugenic sword of Damocles that was hanging over every family living under Hitler's inchoate New Order. Small wonder that rumors began to circulate that the elderly and infirm would one day also be included.

All this is meant to say that whoever tries to imagine the practices that the men of violence pursued with even greater determination after the beginning of World War II should not focus merely on the prominent leaders. For the "ordinary men" (and relatively few women) who were prepared to execute the maxims of Nazi dogma were already waiting in the wings. They shot Jewish women and children in the villages or drove them into the gas chambers. Nurses and physicians gave lethal injections and conducted pseudoscientific and shockingly cruel experiments on camp inmates. Other "researchers," like August Hirt, a professor of anatomy at Strasbourg University, arranged for skulls and skeletons of victims to be forwarded to him for his collections of "non-Aryan" remains, just as skulls of Hereros had been sent to the Reich after the 1904 war in German South-West Africa.[71]

It is difficult to grasp how it became possible that men who often hailed from the educated middle classes and in many cases had earned a doctorate, even taken the Hippocratic oath, participated in these programs of looting and mass murder. However, the utopia of the Nazi New Order propelled not merely the Hitlers and Himmlers, but also many members of the middle strata to whom the wartime conditions had given almost unlimited powers over the lives of thousands of innocent people. As Christopher Browning and others have shown, they, too, were involved in the progressive radicalization not only of the conduct of the war but also of measures against the civilian populations of the occupied territories and the heartland that became inseparable from it.[72]

Just because the policies of exploitation and extermination were not the work of a small minority but kept tens of thousands of Germans busy in research institutes and universities, as bureaucrats in the ministries and party organizations, and as military accessories in camps and rear areas, it would be misleading to view the programs that were begun during the war and would have been completed after a German victory as propaganda. Whereas the officer corps, having absorbed the doctrines of total warfare, first sent millions of civilians in the conquered lands and finally their own soldiers to their death in large numbers, Nazi officials and other civilian collaborators stood ready to implement other parts of a program under which the mass-produced weapons of an industrial society devoured human beings in their millions. There can be little doubt that this New Order would have fundamentally changed the socioeconomic, demographic, cultural, and moral structures of Europe in a direction that was opposite to the principles that the Allies decided to enshrine in the Atlantic Charter in 1941 and other documents.

Fortunately, the utopian ideas of the Axis Powers did not become reality. In 1945, the men of violence suffered a total defeat. Their reign of terror left an even greater chaos than had existed after World War I. However, there emerged from the rubble, at least in Europe west of the Iron Curtain, a civilian consumer society and parliamentary-democratic constitutional systems, whose origins and unfolding will be discussed in the next chapter.

THE DEFEAT OF THE AXIS POWERS first appeared on the horizon in the winter of 1941–42. The lightning war against the Soviet Union that was supposed to be won by the fall ran up against the determined resistance of the Red Army, while the U.S. entry into the war with its superior industrial potential shifted the balance of forces so decisively that an Allied victory was assured. Moreover, there was also an element of self-defeat, certainly with respect to Germany, whose leaders pursued their racist reordering policy with a fanaticism that undermined the purely military war effort.

It is true that the Wehrmacht was able to regain the initiative in the east in the spring of 1942, but with the capitulation of the Sixth Army at Stalingrad a year later the tide had turned for good. Thenceforth it proved impossible to prevent ultimate defeat by relying increasingly on willpower when the Allies used more and more military hardware. The growing numerical inferiority of the German air force now brought these realities home not merely to the soldiers at the front but also to the civilians on the home front. Allied bombers appeared in ever larger numbers over the cities of the Reich, first at night but soon also in broad daylight. They shed their lethal payload not merely, and not even primarily, over the enemy's industrial installations but also over residential quarters, causing some 1.2 million civilian casualties—400,000 dead and 800,000 wounded.

The air war caused further waves of evacuation of women and children to the countryside. Although Speer, the architect, who had become Hitler's minister for armaments, succeeded in pushing the output of tanks and other weapons to new heights as late as the summer of 1944, slowly the provisioning system and people's daily routines broke down. Many, especially the elderly, now spent the day as members of "folding chair squadrons" outside the air raid shelters so that they would be the first to find protection against the next wave of Allied bombers. Feelings of solidarity that had at first existed increasingly gave way to a *sauve-qui-peut* attitude and little chicaneries and nastinesses with which people tried to make life easier for themselves and more difficult for others.[1]

Meanwhile, the situation at the front progressively deteriorated. In the south, Allied troops slowly moved up the Italian peninsula to the north. In June 1944 they were able to open up another front after landing in Normandy. Paris was liberated on 25 August, and by October British and American armies had reached the Rhine valley. However, the bloodiest battles continued to be fought on the eastern front. There, further millions of soldiers and civilians were killed on both sides until the Wehrmacht finally capitulated in May 1945. The retreating Germans flattened the remaining villages and ploughed up the railroad tracks behind them. They left similar devastations in Norway. Total war thus also reached the extreme north of the continent.

As a result of Himmler's resettlement policies countless ethnic Germans from Transylvania and the Baltic states had been sent to the regions of western Poland from which the indigenous farmers had been moved to the *Generalgouvernement*. Now these resettlers uprooted themselves again and fled westward across the Oder River or the Baltic Sea ahead of the advancing Red Army. Nazi orders to hold out to the last bullet proved a double-edged sword. On the one hand, the propaganda about an impending revenge by the Soviets helped increase the Wehrmacht's determination to resist. They had witnessed how German troops had behaved in the eastern occupied territories and knew how much destruction they had left behind. They were therefore not naive about the Soviet troops and their feelings of hatred. On the other hand, the horror stories of what the Soviets would do caused panic among the civilians. They put their few belongings on horse carts, bikes, or tractors to join the great trek to the west, thereby impeding the supply of the troops fighting the Red Army further east. As they moved west they came into the range of Allied fighter bombers that, in strafing the helpless refugees, inflicted further civilian casualties. Whoever was too slow would be overtaken by the Soviets, who raped women of all ages.[2]

Ultimately it was not just ordinary civilians who were affected by the resulting chaos, but also the higher party functionaries and bureaucrats. Recent research has shown that the regime relied not only on their ideological fanaticism in pursuing Nazism's racist aims but also on their corruptibility. As early as 1933, thousands of big and little führers had enriched themselves by taking the property of Jews who had been incarcerated or had left the country. From all we now know about these "Aryanizations," the greed the beneficiaries displayed was incredible. In many cases, they were the same people who were preaching the purity of Nazi aims and methods. Hitler and his entourage were therefore not merely doing very well themselves, but by having party functionaries, bureaucrats, and officers sharing in the loot dragged them ever more deeply into the criminality of the regime.

This also applied to preferential treatment when it came to the allocation of scarce provisions and "luxuries." With the onset of total war, average citizens went hungry and froze in their apartments; those who had influence and "connections" were able to obtain champagne and caviar. In short, it was not just Göring who lived a life of affluence in the five mansions that he had confiscated. Even the generals who pretended to be bound by a "Prussian" ethos of frugality gave in to the temptations that Hitler dangled in front of them. Quite a few of the military leaders of the "glorious" campaigns in the west and later against the Soviet Union were not only rewarded with medals and promotions, but also accepted some large landed estates as gifts. It was thus both their ideological commitment and their corruptness that led them to serve their führer loyally and to issue racist orders of the day to the troops in the war of extermination against the Jews and Slavs.[3]

Now this ideological war was also being lost. Mussolini was rounded up and strung up on a lamppost in his little enclave on Lake Garda. When they faced a similar fate, top Nazis' reactions varied considerably. Some believed they could save their skin by offering their expertise to the advancing Allies. Others raged against "defeatists" up to the last hour and had those sentenced to death by hastily convened military courts mercilessly executed. Men of all ages, soldiers and civilians, even youths who had formed oppositional cells in the big cities, fell victim to the last-ditch draconian practices of the Nazis.[4]

When their power finally collapsed once the Allies appeared outside the city gates, they put on civilian clothes and blended into the army of refugees with false papers and new identities. Others escaped arrest by committing suicide. Many of those who were sooner or later caught by Allied military police demonstrated a remarkable ability to deny they had been involved in anything criminal or even slightly improper. If investigators had known about their activities in 1945 what was revealed in later years or what we know now, many more former Nazis and officers would have ended up in prison or in the gallows. Large numbers of their collaborators in the once Nazi-occupied parts of Europe met a worse fate. If they fell into the hands of resistance groups, they would be summarily executed. Eastern Europe furthermore saw a renewal of ethnic cleansing in reverse. In Volhynia, for example, some 100,000 people were killed, women and children included, whose only guilt was that they were either Poles or Ukrainians who had fallen into the hands of the other side.

The misery and despair that the Nazis had unleashed in the Reich before 1939 and in World War II in the occupied territories did not end with unconditional surrender in May 1945. Former slave laborers and concentration camp inmates, now known as Displaced Persons (DPs), were particularly hard hit. After the liberation of the camps, they had been given back their freedom, but the physical and psychic health of these adults was often ruined forever. Arguably worse off were the children, many of them under ten years of age, whose parents had been killed or could not be found.[5]

Many women and children who had fled the Red Army and were accommodated in camps, in some cases former concentration camps, were malnourished, sick, and traumatized. Their numbers were augmented by those who had been expelled from east-central Europe. These people had often barely escaped death when the Poles or Czechs decided to deprive them of their citizenship and property and pushed them westward across the border. Between 1944 and 1947, some 12.5 million refugees and expellees arrived from the east, among them 8 million from Poland, 3 million from Czechoslovakia, 500,000 from Hungary, and several hundred thousand from Yugoslavia and Romania.[6] As late as the summer of 1945 up to 10,000 people came daily to the temporary shelters that had been set up in Berlin before they were moved to the camps in northern and southern Germany.

We may never know how many people met a violent death after the end of the war or died of disease or hunger. If in World War I and its aftermath more civilians than soldiers had lost their lives, the proportions were even more skewed after 1945. In liberated Western Europe and in Britain, conditions were markedly better and the number of dead correspondingly lower. But in those parts of Europe the war had left a terrible legacy, too: families who had lost loved ones; houses and factories that had been destroyed; illness and rationing cards. As far as Soviet-occupied Eastern Europe is concerned, it is only since 1989 that we have begun to gain a clearer picture of material conditions and the traumatization of millions of people there. The Axis Powers had left nothing but chaos in Europe.

As the Japanese were gradually forced to retreat from their conquests in Asia, the picture of devastation and of massive atrocities that the Empire of the Rising Sun had left behind likewise emerged in its full horror. As in Germany and Italy, the war ultimately came to the Japanese home front. The photos of the moon landscapes left by the two American atomic bombs dropped on Hiroshima and Nagasaki in early August 1945 have been widely circulated. The controversy over whether the Japanese government was ready to capitulate without these devices continues. The first one detonated over Hiroshima left 90,000 inhabitants dead and 40,000 wounded; the Nagasaki bomb claimed 40,000 lives and 60,000 were wounded, many of whom subsequently died a slow death as a result of their exposure to radiation.

The defeat of the men of violence and their attempt to establish industrial warrior states whose mass-produced weapons had "consumed" millions of lives cleared the way for an alternative that now began to assert itself, at least in Western Europe. This alternative had appeared as a possibility on the European horizon before 1914. It was the model of a civilian society that peacefully consumed its mass-produced goods within a democratic-representative order. In the mid-1920s, the United States with its constitutional government and its postulates of liberty and the "pursuit of happiness" had made good progress on the path toward this type of modern industrial society. This system, it is true, still had many imperfections, which are not being minimized here. America's minorities in the rural South or in the slums of the big cities were barely included in the prosperity of the 1920s. But a beginning had been made with the promise that this prosperity was, in principle, for all people. The Europeans had been given a taste of it when Fordism and the idea of a civilian consumer society spread, however briefly and thinly, to their part of the world.

The defeat of the attempt by the Axis Powers to reorder, with the force of arms, the power-political and economic structures of the international system and to revolutionize entire societies and the values on which they were based by means of racist policies reinforced the determination of the United States *not* to repeat the mistake of 1918–19 when they had retreated from world politics. The victory of 1945 was to be seized by Washington in order to assume a leadership role in the postwar international system that was commensurate with its political, economic, and sociocultural power. President Roosevelt and his advisors wanted to shape this system both institutionally and intellectually.

While 1945 became one of the great turning points in the history of Europe under the aegis of America that was now so clearly the hegemonic power of the West, we once more must backtrack a few years to 1941–42 if we want to understand the significance of the war's end. We have seen that this was the high point of German New Order planning but also its end point. It was clear that the Axis would lose the war, even if many of the postwar projects, be they the organization of the Holocaust or architectural construction sites, continued until the advancing Allies forced their cessation. For the Allies, the United States in particular, 1941–42, was the starting point of concrete postwar planning.

The contours of what was to come were first formulated in the above-mentioned Atlantic Charter of August 1941 and were later incorporated into the introduction to the Charter of the United Nations. Both documents enunciated principles that were diametrically opposed to the policies that the Axis Powers had begun to implement in Europe and Asia. In light of what has been said about Nazi occupation practices, it is worth quoting from the UN charter:

> We the Peoples of the United Nations, determined to save succeeding generations from the scourge of war which twice in our lifetime has brought untold sorrow to mankind, and to reaffirm faith in fundamental human rights, in the dignity and worth of the human person, in the equal rights of men and women and of nations large and small, and to establish conditions under which justice and respect for the obligations arising from treaties and other sources of international law can be maintained, and to promote social progress and better standards of life in larger freedom, and for these ends to practice tolerance and live together in peace with one another as good neighbors, and to unite our strength to maintain international peace and security, and to insure, by the acceptance of principles and the institution of methods, that armed force shall not be used, save in the common interest, and to employ international machinery for the promotion of the economic and social advancements of all peoples, have resolved to combine our efforts to accomplish these aims.[7]

Other statements coming out of Washington after 1941–42 were more explicit about both the political and economic framework in which the reconstruction of the international system, and of Europe in particular, was to take place after the defeat of the dictators. The political institutions of postwar Europe were to be rooted in parliamentary-democratic constitutions that guaranteed basic human rights; the region's economic system was to be based on the principles of a liberal capitalism that was competitive and would promote full employment, low inflation, and higher living standards for all. It is not surprising that the political and economic system that had emerged in the United States was to provide the model for what the United States was hoping to create out of the ruins of World War II. But it is no less important to emphasize that they did not expect everyone to copy their system. The British parliamentary system had survived and demonstrated its viability even during the crisis years of 1939–41 when the British Empire faced the Axis virtually alone. Other European states had longstanding constitutional traditions of their own that the occupation had destroyed and that merely needed revival and adaptation. Even the Italians and Germans had practiced parliamentary democracy before the rise of Mussolini and Hitler. In short, there was a good deal of leeway in the shaping of Europe's postwar political institutions as long as they enshrined basic human rights and free elections based on universal suffrage.

Nor did Washington expect the Europeans to adopt the American economic system hook, line, and sinker. Like World War I, the second world conflict had, in the interest of victory, made centralization and government intervention into the economy inevitable. The transition to a peacetime economy had to proceed slowly and take account of national peculiarities. Still, the ideal was that sooner or later the national economies of Europe (and of other parts of the world, including Japan) would have competitive market systems. They would also be integrated into a multilateral world trading system of which Secretary of State Cordell Hull, as a confirmed internationalist, had been an unwavering advocate throughout his term of office even at the height of the economic crisis with its flight into protectionism and economic nationalism. After the experience of unprecedented destruction and the defeat of the warrior societies, the idea was not only to forge swords into ploughshares but also to secure peace and prosperity through trade among politically and economically compatible national systems.

By 1945, American ideas on these matters had been cast into more tangible form by a large number of postwar planning committees. Some of them were official and staffed by experts from various ministries; others, like the Committee on Economic Development (CED), brought officials together with the leaders of industry and finance, the unions, and the academic world. The memoranda and publications they produced offered detailed advice or presented a broad view of postwar economic structures and policymaking. To mention just one example: in 1946, Edward S. Mason, a well-known Harvard economist, published, under the auspices of the CED, his book *Controlling World Trade* in which he examined the contours of a future world trading system and suggested how even a state-run economy like that of the Soviet Union might find a place within it.[8]

While there were indeed some people in the American administration who looked for ways of continuing the wartime alliance with Stalin, it became clear soon after the defeat of the Axis Powers that the ideological and systemic differences between the United States and the Soviet Union, the two superpowers of the postwar world, were just too deep to make this possible. The cold war began, dividing Europe right in the middle between east and west. However tragic the consequences of this division were for the East Europeans who now slowly fell under Stalinist rule, it simplified the task of the Americans. Their efforts of material reconstruction and institutional recasting could concentrate on Western Europe. The growing tensions with the emergent Soviet bloc and the fear of communist expansion made it easier to win over American politicians in Congress and midwestern voters who still had to be convinced in 1945–46 that an American withdrawal from Europe and a refusal to aid in the reconstruction of a devastated continent would mean repeating the mistakes of 1918–19. This is the background to the famous speech that Secretary of State George C. Marshall made at Harvard University in June 1947 and out of which grew the European Recovery Program, the so-called Marshall Plan that was subsequently passed by Congress.

While the means for the material reconstruction of Western Europe thenceforth flowed across the Atlantic, the other lesson from World War I was that European industry must not be allowed again to lapse into attitudes and practices that had prevented its more far-reaching modernization in the 1920s. The industrial and financial structures had to be made compatible with those of the liberal-capitalist Open Door world trading system that the American business elites and politicians in Washington wanted to erect. There were to be no more cartels and syndicates, closed economic blocs, and autarky. For this reason, Washington also became an early promoter of the integration of Western Europe as part of an Atlantic community of institutions and values. Thus, John Foster Dulles, secretary of state under President Dwight D. Eisenhower in the 1950s, suggested in a speech before the National Publishers' Association on 17 January 1947 that the Europeans should form a federation along the lines of the American model. Through such a federation, he added, they would gain the advantages of a market that would be large enough to "justify modern methods of cheap production for mass consumption."[9]

In this vision of creating modern mass-production and mass-consumption industries in destitute Western Europe, the western zones of occupied Germany that were to become the Federal Republic in 1949 played a central role. True, the structures of German industry before 1945 had been adapted to the Nazi concepts of *Grossraumwirtschaft* and *Grossraumkartell*. But Hitler's reckless investments in war production had also resulted in a big modernization push. Allied air raids and postwar dismantling of some machinery, especially by the British, notwithstanding, German industry's capital stock was still 11 percent higher than it had been in 1936. West Germany had the potential to be the motor of postwar economic growth. If its pre-1945 structures could be changed from an anticompetitive authoritarian capitalism to a liberal–free market one, the three zones would not only act as the locomotive of the region as a whole but would also help transform whatever protectionist and anticompetitive practices had survived in France, Holland, or other neighboring states. As the hegemonic occupying power, the United States was of course in a particularly strong position to recast West German industry.[10]

This is what now happened in the wake of the Marshall Plan. Just as Norman Davies had identified Germany in 1921 as the core of any American attempt to revive the economies of Europe after World War I, the East Coast business community, encouraged by the Marshall Plan, came back to invest or restart the production facilities they had established in the mid-1920s. Economic experts in the American occupation authority and from 1949 in the U.S. High Commission encouraged the building of institutions and the introduction of policies that came to be embodied in the "social market economy" of economics minister Ludwig Erhard. In 1957 he published a widely read book with the telling title *Wohlstand für alle* (Prosperity for all).[11] This is exactly what he had been trying to bring about through his ministry.

Looking at the scholarly literature, there have been divergent interpretations of Erhard's concept of social market economy, but in analyzing his many speeches and his practical policies, there can be little doubt that what he wanted to realize in West Germany was *au fond* a Fordist mass-production and mass-consumption society. In this sense he was one of the great "Americanizers" of postwar Europe. But he also knew that this could not be done overnight. The war had so lowered the living standards of millions of people that it would take years before incomes were high enough for a majority of the population to be able to afford more than the basic needs of food and shelter. The war had also left behind millions of widowed women, orphaned children, refugees, and expellees whose income was so low that they had to rely on a social security system that had existed in Germany since the late nineteenth century. In short, it would be wrong to see Erhard as a laissez-faire liberal who merely wanted to unleash the forces of the free market upon West German society. Rather he pursued a carefully calibrated policy of economic liberalization that would enable the country to take advantage of the opportunities afforded to it as a trading nation by the reconstitution of multilateralism, while caring for the weaker sections of the population that needed state help. His market economy had a strong welfare state element, a safety net that he considered vital to the stability of postwar society and politics and whose costs would eventually shrink as prosperity became more widespread.

It is at this point that a clear link can be established with American visions of postwar economic reconstruction. After World War I, there was a vigorous push in the United States to return to a classic laissez-faire liberalism. The subsequent experience of the Great Slump with its eight million unemployed, rising to ten million by 1936, changed all this again. It led to the introduction of sets of legal provisions that allowed Washington to intervene in the economy to an unprecedented degree. Some of these were designed to bring immediate help to those hit hard by the depression. Proclaiming a "New Deal" for all Americans in need, Roosevelt established the Federal Emergency Relief Administration, the Civil Works Administration, and the Civilian Conservation Corps. Altogether some twenty-eight million people benefited from the funds made available under these programs to provide food and jobs. But beyond crisis aid and job creation schemes, laws were enacted that established a permanent social security safety net. Thus, the Wagner and Social Security Acts of 1935 guaranteed retirement pensions and unemployment benefits. Government funding amounted to some three billion dollars in 1935. In short, under the impact of mass poverty and despair, political radicalization, and the threat of proliferating unrest, Washington offered the country a New Deal in domestic politics.

This system was complemented by legislation for stricter regulation and supervision of industry and banking, since the lack of controls and restraints on the capitalist system of the 1920s was blamed for the disaster of 1929. Overall, the aim was a firmer management of the economy in Keynesian fashion. As Robert Collins has shown, the impact of Keynes's ideas was considerable, not only on American policymakers but also on key elements of the business community.[12] Above all, it lasted beyond World War II. Fostered by the pressures of war-economic mobilization and of having to engineer a soft landing and conversion to peacetime production, few wanted to go back to the philosophies of the pre-1914 period. Nor did they want an equally radical dismantling of the legal and managerial instruments of the 1930s, that is, Roosevelt's New Deal with its creation of an American welfare state.[13]

If the meaning of the Fordist dream of a mass-production and mass-consumption society had been enlarged in this way by the American experience of the 1930s and the profound crisis of industrial capitalism in those years, it now also becomes more tangible what the United States had in mind when it held out to postwar Europe its model of how to organize modern political and industrial systems after the second catastrophe of the twentieth century. With American help, the Axis model of building a warrior society whose mass-produced weapons devoured human beings had been obliterated. People yearned for societies that lived by the above-mentioned principles enunciated in the Charter of the United Nations. After the ravages of the war, they also wanted to exploit the benefits of mass production and peacefully consume the civilian goods that were being manufactured. This is what seemed to be happening in the United States, whose GNP had risen from $91 billion in 1939 to $166 billion in 1945, and where after the war some 7 percent of the world population produced and consumed 43 percent of the world's electricity, 57 percent of the steel, and 80 percent of automobiles.

Once the monetary and economic instruments had been put in place and the institutions created under American leadership for the revival of a multilateral world trading system began to function, postwar Western Europe soon experienced a modernization and expansion of its economies similar to that of the United States. By 1951 real growth in the West German economy, in American eyes the locomotive of European reconstruction, reached 10.4 percent. It remained around 8 percent over the next three years, peaking at 12 percent in 1955. Erhard's market economy with its heavy social element was clearly working and delivering its promises. This was what the Americans were offering to the West Europeans, including the defeated Germans, after 1945. With its prospect of full employment, low inflation, and peaceful international trade, it represented one key element of their New Deal. But no less important, it was also a New Deal that, while sharply rejecting the alternative model of a racist and exclusive society that Hitler had almost succeeded in realizing, was not tantamount to a purely laissez-faire Fordist capitalism. It contained a strong dose of Keynesian economic management and a sense of societal solidarity and responsibility toward the weaker sections of the population. This made it possible for the West Europeans to accept, with many modifications, the recipes of postwar reconstruction developed by the hegemonic power across the Atlantic.[14] Consequently, Europe, too, became a region of the world whose societies were civilian-industrial in structure and outlook. It is not that militaristic tendencies disappeared completely. In this sense, we may not have reached a "postheroic" age, but attitudes of most Europeans are certainly very different from what they were in the 1930s.

This analysis of what happened in Europe between the late nineteenth century and 1945 and of how the West Europeans escaped from the men of violence and their brutal policies into an era of political constitutionalism, material prosperity, and social security is not meant to be an uncritical praise of civilian-industrial society of the kind that Gary Cross has recently given.[15] To begin with, it should not be forgotten that the emergence of the Atlantic community as a region of political peace, economic growth, and "prosperity for all" did not end wars and civil wars in other parts of the world. Instead, the violence that had stopped in Europe was reexported abroad. As part of the confrontation between the two superpowers of the postwar world, it hovered over Europe and indeed all of humanity in the shape of a potential nuclear war. Although we all once or twice looked into the abyss of another catastrophe, for example, during the Cuban missile crisis, the east-west conflict never exploded into mass violence. But it also meant that the peoples of Eastern Europe fell under a regime that took their political freedoms and constitutional rights away and, though constantly promising a "consumer socialism,"[16] never came close to securing the kind prosperity that the first world enjoyed. The peoples of the second world had to wait until 1989 for this.

The populations of the third world bore the brunt of reexported violence. Whether as part of the painful process of the slow dismantling of Europe's colonial empires or of internal tensions, wars and civil wars in the non-Western world in the second half of the twentieth century were horrifically costly in terms of human lives. It is estimated that close to 120 million people died as a result of violent conflicts and their consequences since 1945, as compared to the estimated 70 million who were killed in two world wars.[17] No less distressing, millions of those who survived continue to live in abject poverty, with shockingly short life expectancies, often without education and health care, and without the slightest hope of a better future. Around one billion people currently live in slums. It is not that we lack the technical and economic means to solve the problems in these parts of the world. The knowledge and know-how also exist for making third world development sustainable. What seems to be lacking is the political will and a public understanding of how much it is in the first world's interest to offer the third world what the Americans offered the West Europeans and Japan after 1945: a New Deal. This, as Bill Gates has argued, is "the last frontier" of mankind.[18] Only when it has been conquered and the productive capacities of modern technology and sustainable development are shared more evenly will it be possible to discuss the undoubted dangers of civilian consumerism in ways that do not ring hollow in the ears of the peoples in other continents who do not enjoy prosperity, education, medical provision, or basic rights that Europeans and Americans have come to value highly.

However, this was not the main point of this study. Rather it represents an attempt to record the history of the first half of the twentieth century and to highlight the major forces that were unleashed by World War I and subsequently shaped the world. It stresses that the rule of the men of violence never completely dominated during this period. There was an alternative vision of how to organize a modern industrial society. At the same time, it is clear that the Axis Powers came close to realizing their utopia. This book therefore also invites the reader to remember and consider what was ultimately at stake in those decades. Certainly, if the fascists had won, the subsequent course of history would have been very different. It fortunately did not come to this, and in this sense ours is also an effort to explain why it didn't and why this period of European history and the decades after 1945 cannot be understood without the United States.

At the center of this analysis stands what might be called a systemic interpretation. Another very daunting question remains admittedly largely unanswered: how was it possible that the men of violence were capable of the atrocities they committed? Are we all capable of such behavior?[19] There are quite a few analysts of the "human soul" who would say we are. But if this is correct, the social milieu and the ideological and legal context become all the more important.

The militarism that was identified as a central phenomenon of this epoch could assert itself only because of the sociopolitical framework within which it arose permitted and even encouraged violent action. Conversely, where the existing framework criminalizes brutality and the propagation of hatred and prejudice and promotes a viable civil society, the ubiquitous men of violence will be confined to the margins and will have no chance of gaining a dominant position.

However, a society of civilians engaged in peaceful production and exchange will not be viable without a stable and slowly growing economy that is not merely geared to individual freedom and initiative in the marketplace, but also to an ethos of socioeconomic justice and societal solidarity. Where resources are unfairly distributed, where access to a good education, adequate health care, and social security create glaring material inequalities, civil society will be no more than a façade. Worse, it will be vulnerable to the challenge of those who are being left behind and who, in the age of universal suffrage, will turn to the men of violence luring them with the promise of radical change and permanent salvation.

Notes

Introduction

I would like to thank the two reviewers for Princeton University Press for their comments and suggestions that helped improve this book. I am also most grateful to Brigitta van Rheinberg for her expert advice and to Jennifer Backer for her careful copyediting of the manuscript.

1. V. R. Berghahn, *Sarajewo, 28. Juni 1914: Der Untergang des alten Europa* (Munich, 1997), 16ff.

2. E. Hobsbawm, *The Age of Extremes* (New York, 1996); M. Mazower, *Dark Continent* (New York, 1998).

3. Hobsbawm, *The Age of Extremes*, i.

4. Ibid., 5ff.

5. Mazower, *Dark Continent*, IX.

6. Ibid., 403.

7. F. Lenger, *Werner Sombart, 1863–1941: eine Biographie* (Munich, 1994). On Schumpeter, Spencer, and Vagts, see V. R. Berghahn, ed., *Militarismus* (Cologne, 1975), esp. 9ff., 40ff., 102ff.

8. H. Dubiel, "Unzivile Gesellschaften," unpublished manuscript, 2001. 1f. See also, M. Walzer, *Toward a Global Civil Society* (New York, 1997).

9. See below pp. 136ff in this volume. See also, e.g., K. *Maase, Grenzenloses Vergnügen: Der Aufstieg der Massenkultur, 1850–1970* (Frankfurt, 1997); W. Susman, *Culture as History: The Transformation of American Society in the Twentieth Century* (New York, 1984); L. Glickman, *A Living Wage: American Workers and the Making of Consumer Society* (Ithaca, 1997); V. R. Berghahn, *The Americanisation of West German Industry, 1945–1973* (New York, 1986), esp. 26ff.

Chapter 1. Europe before World War I, 1895–1914

1. G. F. Kennan quoted in J. Kocka, "Der gebrochene Bann," in W. Küttler, ed., *Das lange 19. Jahrhundert* (Berlin, 1999) 1:99.

2. M. T. Florinsky, *Russia: A History and an Interpretation* (New York, 1953).

3. M. Rauh, *Föderalismus und Parlamentarismus im Wilhelminischen Reich* (Düsseldorf, 1973); idem, *Die Parlamentarisierung des Deutschen Reiches* (Düsseldorf, 1977); M. L. Anderson, *Practicing Democracy: Elections and Political Culture in Imperial Germany* (Princeton, 2000).

4. Anderson, *Practicing Democracy*, 437.

5. N. Ferguson, *The Pity of War* (New York, 1999), 457ff.

6. Quoted in F. Stern, *Gold and Iron* (London, 1977), 478.

7. T. J. Mason, *Sport in Britain* (London, 1988); R. Holt, *Sport and Society in Modern France* (London, 1981).

8. K. Strohmeyer, *Warenhäuser*, (Göttingen, 1979); G. Crossick and S. Jaumain, eds., *Cathedrals of Consumption: The European Department Store, 1850–1939* (Aldershot, 1999); H. Frei, *Tempel der Kauflust* (Leipzig, 1997).

9. R. Kanigel, *The One Best Way* (New York, 1997); A. Kugler, "Von der Werkstatt zum Fliessband," *Geschichte und Gesellschaft* 13 (1987): 304–39.

10. J. Kocka, *Europäische Arbeiterbewegung im 19: Jahrhundert* (Göttingen, 1983); D. Groh, *Negative Integration und revolutionärer Attentismus*, (Frankfurt, 1973).

11. A. Raeburn, *The Militant Suffragists*, (London, 1973).

12. Quoted in E. R. Tannenbaum, *1900* (Garden City, NJ: 1976), 349.

13. A. von Tirpitz, *Erinnerungen* (Leipzig, 1919), 52.

14. Hobsbawm, *The Age of Empire*; G. Schmidt, *Der europäische Imperialismus* (Munich, 1985).

15. J. Joll, *The Origins of the First World War* (London, 1984), 148ff.

16. A. D. Smith, *Nations and Nationalism in a Global Era*, (Oxford, 1995); E. Gellner, *Nationalism* (London, 1997); E. Hobsbawm, *Nations and Nationalism since 1780* (Cambridge, 1990).

17. M. Hawkins, *Social Darwinism in American and European Thought* (Cambridge, 1997).

18. R. Rürup, *Emanzipation und Antisemitismus* (Göttingen, 1975); P. Pulzer, *The Rise of Political Antisemitism in Germany and Austria* (New York, 1964).

19. R. Owen and B. Sutcliffe, eds., *Studies in the Theory of Imperialism* (London, 1972); V. G. Kiernan, *European Empires from Conquest to Collapse, 1815–1960* (London, 1969).

20. This is graphically portrayed in the movie *Zulu Dawn*.

21. I. Laurien, "'That Homa Homa Was Worse, Child!' Berichte afrikanischer Zeitzeugen über den Maji Maji Aufstand in Deutsch-Ostafrika," in P. Heine und U. van der Heyde, eds., *Studien zur Geschichte des deutschen Kolonialismus in Afrika* (Pfaffenweiler, 1995), 350.

22. A. Hochschild, *King Leopold's Ghost* (Boston, 1998).

23. Quoted in ibid., 132f.

24. H. Arendt, *The Origins of Totalitarianism* (London, 1967), 185.

25. A. Hochschild, "Leopold's Congo: A Holocaust We Have Yet to Comprehend," *Chronicle of Higher Education*, 12 May 2000, p. B4.

26. H. Bley, *Kolonialherrschaft und Sozialstruktur in Deutsch-Südwestafrika, 1894–1914* (Hamburg, 1968), 314.

27. W. U. Eckart, "Medizin und kolonialer Krieg: Die Niederschlagung der Herero-Nama-Erhebung im Schutzgebiet Deutsch-Südwestafrika, 1904–1907," in Heine and van der Heyden, eds., *Studien*, 220.

28. Bley, *Kolonialherrschaft und Sozialstruktur*, 191.

29. G. Krüger, *Kriegsbewältigung und Geschichtsbewusstsein: Realität, Deutung und Verarbeitung des deutschen Kolonialkriegs in Namibia, 1904 bis 1907* (Göttingen, 1999), 64.

30. Quoted in Bley, *Kolonialherrschaft und Sozialstruktur*, 297.

31. Quoted in Eckart, *Studien*, 227.

32. J. Zeller, "'Wie Vieh wurden hunderte zu Tode getrieben und wie Vieh begraben,'" *Zeitschrift für Geschichtswissenschaft* 3 (2001): 226–43, 227. See also T. Dedering, "'A Certain Rigorous Treatment of All Parts of the Nation': The Annihilation

of the Herero in German South West Africa, 1904," in M. Levene and P. Roberts, eds., *The Massacre in History* (New York, 1999), 205–22.

33. Quoted in Eckart, *Studien*, 230.

34. Quoted in Bley, *Kolonialherrschaft und Sozialstruktur*, 102.

35. Quoted in ibid., 224; also for the following quotes.

36. Quoted in ibid., 225; also for the following quote.

37. Krüger, *Kriegsbewältigung und Geschichtsbewusstsein;* "'A Certain Rigorous Treatment,'" 217.

38. Quoted in Krüger, *Kriegsbewältigung und Geschichtsbewusstsein*, 66.

39. Bley, *Kolonialherrschaft und Sozialstruktur*, 314. For another excellent collection of essays on the genocide and its long-term consequences, see J. Zimmerer and J. Zeller, eds., *Völkermord in Deutsch-Südwestafrika* (Berlin, 2003).

40. R. Chickering, *Imperial Germany and a World without War* (Princeton, 1975).

41. H. Spencer, *Man versus the State* (1884; London, 1969), esp. 185ff.

42. V. R. Berghahn, *Militarism: The History of an International Debate, 1861–1979* (Leamington Spa, 1981), 19f.

43. J. Joll, *The Second International* (London, 1955).

44. L. L. Farrar, *The Short War Illusion* (Santa Barbara, CA, 1973).

45. Quoted in I.F. Clarke, *Voices Prophesying War* (1966; Oxford, 1972), 134. See also S. D. Denham, *Visions of War* (Bern, 1992); M. F. Boemeke et al., eds., *Anticipating Total War* (New York, 1999).

46. Quoted in Clarke, *Voices Prophesying War*, 114.

47. G. Best, *War and Law since 1945* (Oxford, 1994), 14ff.

48. H. Morgenthau, *Politics among Nations* (New York, 1960), 242.

49. S. Förster, "Der deutsche Generalstab und die Illusion des kurzen Krieges, 1871–1914," in *Militärgeschichtliche Mitteilungen* 54 (1995): 61–95; idem, "Facing 'People's War,'" *Journal of Strategic Studies* 2 (June, 1987): 209–30.

50. G. Ritter, *Der Schlieffenplan* (Munich, 1956).

51. V. R. Berghahn, *Der Tirpitzplan* (Düsseldorf, 1971), 45ff.

CHAPTER 2. VIOLENCE UNLEASHED, 1914–1923

1. F. Fischer, *War of Illusions* (New York, 1973); I. Geiss, *Der lange Weg in die Katastrophe* (Munich, 1990); Ferguson, *The Pity of War*.

2. G. Schöllgen, ed., *Escape into War?* (Oxford, 1991); K. Hildebrand, *Deutsche Aussenpolitik* (Munich, 1989).

3. Fischer, *War of Illusions*, 231ff.

4. K. D. Erdmann, ed., *Kurt Riezler* (Göttingen, 1972), 182ff.

5. V. R. Berghahn, *Germany and the Approach of War in 1914* (London, 1973), 196ff.

6. Fischer, *War of Illusions*, 584.

7. Quoted in Förster, "Der deutsche Generalstab," 89. See also A. Mombauer, *Helmuth von Moltke and the Origins of the First World War* (Cambridge, 2001).

8. A. von Tirpitz, *Deutsche Ohnmachtspolitik im Weltkriege* (Hamburg-Berlin, 1926), 16ff.

9. J.C.G. Röhl, "Admiral von Müller and the Approach of War, 1911–1914," *Historical Journal* 4 (1969): 670 n. 99: "Splendid mood. The government has been very good at portraying us as the attacked party."

10. Tirpitz, *Deutsche Ohnmachtspolitik im Weltkriege*, 16ff.

11 See, e.g., S. Förster and R. Chickering, eds., *Great War: Total War* (New York, 2000); J. Kocka, *Facing Total War* (Leamington Spa,1984); B. Waites, *A Class Society at War* (Leamington Spa, 1987); P. Fridenson, *The French Homefront, 1914–1918* (Oxford, 1992); B.J. Davis, *Home Fires Burning* (Chapel Hill, 2000); M. Horn, *Britain, France, and the Financing of the First World War* (Montreal, 2002).

12. J. Horne and A. Kramer, *German Atrocities 1914* (New Haven, 2002).

13. J. Keegan, *The First World War* (London, 1998), 119ff. See also D. Stevenson, *Cataclysm: The First World War as Political Tragedy* (New York, 2004).

14. H. Aflerbach, "Die militärischen Planungen des Deutsches Reiches im Ersten Weltkrieg," in W. Michalka, ed., *Der Erste Weltkrieg* (Munich, 1994), 286f.

15. Keegan, *The First World War*, 146.

16. J. M. Winter and B. Baggett, *The Great War and the Shaping of the 20th Century* (New York, 1996), 156ff.

17. J. Keegan, *The Face of Battle* (New York, 1976), 204ff.

18. E. Leed, *No Man's Land* (Cambridge, 1979).

19. Quoted in Keegan, *The First World War*, 213.

20. V. G. Liulevicius, *War Land on the Eastern Front* (Cambridge, 2000), 30. See also N. Stone, *The Eastern Front* (New York, 1975).

21. V.N. Dadrian, *The History of the Armenian Genocide* (Providence, RI, 1997).

22. J. M. Winter, *Sites of Memory, Sites of Mourning* (Cambridge, 1995); R. Whalen, *Bitter Wounds* (Ithaca, 1984).

23. See photos of such injuries in Kunstamt Kreuzberg, ed., *Weimarer Republik* (Berlin, 1977) 77ff.

24. B. Kundrus, *Kriegerfrauen* (Hamburg, 1998).

25. A. Rachamimov, *POWs and the Great War* (Oxford, 2002).

26. S. Fitzpatrick, *The Russian Revolution* (Oxford, 1982); G. Hosking, *A History of the Soviet Union* (London, 1985); R. Pipes, *The Russian Revolution, 1899–1919* (London, 1990); O. Figes, *A People's Tragedy: The Russian Revolution, 1891–1924* (London, 1996).

27. W. E. Williams, "Die Politik der Alliierten gegenüber den Freikorps im Baltikum, 1918–1919," *Vierteljahrshefte für Zeitgeschichte* 2 (1964):147–63; R.G.L. Waite, *Vanguard of Nazism* (Cambridge, MA, 1952).

28. E. Mandsley, *The Russian Civil War* (London, 1987), 205. See also V. N. Brovkin, *Behind the Front Lines of the Civil War* (Princeton, 1994). M. von Hagen, *Soldiers in the Proletarian Dictatorship* (Ithaca, 1990); D. P. Koenker et al., eds., *Party, State, and Society in the Russian Civil War* (Bloomington, 1989).

29. P. Corner, *Fascism in Ferrara* (Oxford, 1975); A. Littleton, *The Sinews of Power* (Princeton, 1988).

30. R. Wohl, *The Generation of 1914* (Cambridge, MA, 1979), 176.

31. M. Kitchen, *The Silent Dictatorship* (London, 1976).

32. F.L. Carsten, *Revolution in Central Europe* (Berkeley, 1972), 127ff.

33. D. Schneider and R. Kuda, *Arbeiterräte* (Frankfurt, 1969).

34. P. Nettl, *Rosa Luxemburg* (Oxford, 1966).

35. L. Morenz, *Revolution und Räteherrschaft in München* (Munich, 1968); D.C. Large, *Where Ghosts Walked* (New York, 1997).

36. K. Theweleit, *Männerphantasien* (Frankfurt, 1977), 1: 76ff.

37. Quoted in ibid., 1: 111.

38. J. Erger, *Der Kapp-Lüttwitz-Putsch* (Düsseldorf, 1967); F. L. Carsten, *Reichswehr and Politics* (Oxford, 1966).

39. Quoted in J.C.B. Gordon, ed., *German History and Society, 1918–1945* (Oxford, 1988), 36.

40. E. Weitz, *Creating German Communism* (Princeton, 1997), 106.

41. M. Sabrow, *Der Rathenaumord* (Munich, 1994); U. C. Hofmann, "Verräter verfallen der Feme!" in *Fememorde in Bayern in den zwanziger Jahren* (Köln, 2000).

42. G. Krumeich, "Die Dolchstosslegende," E. François and H. Schulze, eds., *Erinnerungsorte* (Munich, 2001), 1:585–99.

43. U. Lohalm, *Völkischer Radikalismus* (Hamburg, 1970).

44. H.H. Hofmann, *Der Hitler-Putsch* (Munich, 1961).

CHAPTER 3. RECIVILIZATION AND ITS FAILURE, 1924–1935

1. See above p. 11.

2. F. Costigliola, *Awkward Dominion* (Ithaca, 1984).

3. R. Sobel, *The Life and Times of Dillon Read* (New York, 1991), 145ff.; M. Nolan, *Visions of Modernity* (New York, 1994).

4. M. Harrington, *The Other America* (New York, 1962).

5. M. Bonn, *Das Schicksal des Kapitalismus* (Berlin, 1930), 46ff.

6. J. K. Galbraith, *The Great Crash* (New York, 1954).

7. W. Link, *Die amerikanische Stabilisierungspolitik in Deutschland* (Düsseldorf, 1970).

8. M. Stürmer, *Koalition und Opposition* (Düsseldorf, 1967).

9. S. Street, *British National Cinema* (London, 1997); T. Saunders, *Hollywood in Berlin* (Berkeley, 1994).

10. W. von Moellendorff, *Volkswirtschaftliche Elementarvergleiche zwischen Vereinigten Staaten von Amerika, Deutschland, Grossbritannien, Frankreich, Italien,* 2 vols. (Berlin,1930).

11. W. McNeil, *American Money and the Weimar Republic* (New York, 1985); B. Lieberman, *From Recovery to Catastrophe* (Oxford, 1998).

12. See below p. 65.

13. Costigliola, *Awkward Dominion.*

14. P. Clavin, *The Great Depression in Europe* (Basingstoke, 2000); C.P. Kindleberger, *The World in Depression, 1929–1939* (Berkeley, 1975).

15. J. Hinton, *Labour and Society* (Brighton, 1983); B. Weisbrod, *Schwerindustrie in der Weimarer Republik* (Wuppertal, 1978).

16. C. A. Wurm, *Internationale Kartelle und Aussenpolitik* (Wiesbaden, 1989).

17. V. R. Berghahn, *America and the Intellectual Cold Wars in Europe* (Princeton, 2001), 85ff.

18. P. Gassert, *Amerika im Dritten Reich* (Stuttgart, 1997).

19. J. von Kruedener, ed., *Economic Crisis and Political Collapse* (Oxford, 1990).

20. Sobel, *Dillon Read*, 133ff.

21. Galbraith, *The Great Crash*, 118ff.

22. P. Brendon, *Dark Valley* (New York, 2000), 183; J. Paulmann, "Arbeitslosigkeit und sonst gar nichts?" *Vierteljahrschrift für Sozial- und Wirtschaftsgeschichte* 1 (1992): 1–34.

23. J. M. Winter, *Sites of Memory*.

24. J. M. Diehl, *Paramilitary Politics in Weimar Germany* (Bloomington, 1977); K. Rohe, *Das Reichsbanner Schwarz-Rot-Gold* (Düsseldorf, 1966); V. R. Berghahn, *Der Stahlhelm, Bund der Frontsoldaten* (Düsseldorf, 1966).

25. A. Mohler, *Die konservative Revolution in Deutschland* (Stuttgart, 1950); O. E. Schüddekopf, *Linke Leute von Rechts* (Stuttgart, 1960); K. von Klemperer, *Germany's New Conservatism* (Princeton, 1957); J. Herf, *Reactionary Modernism* (Cambridge, 1989).

26. A. L. Burt, *The British Empire and Commonwealth* (Boston, 1956), 708ff.

27. Berghahn, *Der Stahlhelm*, 11ff.

28. Rohe, *Das Reichsbanner Schwarz-Rot-Gold*, 83ff.

29. K. Demeter, *Das deutsche Offizierkorps in Gesellschaft und Staat* (Frankfurt, 1962); M. Kitchen, *The German Officer Corps* (Oxford, 1968).

30. Diehl, *Paramilitary Politics in Weimar Germany*, 128.

31. E. Jünger, *Der Arbeiter: Herrschaft und Gestalt* (Hamburg, 1932).

32. P. Kluke, "Der Fall Potempa," *Vierteljahrshefte für Zeitgeschichte* 5 (1957): 279–97.

33. E. Nolte, *The Three Faces of Fascism* (New York, 1969); A. J. Mayer, *Why Did the Heavens Not Darken?* (New York, 1988).

34. See above p. 77.

35. G. von Rauch, *A History of the Soviet Union* (New York, 1957), 124ff.

36. W. Orth, *Walther Rathenau und der Geist von Rapallo* (Berlin, 1962).

37. I. Deutscher, *Stalin* (London, 1949), 294ff.; G. Hosking, *The First Socialist Society* (Cambridge, MA, 1985); E.H. Carr, *The Russian Revolution from Lenin to Stalin* (London, 1979). M. Levin, *Russian Peasants and Soviet Power* (London, 1968); L. Viola, *Peasant Rebels under Stalin* (Oxford, 1996).

38. R. Conquest, *The Great Terror* (London, 1968).

39. M. Levin, *The Making of the Soviet System* (London, 1985).

40. D. Stone, *Hammer and Rifle* (Lawrence, KS, 2000), 86ff.

41. See below pp. 82ff.

42. Conquest, *The Great Terror*.

43. See below p. 104.

44. I. Kershaw und M. Levin, eds., *Stalinism and Nazism: Dictatorships in Comparison* (Cambridge, 1997).

45. Conquest, *The Great Terror*, 699ff.

CHAPTER 4. VIOLENCE WITHOUT BOUNDS, 1935–1945

1. Jünger's essay was first published in E. Jünger, *Krieg und Krieger* (Berlin, 1930); all quotes here from idem, *Sämtliche Werke*, essay 1 (Stuttgart, 1980), 7:121–41.

2. Jünger, *Sämtliche Werke*, 7:129ff.

3. H.-P. Schwarz, *Der konservative Anarchist* (Freiburg, 1962); D. Morat, "Die schmerzlose Körpermaschine und das zweite Bewusstsein," *Jahrbuch zur Kultur und Literatur der Weimarer Republik* 6 (2001): 181–233.

4. E. Ludendorff, *Der totale Krieg* (Munich, 1935), 3ff; also for the following quotes.

5. Quoted in J.C.G. Röhl, ed., *From Bismarck to Hitler* (London, 1973), 107f..

6. M. Geyer, *Aufrüstung oder Sicherheit?* (Wiesbaden, 1980).

7. K.-J. Müller, *Das Heer und Hitler* (Stuttgart, 1969).

8. Carsten, *Reichswehr and Politics*.

9. W. Deist, *The Wehrmacht and German Rearmament* (Basingstoke, 1981).

10. G. Schmidt, *The Politics and Economics of Appeasement* (New York,1986).

11. M. Geyer, "Rüstungsbeschleunigung und Inflation," *Militärgeschichtliche Mitteilungen* 2 (1981): 121–86; V. R. Berghahn, *Modern Germany* (Cambridge, 1993), 297 (table).

12. D. F. Vagts, "International Law in the Third Reich," *American Journal of International Law* 3 (1990): 661–74.

13. T. Fleming, "'Willenspotentiale.' Offizierstugenden als Gegenstand der Wehrpsychologie," in U. Breymayer et al., eds., *Willensmenschen: Über deutsche Offiziere* (Frankfurt, 1999), 111–22.

14. Ibid., 118ff. On "Rassenseelenforschung" see also Psychologisches Laboratorium des Reichskriegsministeriums, ed., *Abhandlungen zur Wehrpsychologie* (Leipzig, 1936), 86ff.; on Wehrmacht indoctrination see V. R. Berghahn, "NSDAP und 'wehrgeistige Führung' der Wehrmacht, 1939–1945," in *Vierteljahrshefte für Zeitgeschichte* 1 (1967): 17–71.

15. See below p. 130ff.

16. J. Lacouture, *De Gaulle: The Rebel, 1890–1944* (New York, 1990), 23ff.

17. M. Trachtenberg, *Reparations in World Politics* (New York, 1980).

18. See above p. 90ff.

19. S. Schuker, *The End of French Predominance in Europe* (Chapel Hill, 1976).

20. Lacouture, *De Gaulle*, 67ff.

21. H. Lasswell, "The Garrison State and the Specialists on Violence," *American Journal of Sociology* 47 (1941): 455–68.

22. Lacouture, *De Gaulle*, 137ff. See also R. A. Doughty, *Seeds of Disaster* (Hamden, CT, 1985); E. Kier, *Imagining War: French and British Military Doctrine between the Wars* (New York 1965); E. C. Kiesling, *Arming against Hitler* (Lawrence, KS, 1996).

23. T. Mason, *Nazism, Fascism, and the Working Class* (New York, 1995); R. J. Overy, *War and Economy in the Third Reich* (Oxford, 1994).

24. Quoted in Henry Picker, ed., *Hitlers Tischgespräche im Führerhauptquartier, 1941–1942* (Stuttgart, 1965), 163, 208.

25. F. Bajohr, *Parvenüs und Profiteure* (Frankfurt, 2001); idem, *"Aryanization" in Hamburg* (New York, 2004).

26. Quoted in R. Neebe, *Weichenstellung für die Globalisierung* (Cologne, 2004), 46. See also A. Hitler, *Mein Kampf* (Munich, 1933), recent Engl. trans. by Ralph Manheim (Boston, 1973).

27. Quoted in *Hannoversche Zeitung*, 30 April 1990.

28. P. Padfield, *Himmler* (London, 1990); H. Höhne, *The Order of the Death's Head* (London, 1969); R. L. Koehl, *The Black Corps* (Madison, WI, 1983).

29. P. Brendon, *Dark Valley* (New York, 2000), 390ff. See also, e.g., C. Leitz and D. J. Dunthorn, eds., *Spain in an International Context, 1936–1939* (New York, 1999); H. Thomas, *The Spanish Civil War* (London, 1977); G. Jackson, *The Spanish Republic and the Civil War, 1931–1938* (Princeton, 1965).

30. M. Broszat, *Nationalsozialistische Polenpolitik* (Stuttgart, 1961).

31. Ibid., 53ff.

32. Militärgeschichtliches Forschungsamt, ed., *Das Deutsche Reich und der Zweite Weltkrieg*, vols. 2 and 5 (Stuttgart, 1984); G. Hirschfeld, *Nazi Rule and Dutch Collaboration* (New York, 1988); Alan Milward, *The New Order and the French Economy* (Oxford, 1970).

33. E. Nolte, *Der europäische Bürgerkrieg* (Berlin, 1987).

34. M. Chodakiewicz, "Accommodation and Resistance" (Ph.D. diss., Columbia University, 2000).

35. K. Hildebrand, *The Foreign Policy of the Third Reich, 1933–1945* (London, 1973); B. Leach, *German Strategy against Russia* (Oxford, 1973).

36. H. Buchheim et al., *Anatomie dess SS-Staates* (Munich, 1967), 455ff.

37. C. Streit, *Keine Kameraden* (Stuttgart, 1978); T. J. Schulte, *The German Army and Nazi Policies in Occupied Russia* (Oxford, 1989).

38. A. Dallin, *German Rule in Russia, 1941–1945* (London, 1957); M. Mazower, *Inside Hitler's Greece* (New Haven, 1993); R.-D. Müller and G. R. Ueberschär, *Hitler's War in the East, 1941–1945* (Oxford, 1997).

39. D. Goldhagen, *Hitler's Willing Executioners* (New York, 1996); C. R. Browning, *Ordinary Men* (New York, 1992); O. Bartov, *Hitler's Army* (Oxford, 1991); H. Heer and K. Naumann, *Vernichtungskrieg* (Hamburg, 1995).

40. J. Hürter, "Die Wehrmacht vor Leningrad, 1941–42," in *Vierteljahrshefte für Zeitgeschichte* 3 (2001): 377–440.

41. R. J. Overy, *Russia's War* (New York, 1997), 132ff. See also A. Werth, *Russia at War* (New York, 1964); D. Glantz and J. M. House, *When Titans Clashed: How the Red Army Stopped Hitler* (Lawrence, KS, 1995).

42. M. Harrison, *Accounting for War* (Cambridge, 1996).

43. G. L. Weinberg, *The World at Arms* (Cambridge, 1994).

44. Berghahn, *Modern Germany*, 174.

45. J. Erickson, *The Road to Stalingrad* (London, 1975).

46. U. Herbert, *Hitler's Foreign Workers* (Cambridge, 1997).

47. S. Friedlander, *Nazi Germany and the Jews, 1933–1939* (New York, 1997); R. Hilberg, *The Destruction of the European Jews* (London, 1961); C. Browning, *The Origins of the Final Solution* (Lincoln, NE, 2004); P. Longerich, *The Unwritten Order: Hitler's Role in the Final Solution* (Stroud, 2001); M. Wildt, *Generation des Unbedingten* (Hamburg, 2002); R. Breitman, *The Architect of Genocide: Himmler and the Final Solution* (Hanover, 1991); M. Roseman, *The Wannsee Conference and the Final Solution* (New York, 2003).

48. Weinberg, *The World at Arms*.

49. R. D. Müller, *Hitler's Ostkrieg und die deutsche Siedlungspolitik* (Frankfurt, 1991).

50. H. Mommsen et al., *Das Volkswagenwerk und seine Arbeiter* (Düsseldorf, 1996); W. König, "Adolf Hitler vs. Henry Ford: The *Volkswagen*, the Role of America

as a Model, and the Failure of Nazi Consumer Society," in *German Studies Review* 2 (2004): 249–68.

51. J. Thies, *Architekt der Weltherrschaft* (Düsseldorf, 1976).

52. Picker [note 173], p. 143. See also ibid., pp. 270ff.

53. R. Opitz, ed., *Europastrategien des deutschen Kapitals* (Köln, 1977). See also V. R. Berghahn, ed., *Quest for Economic Empire* (Providence, RI, 1996).

54. A. Sölter, *Grossraumkartell* (Dresden, 1941).

55. Picker, *Hitlers Tischgespräche*, 143.

56. See above p. 22ff.

57. K. Hildebrand, *Vom Reich zum Weltreich* (Munich, 1969).

58. W. W. Schmokel, *Dream of Empire* (New Haven, CT, 1964), 196.

59. D. Mack Smith, *Mussolini's Roman Empire* (New York, 1976).

60. J. Lebra, *Japan's Greater East Asia Sphere in World War II* (Oxford, 1975).

61. R. H. Myers and M. R. Peattie, eds., *The Japanese Colonial Empire* (Princeton, 1984).

62. Berghahn, *Americanisation*.

63. A. T. Steele, *Shanghai and Manchuria* (Tempe, 1977).

64. R. B. Edgerton, *Warriors of the Rising Sun* (New York, 1993); I. Chang, *The Rape of Nanking* (New York, 1997).

65. See above pp. 107ff.

66. P. Weindling, *Health, Race and German Politics between National Unification and Nazism* (Cambridge, 1989).

67. D. K. Peukert, *Inside Nazi Germany* (New Haven, CT, 1987).

68. U. Adam, *Judenpolitik im Dritten Reich* (Düsseldorf, 1972); G. Bock, *Zwangssterilisierung im Nationalsozialismus* (Opladen, 1986).

69. C. Clay, *Master Race* (London, 1995).

70. H. Friedlaender, *The Origins of the Nazi Genocide* (Chapel Hill, 1995); E. Klee, *Euthanasie im NS-Staat* (Frankfurt, 1983); M. Burleigh, *Death and Deliverance: "Euthanasia" in Germany ca. 1900–1945* (New York, 1994).

71. F. R. Nicosia and J. Huener, eds., *Medicine and Medical Ethics in Nazi Germany* (New York, 2003); M. Kater, *Doctors under Hitler* (Chapel Hill, 1989); R. Proctor, *Racial Hygiene* (Cambridge, MA, 1988); B. Müller-Hill, *Murderous Science* (Oxford, 1988); R. J. Lifton, *The Nazi Doctors* (New York, 1986).

72. C. Browning, *Path to Genocide* (Cambridge, 1992), esp. 125ff.

CONCLUSIONS

1. W. Wette et al., eds., *Das letzte halbe Jahr: Stimmungsberichte der Wehrmachtpropaganda* (Essen, 2001); J. Friedrich, *Der Brand* (Berlin, 2003).

2. N. Naimark, *The Russians in Germany* (Cambridge, MA, 1995).

3. Bajohr, *Parvenüs und Profiteure*.

4. G. Paul, *Ungehorsame Soldaten* (St. Ingbert, 1994); N. Haase and G. Paul, eds., *Die anderen Soldaten* (Frankfurt, 1995).

5. G. Sereny, *The Healing Wound* (New York, 2001), 25ff.

6. J. B. Schechtman, *Postwar Population Transfers in Europe, 1945–1955* (Philadelphia, 1961).

7. Reprinted in E. P. Chase, *The United Nations in Action* (New York, 1950), 403ff.

8. E. S. Mason, *Controlling World Trade* (New York, 1946).

9. Quoted in Berghahn, *Americanization*, 108.

10. J. Gillingham, *Coal, Steel, and the Rebirth of Europe* (Cambridge, 1991).

11. L. Erhard, *Wohlstand für alle* (Düsseldorf, 1957).

12. R. M. Collins, *The Business Response to Keynes, 1929–1964* (New York, 1981).

13. L. Cohen, *Making a New Deal: Industrial Workers in Chicago, 1919–1939* (New York, 1990).

14. L. Herbst, ed., *Vom Marshallplan zur EWG* (Munich, 1990); M. Hogan, *The Marshall Plan* (Cambridge, MA, 1988).

15. G. Cross, *An All-Consuming Century* (New York, 2000). See also R. Fox and T. J. Lears, eds., *Culture and Consumption: Critical Essays in American History, 1880–1980* (New York, 1983); S. J. Brommer, ed., *Consuming Vision* (New York, 1989); S. Strasser et al., eds., *Getting and Spending: European and American Consumer Societies in the Twentieth Century* (New York, 1998).

16. Strasser et al., *Getting and Spending*, with relevant contributions by André Steiner and Ina Merkel.

17. M. Kaldor, *New and Old Wars: Violence in a Global Era* (Cambridge, 1999). See Also S. Chesterman, ed., *Civilians at War* (Boulder, CO, 2001).

18. Bill Gates quoted in CAM, 35 (Lent Term 2002), p. 6. See also W. F. Felice, *The Global New Deal* (Lanham, 2002); M. Kaldor, *Global Civil Society: An Answer to War* (Cambridge, 2003).

19. For a multivolume treatment, see W. T. Vollmann, *Rising Up, Rising Down* (San Francisco, 2004). For a brief discussion of the problem, see, e.g., J. Kifner, "Report on Brutal Vietnam Campaign Stirs Memories," in *New York Times*, 28 December 2003, p. 24. See also O. Bartov, "Extreme Violence and the Scholarly Community," in *International Social Science Journal* 174 (2002): 509–18; J. R. Ruff, *Violence in Early Modern Europe* (Cambridge, 2001); J. Waller, *Becoming Evil* (Oxford, 2002); T. Lindenberger and Alf Lüdtke, eds., *Physische Gewalt* (Frankfurt, 1995); D. Schumann, "Gewalt als Grenzüberschreitung," in *Archiv für Sozialgeschichte*, 37 (1997): 366–86; D. Anderson, *Histories of the Hanged* (London, 2005); P. Gleichman and T. Kühne, eds., *Massenhaftes Töten* (Essen, 2004).

Selected Bibliography

Aldcroft, D. H. *From Versailles to Wall Street, 1919–1929*. London, 1977.
Arendt, H. *The Origins of Totalitarianism*. New York, 1951.
Bartov, O. *Hitler's Army*. Oxford, 1991.
Bell, P.M.H. *The Origins of the Second World War in Europe*. London, 1986.
Berghahn, V. R. *Militarism. The History of an International Debate, 1861–1979*. Leamington Spa, 1981.
Boemeke, M. et al., eds. *Anticipating Total War*. New York, 1999.
Bourke, J. *An Intimate History of Killing*. New York, 1999.
Brendon, P. *Dark Valley: A Panorama of the 1930s*. New York, 2000.
Broszat, M. *Hitler and the Collapse of Weimar Germany*. Leamington Spa, 1987.
Browning, C. R. *Ordinary Men*. New York, 1993.
Carsten, F. L. *Revolution in Central Europe*. London, 1972.
Costigliola, F. *Awkward Dominion*. Ithaca, 1984.
Dallas, G. *1918: War and Peace*. Woodstock, NY, 2000.
Dallin, A. *German Rule in Russia, 1941–1945*. London, 1959.
Feldman, G. D. *The Great Disorder*. New York, 1994.
Ferguson, N. *The Pity of War*. New York, 1999.
Fischer, F. *War of Illusions*. New York, 1973.
Fitzpatrick, S. *The Russian Revolution, 1917–1932*. Oxford, 1984.
Friedlaender, H. *The Origins of the Nazi Genocide*. Chapel Hill, 1995.
Friedlander, S. *Nazi Germany and the Jews, 1933–1939*. New York, 1997.
Galbraith, G. K. *The Great Crash*. New York, 1954.
Herrmann, D. *The Arming of Europe and the Making of the First World War*. Princeton, 1995.
Hilberg, R. *The Destruction of the European Jews*. London, 1961.
Hildebrand, K. *The Foreign Policy of the Third Reich*. New York, 1973.
Hobsbawm, E. *The Age of Extremes*. New York, 1996.
Horne, J., and A. Kramer. *German Atrocities 1914*. New Haven, 2001.
Hosking, G. *A History of the Soviet Union*. London. 1985.
Joll, J. *The Origins of the First World War*. London, 1984.
Kaldor, M. *Global Civil Society: An Answer to War*. Cambridge, 2003.
Keegan, J. *The First World War*. London, 1998.
Kershaw, I. *Hitler*. 2 vols. New York, 1999–2000.
Kindleberger, C. P. *The World in Depression, 1929–1939*. Berkeley, 1975.
Kitchen, M. *Europe between the Wars*. London, 1988.
Kocka, J. *Facing Total War*. Leamington Spa, 1984.
Landes, D. *The Unbound Prometheus*. Cambridge, 1977.
Laqueur, W., ed. *Fascism: A Reader's Guide*. Harmondsworth, 1976.
Lebra, J. *Japan's Greater East Asia Sphere in World War II*. Oxford, 1975.
Leed, E. *No Man's Land*. New York, 1979.
Mack Smith, D. *Mussolini's Roman Empire*. London, 1976.

Maier, C. S. *Recasting Bourgeois Europe*. Princeton, 1975.

May, E. *Imperial Democracy*. New York, 1961.

Mayer, A. J. *Politics and Diplomacy of Peacemaking*. London, 1968.

Mazower, M. *Dark Continent*. New York, 1999.

Müller, R.-D. and G.R. Ueberschär. *Hitler's War in the East, 1941–1945*. Oxford, 1997.

Nolan, M. *Visions of Modernity*. Oxford, 1994.

Nolte, E. *The Three Faces of Fascism*. New York, 1979.

Overy, R. *Russia's War*. New York, 1997.

Paxton, R. O. *The Anatomy of Fascism*. New York, 2004.

Stern, F. *Gold and Iron*. New York, 1977.

Stevenson, D. *Cataclysm*. New York, 2004.

Strachan, H. *World War I*. Oxford-New York, 2003.

Thomas, H. *The Spanish Civil War*. London, 1977.

Weinberg, G. *The World at Arms*. Cambridge, 1994.

Winter, J. M. *Sites of Memory. Sites of Mourning*. Cambridge, 1995.

Chronology

May–July 1899	First Hague Peace Conference
April 1900	Paris World Exhibition opens
January 1904	Beginning of war in German South-West Africa
15 June 1907	Second Hague Peace Conference opens
July 1911	Agadir Crisis
12 December 1912	"War Council" of Wilhelm II
30 June 1913	Beginning of Second Balkan War
28 June 1914	Assassination of Archduke Ferdinand and his wife at Sarajevo
5 July 1914	Hoyos Mission to Berlin; Wilhelm II issues "blanc check"
23 July 1914	Austria-Hungary hands ultimatum to Serbia
28 July 1914	Austria-Hungary invades Serbia
30 July 1914	Vienna and St. Petersburg order general mobilization from 31 July
31 July 1914	Berlin issues ultimatum to St. Petersburg to withdraw mobilization
1 August 1914	Germany proclaims general mobilization
4 August 1914	Germany invades Belgium; Britain enters World War I
4 September 1914	Beginning of the Battle of the Marne
14 September 1914	Battle of Tannenberg
20 October 1914	Beginning of Battle of Ypres
16 March 1915	Brusilov offensive
31 May 1916	Naval Battle of Jutland
1 July 1916	First day of the Somme Battle
February 1917	Collapse of the tsarist empire; revolution in Russia
6 April 1917	The United States enters the war
October 1917	Lenin seizes power in Russia
3 March 1918	Treaty of Brest-Litovsk
31 March 1918	Beginning of German spring offensive in the west
9 November 1918	Collapse of Hohenzollern monarchy; revolution in Germany
April–July 1919	Bolshevik republics in Munich and Budapest
28 June 1919	Signing of Versailles Treaty by Germany
16 April 1922	German-Soviet Rapallo Treaty
October 1922	Mussolini seizes power in Italy
11 January 1923	France and Belgium occupy Ruhr industrial region
8–9 November 1923	Hitler-Ludendorff putsch
1 December 1925	Locarno Treaty signed
10 December 1926	Germany becomes a member of the League of Nations
31 January 1927	Dissolution of the Inter-Allied Military Control Commission

7 November 1927	Stalin announces first Five-Year Plan
27 August 1928	Signing of Kellogg-Briand Pact
29 October 1929	Wall Street crash
January 1932	Japanese attack on Shanghai
30 January 1933	Hitler nominated German Reich chancellor
1–3 March 1933	Nazi boycott of Jewish shops
30 June 1934	"Night of the Long Knives"; murder of SA leadership
1 December 1934	Murder of Sergei Kirov in Leningrad
15 September 1935	Proclamation of anti-Semitic Nuremberg Laws in Germany
March 1936	Hitler marches into demilitarized Rhineland
26 April 1937	German air raid on Guernica in Spain
December 1937	Japanese conquest of Nanking
12 March 1938	"Anschluss" of Austria
2–30 September 1938	Munich Agreement negotiated
8–13 November 1938	Anti-Semitic pogroms in Germany
15 March 1939	Germany invades Czechoslovakia
23 August 1939	Signing of Nazi-Soviet Pact
1 September 1939	Germany attacks Poland
15 May 1940	Capitulation of Holland
14 June 1940	German troops occupy Paris
13 September 1940	Italy attacks Egypt
28 October 1940	Italy attacks Greece
6 April 1940	Germany invades Yugoslavia
6 June 1941	Germany issues Commissar Order
22 June 1941	Germany invades the Soviet Union
3 August 1941	Bishop von Galen criticizes "euthanasia" program
12 August 1941	Proclamation of the Atlantic Charter
28–30 September 1941	Mass murder of Jews at Babi Yar by Germany
8 October 1941	Construction of Auschwitz-Birkenau
18 November 1941	British counteroffensive in North Africa
7 December 1941	Japan attacks Pearl Harbor
11 December 1941	Germany and Italy declare war on the United States
20 January 1942	Wannsee Conference on "Final Solution"
15 February 1942	Japan conquers British Singapore
November 1942	Beginning of Stalingrad Battle
14–26 January 1943	Casablanca Conference
2 February 1943	Red Army reconquers Stalingrad
18 February 1943	Goebbels's speech on total war
28 April 1943	Warsaw ghetto uprising
10 July 1943	Allies land in Sicily
27 July 1943	Mussolini toppled
May 1944	Deportation of Hungarian Jews to Auschwitz begins
June 1944	Allied landing in Normandy
10 June 1944	Murder of the inhabitants of Oradour by Germans
1–22 July 1944	Bretton Woods conference
20 July 1944	Stauffenberg fails to assassinate Hitler

1 August–2 October	Warsaw uprising
13–14 February 1945	Massive air raid on Dresden
24 April–26 June 1945	San Francisco conference; founding of the UN
4 May 1945	Germany capitulates
17 July–2 August 1945	Allied conference at Potsdam
6 and 9 August 1945	Atomic bombs dropped on Hiroshima and Nagasaki
2 September 1945	Japan surrenders

Index